RAVE REVIEWS

ABOUT THE BOOK

"Finally from the world of psychological psychobabble comes a BOOK OF SUBSTANCE! This is not a fad, and its concepts offer us a solid surface upon which we can begin to understand ourselves and the others with whom we interact. What a TIMELESS GIFT OF INSIGHT. If you only read one book this year, do yourself and the rest of us a favor—READ THIS BOOK! You will never see yourself or others the same again."

—Howard Alper, CEO, Chicago, Illinois

"I will never understand how Oprah Winfrey missed this one. If anything can improve the quality of our lives at every level, THIS IS IT!"

—Paul Beidler, Mission Viejo, California

"It's really very easy. If you don't get this book, you don't get life!"

—Diane Anderson, Corona Del Mar, California

"The CLARITY and VISION of *The Color Code* is PHENOMENAL. The book sits on my nightstand right next to my Bible."

—William Crowder, M.D., Conroe, Texas

"Some people might think this is just lightweight fun. Don't kid yourself. *The Color Code* is a lot like Disneyland. It reads with such an unassuming style and possesses such a uniquely inviting charm that one easily forgets its POWERFULLY CRAFTED, UNPARALLELED ACCURACY."

—Daniel Morse, Fox Point, Wisconsin

"This POWERFUL PERSONALITY MODEL is heads and shoulders above every other personality profile out there. I've used them all from Myers-Briggs to Wilson Learning and there is NO COMPARISON. Once you have used this model, you will never use the others again."

—Donalie Hartwell, San Luis Obispo, California

ABOUT THE AUTHOR

"In a day and age when whining for the spotlight and shameless notoriety are often confused with earned fame, Taylor Hartman strikes you, instead, as the GENUINE ARTICLE. He is WARM, CHARISMATIC, and CHARMING. He is a much sought after and spellbinding speaker, and literally hundreds of thousands of people have felt the force of his unconditional love and improved their lives as a direct result of his work. He embraces life absolutely and is a remarkable, life-enhancing figure. Dr. Taylor Hartman is DESTINED TO IMPACT THE WORLD IN A WONDERFUL AND PROFOUND WAY!"

—Brad Willis, Provo, Utah

D0167824

"Dr. Hartman's WEALTH OF WISDOM, which he shares using his humor, compassion, and strength—in fact, his whole personality—causes me to call it as it is: There are other psychologists, and then there is Dr. Taylor Hartman."
—Frederick Knauss, Sacramento, California

AS A CONFERENCE KEYNOTE SPEAKER

"I've been in this field a long time and heard it all, and believe me, it doesn't get any better than this! The feedback and cheers are still coming in confirming your work as the BEST, MOST INFORMATIVE, GREATEST INSPIRATION, AND MOST BENEFICIAL OF ALL CONVENTIONS TO DATE!"
—Jim Hennig, Ph.D., President, National Speakers Bureau, Phoenix, Arizona

"Extremely effective keynote address! You got rave reviews! You are a special gift and you played a major role in this hugely successful conference."
—Jayne Felgen, Senior Vice President, E.C. Murphy Ltd., Amherst, New York

"In all my twenty-six years of attending and chairing conferences, nothing prepared me for Dr. Taylor Hartman. He is a conference chairman's worst nightmare! People would drag in chairs, sit against the walls, and block the doorways to simply hear his presentation. Participants from the United States Department of Corrections are not easily impressed, but they raved that he was the BEST SPEAKER and his message was the MOST BENEFICIAL INFORMATION they ever heard. At every conference his packs the house and then some, leaving the standing-room-only audience wowed and grateful they attended. Those who have read his work can't hear him often enough!"
—Kimball Bird, Chief, Salt Lake City, Utah

POWERFUL PRAISE FOR BUSINESS APPLICATION

"Dr. Taylor Hartman has become a leading business resource to the Young President's Organization (YPO) companies for improving operational efficiencies as well as personal relationships. Taylor has produced SPECTACULAR RESULTS with each of my companies. His methods have done more to create a productive team environment than anything I've experienced."
—Robert M. Irwin II, CEO, Long Beach, California

"I've been trained in some of the most sophisticated aircraft in the world, gone to over forty months of training in Air Force schools, and taken three years of graduate-level college courses, so I can speak with some authority when I say THIS IS THE BEST ONE-DAY TRAINING PROGRAM I HAVE EVER SEEN . . . COLOR-CODING WORKS! IT'S SIMPLE, EASY TO UNDERSTAND, AND POWERFUL IN RESULTS!"
—Seminar Participant, Tom Bay Speaks Up, Newport Beach, California

"Whoever latches on to this man and his message will have their own personal golden goose! He has an electric personality and his love for all people literally shines through. This man WALKS HIS TALK! I have used him and his books in my business and family life—both with tremendous success. At work, I am much more effective at retaining key people and nurturing team work, driving up our sales a record 30 percent. At home I am more compassionate and centered. I LOVE THIS MAN AND HIS MESSAGE FOR WHAT HE HAS DONE IN MY LIFE AND THE LIVES OF THE PEOPLE AROUND ME."

—Chet Fortney, CEO, Covina, California

"The Hartman Personality Profile from *The Color Code* is BY FAR THE MOST IMPORTANT ASPECT IN HIRING PERSONNEL. Using this creative instrument consistently leads to hiring better employees. This POWERFUL, REVOLUTIONARY THEORY will change the way businesses hire, fire, and educate employees. Giving copies of this book has become my all-time favorite gift!"

—Chuck Davis, CEO, Huntington Beach, California

"*THE COLOR CODE* IS UNEQUALED in its ability to answer the difficult questions about people in the business world. Its concepts offer clarity in successful hiring, placing and/or firing of personnel, effective communication techniques, conflict-resolution strategies, team-building, stress management, and how to make employees and customers happy and loyal."

—Roger Jaska, CEO, Upland, California

ACCOLADES FROM EDUCATORS

"Dr. Hartman's work is DYNAMIC, HUMOROUS, CLEARLY EFFECTIVE AND MOTIVATING! People find his message so easy to embrace because he is genuine, honest, and sincere. This personality model really works. What a gift!"

—Karen Cummings, Las Vegas, Nevada

"*The Color Code* ignites enthusiasm in audiences from all walks of life! High school students, faculties, and parents are going wild over *The Color Code!* Watching students, faculty, and parents embrace personality diversity has become a LIFE-CHANGING ADVENTURE FOR US ALL!"

—Anna Valasco, Aica, Hawaii

"I am a professor of Marketing and Business Education at Central Washington University. Prior to discovering *The Color Code,* I used other inventories such as the Strong-Campbell and the Myers-Briggs. After reading *The Color Code* and applying it to virtually everyone I know, I feel that its simplicity and its motivation-based perspective make it more accurate, more effective, easier to understand, and therefore more practical than any other inventory."

—Bill Chandler, Professor, Olympia, Washington

ON RELATIONSHIPS

"WHAT A LIFE-CHANGING EXPERIENCE! I LEARNED MORE ABOUT MYSELF IN THREE DAYS WITH *THE COLOR CODE* THAN IN A DECADE OF COUNSELING. I can't thank you enough for your gift. I look forward with delight to having the healthiest and most intimate relationships, and owe you a huge debt of gratitude."

—Paul Newman, Alta Loma, California

"The benefits of *The Color Code* are LIMITLESS! Gaining this knowledge allows me to work with an endless variety of people much more comfortably. I now understand why we do what we do, thus allowing me to relate much more effectively with others on an entirely new level. IT HAS CHANGED THE QUALITY OF MY LIFE FOREVER!"

—Starla Lewis, Seattle, Washington

"*The Color Code* COMPLETELY ERASES RACIAL, RELIGIOUS, AND CULTURAL BIAS! The Personality Colors presented in this book are the single most effective tool for helping the various groups to see each other as the individuals they truly are rather than the bland, generic factions they often appear to be."

—Patty Vogen, Tonga

"Why didn't someone explain psychology like this when I was younger? Everyone else talks about 'behavior' while Dr. Hartman has found the key in *The Color Code* with his explanation of 'MOTIVE.' I initially learned more about myself and my relationships in one hour with this book than I ever learned in the last thirty-three years. And after rereading this book, I can't believe how deep it goes. I can't imagine dating long-term, let alone marrying or hiring someone, without knowing their personality color. This is the best relationship model I have ever discovered."

—Johnny Simms, Charlotte, North Carolina

Also by Taylor Hartman, Ph.D.

THE CHARACTER CODE

THE
COLOR
CODE

A New Way to See Yourself,
Your Relationships, and Life

Taylor Hartman, Ph.D.

A FIRESIDE BOOK
PUBLISHED BY SIMON & SCHUSTER

FIRESIDE
Rockefeller Center
1230 Avenue of the Americas
New York, NY 10020

Copyright © 1987, 1998 by Taylor Hartman

FIRESIDE and colophon are registered trademarks of Simon & Schuster Inc.

DESIGNED BY ERICH HOBBING

Set in Sabon

Manufactured in the United States of America

17   19   20   18   16

Library of Congress Cataloging-in-Publication Data
Hartman, Taylor.
The color code : a new way to see yourself, your relationships, and life / Taylor Hartman.
        p.   cm.
1. Typology (Psychology) 2. Color—Psychological aspects.
        I. Title.
        BF698.3.H37   1998
    155.2'64—dc21   97-44594
                CIP
        ISBN-13: 978-0-684-84376-6
        ISBN-10:   0-684-84376-5
        ISBN-13: 978-0-684-84822-8 (Pbk)
        ISBN-10:   0-684-84822-8 (Pbk)

FOR J*EAN*

ACKNOWLEDGMENTS

It takes a lot of colors to make a rainbow. It takes a lot of people to make a book.

My professional life is filled with remarkable friends, family, professors, and mentors who have continually colored my world with truths, passions, and love.

This manuscript is the result of six Reds who continually invited me to stretch in bringing this whole project from a mere dream to a powerful reality. Dr. Linda Burhansstipanov, Charles Hansen, Tish Whitney, and Pierre Drouhay inspired me and demanded that I perspire as well. (So it goes with Reds, right!?!)

My literary agent, Margret McBride, and my publisher/editor, Susan Moldow, picked up ten years later and introduced me to a level of professionalism I had never known in the literary world. They have always believed in me and my work.

Finally, my patients (all colors) freely assisted in my research by inviting me to share so fully in their lives. I love and appreciate you all.

CONTENTS

CONTENTS

Part Four: Building Character

FOREWORD

How do I introduce this man? At first my thoughts turn to his many degrees and professional credentials, but he has experienced so many things and enriched the hearts of so many people, those degrees and credentials can't describe the *real* Taylor Hartman.

When I think of his doctoral degree at the United States International University in San Diego, California, what I remember is the way he kept up with his commitment to his family and community obligations despite his heavy career and education schedule. Taylor has enjoyed many professional and civic responsibilities, and yet he always lets us know that we are the most important people in his life.

Taylor is a lover. He loves people so easily that one would almost have to live with him as I do to appreciate how sincere his love is.

Taylor has always been committed to improving the quality of life—not only his but that of all those he encounters. And yet he remains very playful and loves to live in the present.

Taylor is as comfortable playing "horsie" and "duck-duck-goose" in our family room as he was addressing the International Congress of Psychologists in Austria. In fact, his playful behavior has often provided a creative outlet for our family. He "dated" each of our five children once a month as they grew up, and continues to romance me with frequent surprises and adventures.

Despite Taylor's busy professional counseling and consulting business, he still maintains that the highest compliment he ever received was from his nine-year-old daughter. She told her schoolteacher that she didn't mind having personal problems, because Dad would always take time to give her private counseling.

The question I am most often asked about Taylor is: "What is it *really* like to live with him?" Perhaps the easiest and most accurate answer is to simply say: "He's a man who practices what he preaches."

The Color Code is a special gift from a very special person. He cares. This book will help you understand:

- the mysteries of yourself,
- the miracle of your relationships, and
- the magic of living.

Taylor Hartman will touch your heart. . . . This book will change your life.

Jean Hartman, 1997

PREFACE

It happens to all of us. In social, business, and even family encounters, we meet some people and instantly establish a rapport—laughing at the same things, concerned about the same issues, discovering, perhaps, that we have had similar life experiences. Then we meet others and just making conversation is a struggle—we're on guard, uncomfortable, inexplicably hostile.

Why?

In *The Color Code*, I group various aspects of personality and behavior into four color categories: Red, Blue, White, and Yellow. While few of us are completely one color or another—we are potential rainbows within—these categories represent a useful guide to personality types.

I use color codes for personality because color is already an established metaphor for emotion and behavior. We "see red" when we're angry. We "feel blue" when we're sad.

Using this color guide to personality, readers will be able to "see" the motives behind their own and other people's behavior, which will help anyone establish and maintain relationships with greater ease. They will be able to accept others for what they are. And, most important, they will learn to incorporate within themselves the best of all the colors of life.

INTRODUCTION

FEBRUARY 14, 1986

Ambulances and fire engines with flashing red lights and blaring sirens raced to the scene of our head-on collision. It was raining heavily that night. My wife and I had been out to dinner for Valentine's Day. She had reminded me to fasten my seat belt for the drive home. I had never been happier in my life. I knew who I was and where I was going. I felt committed to life and able to contribute much to my family, friends, and profession. Not more than three months earlier we had moved to our dream home in the country in southern California. Our children were happy and healthy. My wife was creatively decorating our home and making new friends. My private practice was thriving, and my tennis game was at its peak.

Twenty-five minutes later, I lay unconscious in my wife's lap while the firefighters cut through the car door in an effort to free us and transport us to the hospital. I knew no one and nothing about myself. I no longer enjoyed the security of an identity. The only evidence that I was in fact alive were the headaches.

For weeks, I struggled to find me. I felt depressed and valueless. I had no core of personality from which to establish an identity. Gone were my humor and patience with children. Gone were my emotional connection to my wife and my memory of my patients. I had lost the first great gift life offers. I had lost a sense of myself.

For the first time in my life, I recognized how enviable it is to be somebody—to feel truly unique and alive. I desperately needed my sense of identity. I felt desperate and lost without my personality.

As the weeks and months went by, I began to regain some of my memory. Numerous phone calls and cards from people helped me

19

remember the warmth of our friendships. Tears came to my eyes many times when I realized I could still hold my "Blue" wife and feel her committed love. The noise my children made began to excite me again as a reminder of how lucky I was to be alive to watch them grow up. Once again I began to see how unique their personalities were. My oldest "Red" daughter, Terra, who moved so confidently, demanded that I reconnect with her, while Summer, "White," waited and watched patiently for my return. My "Yellow" daughter, Mikelle, hugged me freely, told me she loved me, and went off to play, confident that I would once again be well. My little "Red" three-year-old, BreAnne, continued her independent play, unfazed by her daddy's recent confusion. It was as if my identity returned, and with this new identity came my commitment to live again.

Actually the identity wasn't new. I had merely found the old me again. After wandering for months in depression and severe memory loss, I felt new. I began to laugh and tease friends. I felt myself beginning to get comfortable with life, much the way a guest who stays long enough in a home begins to feel like family. I was once again comfortable with my life because I had found my personality—my identity.

My renewed self-awareness and the recognition of my family's diverse personalities reminded me of the book I had been working on prior to the accident. Difficult as the accident and its aftermath were, no experience could have been more timely. It convinced me of the incredible purpose our personalities play in our lives. It reminded me of my character strengths and limitations. It brought *me* back to *me*.

I am more sensitive today than I was before the accident. I had become too busy to play. I had become too busy to do the things I enjoyed most in my profession—time to call patients, create team-building strategies with corporate clients, and deliver exciting keynote speeches. Now I take the time to go to lunch with friends and laugh until we must leave. Now I take the time to call my wife during the day just to say "I love you." Now I take the time to play baseball with my children. Now I take the time to live and to love.

This close brush with death brought refreshing perspective to my life. All of us, in some way, experience our own crises. Perhaps they afford us the luxury we might otherwise never afford ourselves—the sudden sense of who we really are and what we're really all about.

You, the reader, do not have to experience a serious accident to discover your own identity. You can be awakened to your identity with a carefully designed profile that will aid you in identifying your personality traits. Each personality, with its strengths and limitations, will be fully explained. You will be offered suggestions on how to develop your character and your personality to be your best self. Relationships between the personality styles will also be discussed. You will be guided in assessing how to succeed in your various relationships at work, at home, and with friends.

We all have a personality and character. It is not determined at birth what we will do with either of them. Unfortunately, many people simply grow old rather than ever growing up. This is your opportunity to understand the difference. It is my hope that *The Color Code* will be your guide to understanding and appreciating various personality types. Using the color-coded system described in the following chapters, you will learn how to improve your relationships, including the most important relationship of all—your relationship with yourself.

Part One

PERSONALITY IN PERSPECTIVE

Chapter One

THE ELEMENTS
OF PERSONALITY

Every woman who has given birth
to more than one child
would tell you that each comes
with a unique personality at birth.

PERSONALITY IS INNATE

Every child is born with a unique set of personality traits. Ask any woman who has given birth to two or more children and she will attest to the fact that while still in the womb her children showed marked differences in their behavior. One "demands" more room to move, chews on the umbilical cord, and refuses to accept a variety of foods Mom selects. Another settles in quietly, pleased there is no bed to make or food to cook, and thinks, "Hey, maybe I can get a twelve-month ride out of the old girl!"

Everyone knows that no two sets of fingerprints are alike. How could we possibly believe that human personalities are any less individual than fingerprints?

There are psychologists who theorize that a child's personality is not completely formed until the age of five. Others go further—they say personality develops slowly through a lifelong process of discovery and maturation. I disagree. I think when some of my colleagues use the word *personality* they really mean "personal history."

I believe that each personality is complete at conception and comes in the soul of every child. It is present along with various genetically inherited traits, such as hair color and blood type, although personality itself is not inherited from one's parents. Nor is it shaped by environment. Science has not yet discovered all the factors that determine our prenatal makeup. But this should not deter us from using what we *do* know to improve ourselves and our relationships.

> *Personality is a solid core of traits*
> *reflecting the unique essence*
> *of a particular human being.*

Personality is a solid core of traits reflecting the unique essence of a particular human being. Attempts by social scientists to explain personality in terms of genetics or environmental influences merely limit our understanding of the true nature of personality. By confining themselves to the old nature versus nurture argument, such attempts to explain personality doom themselves to failure. Personality is not black and white. Personality is a kaleidoscope. We can understand personality—and ourselves—only by opening our eyes to a whole new kind of understanding.

Since the beginning of time, humans have been trying to learn what it is that makes them tick. Greek myths abound with spellbinding stories of men and women who were changed by their interactions with one or more of the gods. Such mythology was an early way of trying to explain personality. The suggestion was that people had unique strengths and limitations because of the influence of deities. Astrologers embraced the twelve signs of the zodiac as the determining factors in personality, substituting planetary power for the powers of the gods. Chinese tradition associated personality with the year a child was born.

Later theoreticians turned to the environment to explain personality differences. They categorized personalities according to four dominant aspects of nature—earth, air, fire, and water. This theory of the elements provides us with an interesting starting point from which to proceed in our understanding of personality. It is simple, it is memorable, and it is rooted in fertile historical ground. I'll expand on this idea later. For the moment, the important thing to understand is that, from my point of view, your personality is formed before you take your first breath.

Now let's explore the meaning of personality. What does it do? How does it affect our lives?

> *Personality is not black and white.*
> *Personality is a kaleidoscope.*

PERSONALITY IS AN INTERPRETATION OF LIFE

Some people see the world through rose-colored glasses. Others see it through dark glasses. But we can't try on personalities the way we try on glasses. Personality is built in.

Your personality determines whether you are easily depressed, casual, formal, careful, or carefree. It determines whether you are passive or assertive. Do you dash off at the last minute for an appointment, or always arrive with time to spare? Do you prefer deep, meaningful conversations, or would you rather dance the night away? Are you most comfortable being entertained, or do you prefer to entertain others? Your personality is the key to how you react to these and all other situations. Your personality is more than just an "attitude." It is what causes you to act and react the way you do.

PERSONALITY IS A CODE OF BEHAVIOR

Personality is that core of thoughts and feelings inside you that tells you how to conduct yourself. It's a checklist of responses based on strongly held values and beliefs. It directs your emotional as well as your rational reactions to *every life experience*. It even determines which type of reaction—emotional or cerebral—you're likely to have in any given situation. Personality is an active process within each person's heart and mind that dictates how he or she feels, thinks, and behaves.

> *You can never change your core color.*
> *Learn to nurture your strengths*
> *and overcome your limitations.*
> *Perhaps the greatest human tragedy of all*
> *is watching someone abandon their innate personality*
> *and simply discard themselves*
> *along the side of life's road.*

Your personality watches over and guards you like a parent. Without clear-cut personality traits to mark our paths through life, we would become lost. This is what personality fears most. It is what makes you different from everyone else, and so it is rigid and quite resistant to change. Personality protects itself. It does not easily venture out to experience or understand other types of personalities. It accepts you—that is, itself—quite readily but is much less flexible with others. And, as sometimes happens between parents and children, your personality may give you problems from time to time. But let an outsider do or say something threatening, and our personality, like a parent, reacts defensively and lashes out.

Personality points each of us in a particular direction and makes us feel uncomfortable when we deviate from it. The moment we stray from its prescribed plan, it makes us feel disoriented. When we try to deny or explain away unusual thought processes, we feel emotional fatigue and a vague sense of fear. We suffer spiritual pain that we cannot understand. We feel confused and overwhelmed by our inability to figure out our seemingly irrational behavior.

> *I believe that life is the most entertaining journey of all.*
> *It can be a better journey than you ever dreamed,*
> *if you know where you've been and where you're going.*

For each of us, the core of our personality—its type, the direction in which it points us—is vitally important in explaining us to our ourselves. Without it, we would be truly lost. Each of us needs a personal code of behavior, a personality, but it makes for rough going if we want to change, to grow. And if we do not understand our personalities well enough to exert some control, we can never grow into healthier, happier human beings.

PERSONALITY IS A MYSTERY

Sadly, few of us really know the reasons why we think and act as we do—perhaps none of us ever finds *complete* answers. Still, we can try. For many people, their own personality is the greatest mystery of all. They are puzzled and frustrated when they do not understand the basis for their actions and reactions. Trying to understand our personalities is the only way to grow. Step by step, bit by bit, we can gather enough knowledge about ourselves to begin to take control of our lives. I believe that life is the most exciting journey of all. It can be a better journey than you ever dreamed, if you know where you've been and where you're going.

This book is designed to guide you in your journey of self-

> *Trying to understand our personalities*
> *is the only way to grow.*

discovery. Knowledge is power. The knowledge you gain from this book will give you the power to change your behavior, if you so choose, and to understand the behavior of others.

PERSONALITY IS A RAINBOW

Let's return to the idea that the elements can be used as a metaphor for personality. Thousands of years ago, when the "known elements" were earth, air, fire, and water, it was thought that there were also four distinct personality types. In this book I will borrow and expand upon the ancients' metaphor. In my color code, fire becomes the color Red, Blue reflects the earth, White represents water, and air is symbolized by Yellow.

Each color stands for a collection of traits, strengths, and limitations. But far from being limited to explaining only individual personalities, this color symbolism also clarifies relationships between people and the impact that various personalities have on one another.

In order to understand the power of interactions among the four personality types, we can carry the nature analogy one step further. Earth without water is parched and desolate. And fire cannot exist without air. Symbolically, we see that each personality can best define itself through its relationships with other personalities.

You should understand that the four primary personalities identified with the four colors are the personality types found in every culture in the world, in every age group, in every religion, race, and sex. They belong to and describe everyone. They identify innate strengths as well as innate limitations. They influence every action and reaction.

Of course, every person develops unique strengths and weaknesses—this makes for numerous variations within the four primary color groups. Also, some behavior patterns are not caused by inherent personality at all but instead reflect cultural biases—such as, for instance, the submissive role played by women in some countries. We must always look beyond culturally induced behavior to see the innate, natural personality of any individual.

Despite variations and exceptions, however, we can each identify most clearly with only one of the personality colors. If we can each find our own personal color, learn its characteristics, and discover how to accentuate its strengths and work within its limitations, we will be better prepared to understand ourselves and cope with the everyday problems of life.

To help you accomplish this, a simple and enjoyable profile appears in the next chapter. It will enable you to discover your personality color. I urge you to take the profile now, before reading on, first, so that you can understand and identify with the material in the rest of the book and, second, so you can learn to harness the strengths of your personality and enhance the rest of your life.

Chapter Two

THE HARTMAN
PERSONALITY PROFILE

*Since your personality is innate
and comes with you at birth,
answer each possible question
from your earliest recollection.*

Now it's time to discover your own personality type—your own "color." Perhaps you will learn things about yourself that you were not aware of, or find out why you have certain tendencies or reactions you have never been able to understand. In time, you will probably be able to identify the colors of some other people as well. This will help you to understand them better, and pave the way to more meaningful relationships.

It's unlikely that your color will prove to be a "pure" one—100 percent Red or Blue or White or Yellow. Nature isn't that simple. Instead, even those individuals with a strong affinity for one particular color will find it tinged with traces of others. When your test results reflect high scores in more than one personality area—that is, when two colors are almost equal in strength—you may at first find it difficult to identify the stronger one. Don't worry. As you read further, the motives and characteristics of each personality type will become clear, and you should have little trouble determining your primary personality color.

As you seek your true identity, you may begin to see yourself differently—and more accurately. You will become aware of your many strengths. And though some of your negative suspicions about yourself may also be verified, you will be comforted in knowing that you are not alone—we all have a balance of strengths and weaknesses in our personality makeup. Don't be discouraged by any weaknesses you have. In the later chapters of the book, I will show you how to turn limitations into assets.

In taking the Hartman Personality Profile, be as honest as you can. There's no point in deceiving yourself about who you really are. Dishonesty will only limit your knowledge of yourself and confuse your relationships with others.

Here are some other suggestions that will assist you in completing the profile:

1. Unless otherwise directed, answer every question from your earliest recollections of how you were as a child. Since your personality is innate and comes with your soul, this will provide a more accurate perspective on who you innately are as opposed to who you have become.
2. At first, mark the choices that come to you most readily. Skip the more difficult questions, but return to them later.
3. Do not hesitate to ask others for feedback—especially people who may not agree with you. Their opinions can help you balance your self-assessment.
4. Strive to choose answers that are most often typical of your thoughts and/or actions. Subconsciously, you may want to avoid identifying—or facing—the real you, but tough it out. Don't cheat yourself by prettying things up. The potential rewards for honesty are too great.
Now, enjoy the profile. You are about to determine your true color.
5. Some of you may consciously seek ways to "beat" the profile and actually look for patterns in order to skew the profile results. Others may perceive the profile design to be oversimplified. I caution you not to be fooled. The profile has been successfully used by hundreds of thousands of readers for over ten years in producing reliable insights. The results have reinforced my confidence that your honesty and the profile's simplicity are a tough team to beat.

THE HARTMAN PERSONALITY PROFILE

Directions: Mark an "X" by the one word or phrase that best describes what you are like *most of the time*. Choose only one response from each group. After you've finished question 30, total your scores for each letter.

PERSONALITY STRENGTHS AND LIMITATIONS

1. a) __ opinionated
   b) __ nurturing
   c) __ inventive
   d) __ outgoing

2. a) __ power-oriented
   b) __ perfectionist
   c) __ indecisive
   d) __ self-centered

3. a) __ dominant
   b) __ sympathetic
   c) __ tolerant
   d) __ enthusiastic

4. a) __ self-serving
   b) __ suspicious
   c) __ unsure
   d) __ naive

5. a) __ decisive
   b) __ loyal
   c) __ contented
   d) __ playful

6. a) __ arrogant
   b) __ worry prone
   c) __ silently stubborn
   d) __ flighty

7. a) __ assertive
   b) __ reliable
   c) __ kind
   d) __ sociable

8. a) __ bossy
   b) __ self-critical
   c) __ reluctant
   d) __ a teaser

9. a) __ action-oriented
   b) __ analytical
   c) __ easygoing
   d) __ carefree

10. a) __ critical of others
    b) __ overly sensitive
    c) __ shy
    d) __ obnoxious

11. a) __ determined
    b) __ detail conscious
    c) __ a good listener
    d) __ a party person

12. a) __ demanding
    b) __ unforgiving
    c) __ unmotivated
    d) __ vain

13. a) __ responsible
    b) __ idealistic
    c) __ considerate
    d) __ happy

14. a) __ impatient
    b) __ moody
    c) __ passive
    d) __ impulsive

15. a) __ strong-willed
    b) __ respectful
    c) __ patient
    d) __ fun-loving

16. a) __ argumentative
    b) __ unrealistic
    c) __ directionless
    d) __ an interrupter

17. a) __ independent
    b) __ dependable
    c) __ even-tempered
    d) __ trusting

18. a) __ aggressive
    b) __ frequently depressed
    c) __ ambivalent
    d) __ forgetful

19. a) __ powerful
    b) __ deliberate
    c) __ gentle
    d) __ optimistic

20. a) __ insensitive
    b) __ judgmental
    c) __ boring
    d) __ undisciplined

21. a) __ logical
    b) __ emotional
    c) __ agreeable
    d) __ popular

22. a) __ always right
    b) __ guilt prone
    c) __ unenthusiastic
    d) __ uncommitted

23. a) __ pragmatic
    b) __ well-behaved
    c) __ accepting
    d) __ spontaneous

24. a) __ merciless
    b) __ thoughtful
    c) __ uninvolved
    d) __ a show-off

25. a) __ task-oriented
    b) __ sincere
    c) __ diplomatic
    d) __ lively

26. a) __ tactless
    b) __ hard to please
    c) __ lazy
    d) __ loud

27. a) __ direct
    b) __ creative
    c) __ adaptable
    d) __ a performer

28. a) __ calculating
    b) __ self-righteous
    c) __ self-deprecating
    d) __ disorganized

29. a) __ confident
    b) __ disciplined
    c) __ pleasant
    d) __ charismatic

30. a) __ intimidating
    b) __ careful
    c) __ unproductive
    d) __ afraid to face facts

Strengths and Limitations Totals

___Total a's   ___Total b's   ___Total c's   ___Total d's

Enter your totals in the proper spaces. Now let's see if you respond the same way to the following situations as you did to groups of descriptive words. Again, pick only one answer, and record your totals for each letter at the end of the section.

SITUATIONS

31. If I applied for a job, a prospective employer would most likely hire me because I am:
    a. Driven, direct, and delegating.
    b. Deliberate, accurate, and reliable.
    c. Patient, adaptable, and tactful.
    d. Fun-loving, spirited, and casual.

32. When involved in an intimate relationship, if I feel threatened by my partner, I:
    a. Fight back with facts and anger.
    b. Cry, feel hurt, and plan revenge.
    c. Become quiet, withdrawn, and often hold anger until I blow up over some minor issue later.
    d. Distance myself and avoid further conflict.

33. For me, life is most meaningful when it:
    a. Is task-oriented and productive.
    b. Is filled with people and purpose.
    c. Is free of pressure and stress.
    d. Allows me to be playful, lighthearted, and optimistic.

34. As a child, I was:
    a. Stubborn, bright, and/or aggressive.
    b. Well-behaved, caring, and/or depressed.
    c. Quiet, easygoing, and/or shy.
    d. Too talkative, happy, and/or playful.

35. As an adult, I am:
    a. Opinionated, determined, and/or bossy.
    b. Responsible, honest, and/or unforgiving.

    c. Accepting, contented, and/or unmotivated.

    d. Charismatic, positive, and/or obnoxious.

36. As a parent, I am:
    a. Demanding, quick-tempered, and/or uncompromising.
    b. Concerned, sensitive, and/or critical.
    c. Permissive, easily persuaded, and/or often overwhelmed.
    d. Playful, casual, and/or irresponsible.

37. In an argument with a friend, I am most likely to be:
    a. Verbally stubborn about facts.
    b. Concerned about others' feelings and principles.
    c. Silently stubborn, uncomfortable, and/or confused.
    d. Loud, uncomfortable, and/or compromising.

38. If my friend was in trouble, I would be:
    a. Protective, resourceful, and recommend solutions.
    b. Concerned, empathetic, and loyal—regardless of the problem.
    c. Supportive, patient, and a good listener.
    d. Nonjudgmental, optimistic, and downplaying the seriousness of the situation.

39. When making decisions, I am:
    a. Assertive, articulate, and logical.
    b. Deliberate, precise, and cautious.
    c. Indecisive, timid, and reluctant.
    d. Impulsive, uncommitted, and inconsistent.

40. When I fail, I feel:
    a. Silently self-critical, yet verbally stubborn and defensive.
    b. Guilty, self-critical, and vulnerable to depression—I dwell on it.
    c. Unsettled and fearful, but I keep it to myself.
    d. Embarrassed and nervous—seeking to escape the situation.

41. If someone crosses me:
    a. I am angered, and cunningly plan ways to get even quickly.
    b. I feel deeply hurt and find it almost impossible to forgive completely. Generally, getting even is not enough.
    c. I am silently hurt and plan to get even and/or completely avoid the other person.
    d. I want to avoid confrontation, consider the situation not important enough to bother with, and/or seek other friends.

42. Work is:
    a. A most productive way to spend one's time.
    b. A healthy activity, which should be done right if it's to be done at all. Work should be done before one plays.
    c. A positive activity as long as it is something I enjoy and don't feel pressured to accomplish.
    d. A necessary evil, much less inviting than play.

43. In social situations, I am most often:
    a. Feared by others.
    b. Admired by others.
    c. Protected by others.
    d. Envied by others.

44. In a relationship, I am most concerned with being:
    a. Approved of and right.
    b. Understood, appreciated, and intimate.
    c. Respected, tolerant, and peaceful.
    d. Praised, having fun, and feeling free.

45. To feel alive and positive, I seek:
    a. Adventure, leadership, and lots of action.
    b. Security, creativity, and purpose.
    c. Acceptance and safety.
    d. Excitement, playful productivity, and the company of others.

Situations Totals

___Total a's   ___Total b's   ___Total c's   ___Total d's

Now add your totals from numbers 1–30 to those from numbers 31–45 to get grand totals. At this point, the four personality color types are assigned to each of the letters: Red for "a," Blue for "b," White for "c," and Yellow for "d."

GRAND TOTALS

Red (a) ___   Blue (b) ___   White (c) ___   Yellow (d) ___

INTERPRETING THE SCORES

The letter with the greatest total reflects your natural personality. The number of responses from multiple columns suggests the amount of blend your personality represents. You have only one basic personality, but you may be a strong blend (behaviorally) of two personalities, depending on your responses. However, your motive (not your behavior) determines your primary personality (we'll get to that in Chapter 3).

If the totals from the word-choice section do not substantially agree with the totals from the situations section, you will find further guidance in later chapters on the various colors and their motives.

A NEW IDENTITY

How does it feel to have a new identity and immediate membership in an elite group of people with the same color? Of course you are unique, but there is a strong bond of similarity between you and everyone who shares your distinct color characteristics.

You must consider this color profile a guide, not a directive engraved in stone. Few people are completely represented by just one personality type. Your color reflects your primary personality, but, like most people, you are probably a mixture of types. The degree to which you have marked responses other than those of your main color reflects this. You are, however, *always* predominantly one color, one personality. Even if your scores seem close now, by the time you've studied the whole book, you should be able to glean your primary color.

As a result of taking the Hartman Personality Profile, you have discovered the first important truth about yourself. You are either a *purist* (predominantly one color, totaling 30 or more responses to a single letter) or a *mixed personality* (two or more colors representing almost equal totals).

Suddenly, you have a new identity—perhaps an unexpected one. You did not choose it, study for it, or acquire it through conscious effort. Nor can your parents claim genetic responsibility for it. Your personality is uniquely and refreshingly *you*.

> *Do what comes naturally.*
> *That is the straightest path*
> *to inner peace.*

SECONDARY COLORS

While purists find it easy to relate to examples that reflect primary colors, individuals with strong secondary colors do not. They are more complex. The characteristics of their behavior and their motives are harder to pin down. Once you have reviewed each of the primary core colors, Chapter 9 will delve deeper into secondary colors. For now, let me offer brief insights into the common personality blends.

The most difficult color combination within one individual is the mixture of Red and Blue. If you are strong in both categories, you will often find yourself stepping on someone's toes to get a task completed (Red), but feeling guilty afterward for making that person unhappy (Blue). Chapter 3, about motives, will help you understand your constant struggle between seeking power and searching for intimacy in relationships.

Red-White combinations are difficult to read because they can be aggressive and determined one minute (Red), then quietly passive the next (White). If you fit this category, your guiding motive is power or peace rather than intimacy, which spares you the intense struggle of the Red-Blue combination. You are likely to be misunderstood because your behavior is inconsistent, and you don't easily allow others to figure you out.

If you're a Red-Yellow, you are a natural leader and find yourself in a comfortable blend. The Red dynamically directs your life, while the Yellow charismatically invites others to enjoy your friendship.

If you're a Blue-White combination, you are comfortable. You express yourself softly and sincerely. People find you determined, yet flexible. You are someone with whom almost anyone can get along.

Blue-Yellows are fun to tease. I call them my dual personalities because they can be footloose and carefree one minute, then suddenly turn very serious the next. They may pack the neighborhood kids in the van and race to the beach for a day of sun and fun. But once there, they'll start to worry about all the things they should be doing at home.

If White and Yellow are your two strong colors, you possess the best people skills of all the personalities. You are relaxed and usually take the path of least resistance. You do not experience much conflict between your colors, despite the different motives represented by each. You are comfortable with your blend and present an inviting atmosphere to those around you.

Ultimately—whoever *you* are—you are driven by one basic personality. You must find your driving core motive, even though it may be concealed by a mixture of two or more colors. All individuals have just *one* primary personality; therefore it is essential that you determine your basic color. A person with one watch knows the time, but a person with two or more is never sure.

You will find clues to your primary personality—no matter how much of a blend you may be—in the following chapter on motives. As you read, remember that you should always defer to your natural personality strengths. Do what comes naturally. This is the straightest path to inner peace.

Now let's continue—as Reds, Blues, Whites, and Yellows. We will begin by identifying and exploring the needs, desires, and motives of each of the colors in the complex and fascinating rainbow of personalities.

DEMOGRAPHICS AND PERSONALITY

Every group of people provides different demographics with the number of Reds, Blues, Whites, and Yellows they will find among them. Sales organizations are usually strong in Reds and Yellows, while finance departments are high in Blues and Whites. The general breakdown suggests that 35 percent are Blue, 25 percent are Red, 20 percent are White, and 20 percent are Yellow. While sexual identity and cultural diversity modify the appearance of a greater majority of any given color, the truth is that innately there are as many Red women as Red men, but society skews it to appear as if there are more Red men and Blue women. Many countries promote different colors through their cultural biases, but when one looks at individuals within the culture, the general breakdown remains the same around the world.

PERSONALITY FILTERS

I am often asked what role other factors play in determining one's core personality. Equally curious to people seems to be the fact that I can categorize everyone into only four core personalities. Before delving into the focus of my work, let me address these important questions.

Nothing exists in a vacuum. While *personality* is the most critical factor in determining how you will face life, it is clearly influenced by a myriad of other significant factors.

Many factors influence our personality. However, keeping it all in

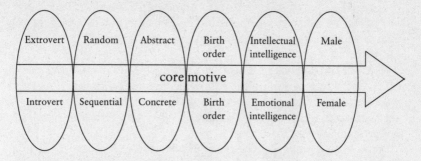

Extrovert	Random	Abstract	Birth order	Intellectual intelligence	Male
		core motive			
Introvert	Sequential	Concrete	Birth order	Emotional intelligence	Female

perspective, it is more critical to identify our driving core motive than any other factor. Once that is accurately identified, we begin to assess how the many other influences impact our driving core motive. This also speaks to the issue of how I can categorize the masses into only four primary personality groupings.

No two people are exactly alike. However, I guarantee that every individual with a Yellow personality is driven by the same core motive of *fun*. That's the magic of color coding. For example, one of my very best friends is a Yellow. We share many similar attitudes due thanks to our mutual personality. However, he is an introvert who primarily derives his energy from within. He prefers riding horses alone in the country, while I am an extrovert and primarily derive my energy from others—I prefer the interaction of many people.

I come from a family of seven children, three of whom have Yellow personalities. I have a Yellow sister and a last-born Yellow brother, and I am a middle child. While both birth order and gender clearly influence us, creating differences in our personalities, we all share the same driving core motive of *fun*.

The human face, with its limited number of variables (i.e., eyes, nose, chin, ears, hair), never produces exactly the same look. The same is true with personality. Limited to four core motives, no two people are exactly the same because of numerous personality filters.

Chapter Three

COLOR-CODED
MOTIVES

*Learn to speak
four languages fluently!*

You have just completed a profile that has revealed your personality color. The profile listed many *behaviors*. Behaviors are determined by *needs* and *wants*. For example, if a Red needs to be right, his or her behavior is likely to be opinionated. And if a Red wants a leadership position, his or her behavior is likely to be assertive and/or bossy.

Many of us are familiar with the *Peanuts* cartoon strip that features Lucy, a Red child who *needs* to be right and *wants* to lead. As a result, her behavior is dominant and bossy ("crabby" in Charlie Brown's terminology).

Just as behavior is directed by needs and wants, needs and wants are determined by *motives*. Motives are our innermost reasons. They explain *why* we think and behave as we do. They are the driving force behind our personalities. Motives are to our personalities what engines are to our cars.

Motives are the principal means of identifying a personality color.

Each color stands for one particularly strong motive. Red is for power. Blue is for intimacy. White is for peace. Yellow is for fun.

I am reminded of a White male patient of mine. (Remember: "White" is his personality color, not necessarily his race. When it comes to race, we should all be colorblind.) For five years, this patient carried on an affair with a woman he loved, while staying in a marriage that was based solely on social obligations and pressures. There was no love or companionship in his marriage. Many other men might have moved out, divorced their wives, and gone off with the other woman. But this man, a White personality, had peace as his primary motive. He didn't want to rock the boat. He wouldn't—or couldn't—confront his wife. He had great need to feel good inside, and a confrontation would have been painful. He sought to please both himself (by having an affair) and others (by staying married to his wife). At this point, his motives, needs, and wants were pulling him in different directions. It is no surprise, then, that an unhealthy behavior pattern followed. He was unhappy, and he made those around him unhappy, too.

Motives, needs, and wants are neither good nor bad. They are neutral. They become healthy or unhealthy depending on how they relate to the truth. (I will discuss truth in more depth in Chapter 14.)

The White motive of peace can be healthy if it benefits everyone involved. In the case of the married man, the White motive of peace was selfish. His unwillingness to be honest with his wife and face the consequences of his behavior kept her from finding someone else to love. It kept his girlfriend from enjoying the true intimacy that would have come from sharing his warmth and companionship on a full-time basis. And it kept him from developing his character and pursuing his needs and wants in any positive way. His motive—peace—was neutral, but his actions were unhealthy, dishonest, and selfish. He made a mess of his life and the lives of everyone involved with him.

My White patient's story has a happy ending. He learned to develop his character and clean up his motives. He scraped up enough courage to be honest with his wife. He moved into an apartment of his own—which was difficult and uncomfortable, especially for a comfort-loving White personality—and remained alone until he could decide which woman to live with. Ultimately, he chose his girlfriend. As difficult as this process was, it freed all concerned to pursue healthy and fulfilling lives. His decision was the first step in getting his motives in line with the realities of his life.

This man hit upon the key to success, no matter what the personality color. He examined his motives, realized what hardship he was creating in pursuing them in an unhealthy way, and put them in a new, positive, and healthy perspective. Being White, he still desired peace, but he recognized that he could never find real peace until he faced the truth about his behavior. By facing the truth, he defied his innate personality limitations (passiveness, indecisiveness, and the need to avoid confrontation at all costs), and developed a healthy sense of his own character. He eventually achieved tremendous success in all his personal relationships—because of his new willingness to align his motives, needs, wants, and behaviors with truth.

This brief example illustrates the strengths and limitations of the White personality, but each color has its own unique set of needs, wants, and behavior patterns, all sparked by a unique set of motives. Now that you know your own personality color, what are *your* particular motives, needs, and wants? What does *your* true color reveal about you?

Remember that while every individual has only one driving core motive, high secondary colors create blends in someone's needs, wants, and subsequent behaviors. Seek now to gain a simple and clear perspective on your core color as defined by your driving motive. In Chapter 9 we will address the more complex nuances of secondary colors and blended personalities.

REDS

Reds Are Hungry for Power

Simply stated, Reds want their own way. If they have been raised in environments where they were able to manipulate their parents and siblings, they become difficult to manage as they get older. When they have gotten their way for too long, Reds find it almost impossible to relinquish their power and freedom when they meet authorities in society (teachers, bosses, police, clergy, military officers) who refuse to grant them the total control they demand.

Reds Want to Be Productive

Reds like to work—in school, in their careers, and in their relationships. Just don't expect them to attach the same importance to things other people care about—like other people's schooling, careers, and marriages. But give them a reason to produce, and watch them take off. Reds like to get the job done. They are often workaholics. They will, however, resist being forced to do anything that doesn't interest them.

Reds Want to Look Good to Others

Reds need to appear knowledgeable. They crave approval from others for their intelligence and insight. They want to be respected even more than they want to be loved. They want to be admired for their logical, practical minds. When you deal with a Red, be precise and factual. Reds are unmoved by tears and other displays of "weakness."

Reds Shouldn't Be Taken Too Seriously

Reds are often just stating the facts as they see them, despite their antagonistic demeanor. They seldom say "in my opinion" before stating their opinions. I have seen too many Blues, Whites, and Yellows become greatly concerned over issues raised by Reds, only to discover later that the Reds were simply interested in debating. Reds enjoy a good power play. But once you get emotionally involved arguing issues, you may be disappointed and frustrated to find that a Red is no longer interested.

Reds Seek Leadership Opportunities

Despite the rigidity of the military, many young Red men and women select it as a career in order to experience leadership. Reds are often called "control freaks." They like to be in the driver's seat. Red children are often frustrated in school because teachers (often Blue personalities) won't let them take charge. If a Red can get the upper hand, he or she will. Reds are willing to pay any price for an opportunity to lead.

BLUES

Blues Are Motivated by Altruism

Blues love to do nice things for others. They look for opportunities to give up something in order to bring another person happiness. Selflessness rather than selfishness is their guiding philosophy. Many Blues are uncomfortable doing things solely for themselves. They hold doors open for people, offer rides when someone's car breaks down, contribute to charities, even devote their entire lives to helping others.

Blues Seek Intimacy

More than anything else, Blues want to love and be loved. A true Blue will sacrifice a successful career to improve an important relationship. Once considered solely a female characteristic, this nurturing is more accurately understood as a Blue personality trait.

Blues Crave Being Understood

Blues are gratified when they are listened to, when they feel understood and appreciated. They are notorious for revealing their inadequacies, because they value being known and understood so much. In the eyes of a Blue, being vulnerable is a small price to pay for the chance to connect emotionally. Blues may have their hearts broken more than most people, but they also spend much more time in love.

Blues Need to Be Remembered and Appreciated

With Blues, a simple pat on the back will not suffice. Blues expend such great effort in making the world a better place that sometimes they need to be told how wonderful they are. They need to be thanked and specifically remembered for their good deeds. They need sincere gratitude. They delight in being remembered on birthdays and other special days, especially if the remembrance is personal—a homemade anniversary card, a welcome home party, a special day that isn't on the calendar. Blues need tender loving care.

Blues Are Directed by a Strong Moral Conscience

Blues are motivated to behave in a proper, appropriate manner. They have a moral code that guides them in their decision making, their value judgments, even their leisure time. Blues enjoy being "good." Of all the personality colors, Blues come equipped with the strongest sense of integrity. A Blue would rather lose than cheat. Blues are trustworthy. Ethically, Blues are the people who should be in positions of power, but seldom are.

> *The best thing about acknowledging limitations*
> *is that, once understood, they can be turned into strengths.*

WHITES

Whites Are Motivated by Peace

Whites will do almost anything to avoid confrontation. They like to flow through life without hassle or discomfort. *Feeling* good is even more important to them than *being* good.

Whites Need Kindness

While Whites respond beautifully to thoughtfulness and amiability, they have a strong, silent stubbornness that surfaces when they are treated unkindly. They resent being scolded. They dislike harsh words. They open up instantly to people who are kind, but Whites recoil from those who are hostile. They are motivated by kindness—and can't understand why other people are unkind.

Whites Prefer Quiet Strength

Whites enjoy their quiet independence. What appears to some people as quiet desperation can show itself to be bullheadedness. Those who misinterpret the peace-loving nature of a White as an invitation to be demanding and bossy will soon meet a wall of passive resistance. Whites are tougher than people think.

Whites Like to Keep a Low Profile

Whites like to be asked their opinions. They won't volunteer them. They value the respect of others, but they rarely go out of their way to seek it. They need to be coaxed to talk about their skills, hobbies, and interests.

Whites Are Independent

Unlike Reds and Blues, who want to control others, Whites seek only to avoid being controlled. They simply refuse to be under another's thumb, especially when treated without the respect they feel they deserve. Whites want to do things their own way, in their own time. They don't ask much of others, and resent it when others demand things from them. They often comply with unreasonable demands—just to keep peace. They will express their anger and frustration only when they can no longer stand being bossed around. Whites don't like to be pushed, and they can be fearsome when they finally "blow up."

Whites Are Motivated by Other People's Desires

Whites are open to the recommendations of others on ways to resolve any and all situations. White executives value new management ideas from employees. White children welcome help—they are receptive students. Whites make agreeable dates. They are interested in making sure the other person has a good time, and are willing to do whatever the other person wants. Whites, however, want suggestions—not demands.

YELLOWS

Yellows Value Play

Yellows consider life to be a party. And they're hosting. One father (Blue) was disappointed when his son (Yellow) preferred spending time with friends instead of with him. I reminded the father that his son was motivated by fun, and suggested that he should try to come up with activities that his son felt were exciting. It was the "better offer" principle—and it worked. Yellows just want to have fun.

Yellows Welcome Praise

Yellows need to be noticed. Little else improves a relationship with a Yellow more than praise. Yellows need to know they are valued and approved of. Yellows often act as though they have the world by the tail, but they do have their fears and frustrations—which they rarely confide until they know they are emotionally safe. Safety is most effectively evidenced to Yellows through praise.

Yellows Need Emotional Connections

Yellows often appear so nonchalant that people think they don't care about anything. Nothing could be further from the truth. Yellows need a great deal of attention. They need to be stroked. Yellows enjoy touching. To them, physical contact is often the most direct, comfortable intimate connection.

Yellows Want to Be Popular

Yellows like to be center stage. Social acceptance is very important to them. Friendships command a high priority in their lives because popularity answers one of their basic needs—the need for general approval. Yellows are highly verbal. They relish good conversation, but they can also simply go with the flow. Yellows can superficially chitchat with the best of them.

Yellows Like Action

Easily bored, Yellows seek adventure. They can never sit still for long. They choose friends who, like them, refuse to allow the "boring details" to get in the way of the most important thing in life—play. Ironically, numerous people are currently misdiagnosed as having ADD (Attention Deficit Disorder) when, in fact, they are merely Yellow personalities struggling with their innate inability to sit still very long and/or stay focused.

PERSONALITY OVERVIEW

Now that you are familiar with the motives, needs, wants, and behaviors of each personality color, let's get an overview of the basics.

	RED	BLUE	WHITE	YELLOW
MOTIVE	Power	Intimacy	Peace	Fun
NEEDS	To look good (technically)	To be good (morally)	To feel good (inside)	To look good (socially)
	To be right	To be understood	To be allowed their own space	To be noticed
	To be respected	To be appreciated	To be respected	To be praised
	Approval from a select few	Acceptance	Tolerance	Approval from the masses
WANTS	To hide insecurities (tightly)	To reveal insecurities	To withhold insecurities	To hide insecurities (loosely)
	Productivity	Quality	Kindness	Happiness
	Leadership	Autonomy	Independence	Freedom
	Challenging adventure	Security	Contentment	Playful adventure

Having identified all four personalities, the motives behind them, and personality filters, we will continue in the following chapters to examine the strengths and limitations of each personality color. Remember that all of the characteristics of *your* primary color may not reflect your own personality. But the motives, needs, and wants behind those characteristics do influence you.

You will notice that occasionally the same characteristics appear in two different personalities. This is due to the fact that there are similarities as well as differences between the colors. Generally, however, you will find one color that fits your behavior better than any other.

As you identify your strengths, you can get acquainted with your limitations at the same time. Limitations are nothing to be afraid of. Each color has much to learn from the others. But we are most effective in understanding other people when we see them whole— treating them as complete personalities rather than focusing on either their strengths or limitations.

Reading about one's limitations can be painful. It can be very difficult to acknowledge areas in which we are weak. (Especially you Reds!) We prefer to shield ourselves from that information. So prepare yourself for a little discomfort. "It will only hurt for a moment," as the doctor says. Take stock in the fact that the cure is better than the disease. And, in this case, the cure is knowledge. The best thing about acknowledging limitations is that, once understood, they can be turned into strengths.

> *We are most effective in understanding other people*
> *when we see them whole—treating them as*
> *complete personalities rather than focusing on either*
> *their strengths or limitations.*

Chapter Four

PERSONALITY
IN PERSPECTIVE

*To experience passion, one must have
an accurate sense of oneself and feel
a congruence between who one is
and the life one lives.*

The Hartman Personality Theory identifies three essential dimensions that must operate in unison for an individual to be fully human—fully alive. All three play distinctly different albeit highly integrated roles in creating a complete person.

THE PERSONALITY

The personality plays the central role of the three critical elements. Each personality is driven by a core motive, which you have just identified after completing the Hartman Personality Profile. It represents each individual's innate wants, needs, and natural behaviors. While no individual is limited from embracing any strengths or limitations of all personalities, he or she can never abandon their innate core personality. Even when people strive to alter their core personality by purposely choosing behaviors of another personality, their very being cannot deny who they innately are.

   I was conducting a business retreat in Oxnard, California, with a small group of twenty executives on a weekend team-building retreat. Monica listened intently with the others while I presented the basics of the Color Code. Just prior to our first morning break, she blurted out, "I am her! I can't believe this! After all I've done to free myself of her distasteful memory, I am, in the end, *her!*"

As we discussed her sudden awareness, Monica explained that the "her" she referred to was her mother, for whom she felt no love and, indeed, very little regard at all. She had pledged never to be like this woman who had proved such a destructive force in her childhood. On the other hand, she adored her father and had spent endless hours mimicking his strengths and choosing a lifestyle similar to his own.

The accuracy and simplicity of the Color Code makes it relatively easy to identify your own true core personality and the personalities of others with whom you interact as well. Monica quickly identified that she and her mother shared the same core Blue personality, while her father was a Red. In distancing herself from her mother, she had also painfully detached from herself. Developing the positive Red strengths of her father was extremely positive but *not* with the negative motive of replacing her own innate Blue strengths. Monica could have replaced her own innate Blue limitations that she shared with her mother, but her core motive of intimacy could never be completely ignored. Subsequently, it haunted her and, despite all her efforts, the minute she heard my presentation, she recognized her true identity. Our personality comes with each of our individual souls and must be respected and nurtured as vital to our being.

DEVELOPING CHARACTER

Character breathes substance into the personality. My next book, *The Character Code*, brings a tremendous integrity to the Color Code. While the miracle of accurate self-identity is awe-inspiring, it is essentially just the beginning of knowing ourselves and what we're all about. For example, after completing the Hartman Personality Profile, you now know your core personality complete with driving core motive, wants, needs, and natural behaviors. You cannot, however, identify the ratio of your strengths to your limitations.

Without the Character Code, you cannot easily identify what behaviors you need to develop from the other personalities. You cannot readily see which of your limitations create difficulties for you when interacting with others and why. This requires a process called "charactering" and will be introduced using an instrument called the Hartman Character Profile in my next book. In order to complete the process of becoming your best self, you must identify and develop the personality traits unnatural to your innate personality, while maintaining and nurturing your own driving core motive.

Charactering is a challenging adventure. It is never easy to balance accepting yourself as you are, while simultaneously stretching to embrace new gifts to replace current deficiencies. If you think this is easy, you have probably never personally engaged in the process of charactering yourself. It requires a lifelong effort.

For now, a simple illustration will have to suffice. It will help you see the strong correlation between personality and character. There are four general ways to identify the different levels people can operate on.

Charactered	Healthy	Unhealthy	Sick
+ positive traits of each personality other than their own innate color	+ positive traits within your own innate personality	− negative traits within your own innate personality	− negative traits of each personality other than your own innate color

The *charactered* dimension represents people who use the positive strengths of each personality outside their own innate color. While the Color Code clearly requires that you accept your core driving motive as innate and unchanging, it also embraces the reality that you can choose to develop every positive gift the other personalities provide.

The *healthy* dimension identifies people who use the positive gifts they were naturally born to exude. My professional experience indicates that most people could comfortably survive their entire lifetime by simply relying solely on their own innate personality strengths, rather than having to develop outside gifts.

The *unhealthy* dimension categorizes people who go through life using the innate limitations of their natural personality. Most people have more limiting behavior traits in their own innate core color than in any other personality.

The *sick* dimension represents the ultimate in poor mental health. People who use the negative behavior traits of any (and sometimes every) other personality than their own are extremely difficult to identify accurately, let alone relate well with. Whenever I ask a seminar participant to identify the core color of an ex-spouse where there has been extreme abuse or dysfunction, they will often shake their head and say, "Can I use the color Black?!" They can't readily see the ex-spouse's core personality color because they can remember only their various limitations from multiple personality sources.

Most people operate in one of the following dual dimensions: The charactered-healthy dimension, healthy-unhealthy dimension, or unhealthy-sick dimension. One of the positive dynamics of becoming charactered is that if you struggle with a limitation outside your core color (sick dimension), you can focus on a strength of another color (charactered dimension) to overcome it. In so doing you can leap from the sick dimension to becoming charactered without having to move individually through the other dimensions as well. Developing unnatural strengths requires arduous work and tremendous humility in order to succeed.

CREATIVE PASSION

Finally, passion breathes life into both personality and character. With personality and character you can see the lights on in the house, but there is no guarantee anybody's home. Passion turns the light on when the person is home, creating a powerful synergy between the two. Passion cannot be forced. It must be genuine and flow from one's very being. No one can develop your passion. It is like breathing. You must do it on your own or you will die. Sadly, we live in a society where far too many people die years before they are buried. Passion makes the difference in why people get out of bed in the morning and how they feel about themselves when they fall back into bed at night. **To experience passion, one must have an accurate sense of oneself and feel a congruence between who one is and the life one lives.** If this aspect of the color method interests you particularly, you will want to find a copy of *The Character Code* when it is widely available.

Having put personality in its proper perspective against the backdrop of the added elements of character and passion, let's refocus on identifying our core personalities. That's where it all begins and, like constructing a building, unless we get the foundation correct, nothing is going to line up properly later on. Our personalities are rooted in our innate driving core motives and offer powerful insights into our wants, needs, and natural strengths and limitations.

Part Two

✖✖✖

THE
COLORS

Chapter Five

REDS:
THE POWER WIELDERS

Reds have the most dominant, intimidating personality.
Expressing themselves emotionally is uncomfortable
and creates the vulnerability they typically avoid.

ACTIVE AND PRODUCTIVE

The Red personality moves forcefully through life. As Helen Keller said, "Life is either a daring adventure or nothing at all." Reds are highly committed to causes, and find themselves determined to accomplish whatever life places before them. In fact, they seek challenges, and, with rare exception, they rise to the occasion. As a result of their tenacious nature, Reds often are successful. Their success comes primarily from business and task-oriented activities, while Blues, for example, usually experience their success through deep interpersonal relationships or in highly creative fields. Reds seek action and results. They crave productivity. They measure their success by how much (versus how well) they accomplish. Simply stated, Reds get things done.

VISIONARY

I would gladly follow a healthy Red to the ends of the earth. They are always looking toward the future and putting puzzle pieces together in their heads. People often accuse Reds of simply acting without giving their actions a second thought. In fact, the opposite is true! Reds hate to fail. Therefore, they always ask the question of themselves, "What if I fail?"

Rob is a Red CEO and the youngest brother in a family-owned business. His two older brothers are Blue and constantly worry about details such as petty employee complaints and current cash flow. Meanwhile, Rob is focused on the future by creating new companies as spin-offs of their already successful business and developing personnel for stronger leadership roles as the companies evolve. Reds instinctively see the future and take the steps necessary to successfully take them there.

While most other personalities (Blues in particular) usually stop right there with the realization that they, indeed, might fail, Reds have already instinctively developed an alternate plan. They think to themselves, "Now if the original plan fails, I will do this or even that." While others stop because of fear, Reds offset their fear with rational alternatives and simply do what needs to be done.

INSENSITIVE AND SELFISH

Reds are so clearly defined that one finds it difficult to believe they would not instantly recognize the color of their personality. Many do. But often the most critical stumbling block for Reds in identifying themselves is denial. Reds are proud and known to parade their values and opinions in the faces of all others. They can present themselves in a distant and insensitive manner. A mother had promised to take her Red teenaged daughter to the library in order to study for a school report. Just before they were to leave, the mother and father engaged in a traumatic argument, and the father threatened divorce. The daughter witnessed the entire one-hour ordeal. The mother was devastated and crying uncontrollably when her daughter said matter-of-factly, "Mom, will we still be able to get to the library before it closes tonight?!" Only Reds can be so insensitive to the feelings of others! This weakness may explain why Reds are more successful at developing and promoting ideas, events, and business ventures than quality relationships.

"KING OF THE JUNGLE"

Considering their productive and tenacious natures, it is no wonder Reds exude incredible self-confidence. They appear strong and certain of themselves. As such, few people are willing to confront them. This strength bestows on them the most feared status of all personalities. They are "King of the Jungle." When people seek advice and direction, they find Reds are most helpful. Reds have a sense of what is right, and often express themselves in a manner few people can logically refute. Many Reds are notably intelligent and skilled in making good decisions. Subsequently, others choose to follow. And why not? When you find a good doctor, why seek another? It is their uncanny and enviable ability to be right so often that influences others to place them in leadership positions. It is the Reds' natural gift and desire to lead that drives them to select opportunities for advancement to the top of many organizations, businesses, and other affiliations.

> *Lead, follow, or*
> *get out of the way.*

Perhaps the most intriguing complexity of Reds' apparent self-confidence *and* frustrating arrogance lies in their deep insecurity. They seek the very acceptance and understanding they often refuse to give others. However, this need is placed so deeply within their hearts where they can skillfully protect it, that it is often well hidden from their rational mind's eye. Deferring to their logic, they refuse to acknowledge emotional vulnerability. As youths, while yet somewhat sensitive to emotions, their insecurities are more clearly viewed. Unfortunately, with age and increased skill at logic, they usually keep their deep emotional insecurities adeptly disguised from others. With time, they often lose an accurate perspective and actually believe they have no need for emotion. The irony is that in order for Reds to experience a full and intimate life, they must expose themselves to perhaps their greatest fear—their emotional insecurity and need to be loved and accepted.

DEMANDING AND CRITICAL

Reds are highly critical of other people. Most Reds are verbally critical, while some remain quietly dissatisfied with others' performance in life. They are rather impatient with human inadequacy, and feel nothing short of efficiency should be tolerated. While Reds are not as perfectionistic as Blues (thank our lucky stars), they do want a job done right and expediently. They have no tolerance for mental dullness, lack of common sense, or unpreparedness. They expect results, and spare little time reminding others of their expectations. They can be highly biased and reactionary in their judgments of others. The irony lies in how emotionally based this behavior is, when one realizes the logical rigidity that permeates the thinking and behavior of most Reds.

INSECURE

Reds can bury their own personal insecurities deep enough so as to not consciously feel the pain of their exposure. Subsequently, they are often insensitive to the raw nerves they touch in others who are less willing (or able) to hide their vulnerability. Reds mean no harm to others as long as the Red's productivity is enhanced and they are proved to be right. Reds have little sympathy for obstacles to progress, regardless of the source—be it employees, children, spouses, or friends.

MUST BE RIGHT

Driven by their need to hide emotional insecurities, they demand to be right. They do not ask whether they are perceived by others as right. They simply state that they *are* right 100 percent of the time. Even after evidence dictates that Reds are inaccurate, they often brush their error aside as a misunderstanding or misinterpretation.

> *Reds are so decisive.*
> *If they make 51 percent of the decisions right*
> *they're happy, because they know the other 49 percent*
> *would have worked, but you screwed up.*

A family was looking for an office building but didn't know the exact address. One teenager remarked, "I think it's near the corner of Moody and Lincoln." Her Red older sister, Ginny, replied, "Oh, no it's not. It couldn't be there. I know all the buildings over there." Ginny was driving and ignored the suggestion. One hour later, after several telephone calls, they pulled up in front of the office building right on the corner of Moody and Lincoln. When they arrived home, their mother suggested that in the future perhaps *all* suggestions should be entertained with an open mind. To this Ginny scoffed, "I know she didn't say Moody and Lincoln. She must have said somewhere else. After all, I'm the one who finally found it, didn't I?!"

COMPETITIVE AND BOLD

Reds are daring and bold—both traits luring them away from the business world or home duties to excel in adventures such as mountain climbing, hang gliding, or building their own homes. However, Reds can also find great excitement in promoting an innovative concept or gaining the competitive edge in the business world. Combining their brave and competitive strengths, Reds are bold within organizational structures as well as in personal settings.

In business, at home with friends, or engaged in hobbies, Reds are certain to get their share of the pie. Simply stated, they are typically selfish. They know what they want and often control events and people in order to achieve it. They are not much concerned with guilt feelings or compassion for others. Ironically, very insecure Reds seek attention and make certain that whatever inconvenience they must endure (e.g., illnesses or accidents) is shared by others in their life.

TENACIOUS AND TAXING

Whether ill or in good health, a Red is a taxing personality. They are so tenacious and bossy that they begin to wear you down rather rapidly. Reds remind me of houseguests who want the household schedule adapted to *their* personal schedule. After a short period of time with this overbearing personality, a change and a breath of fresh air is not only welcome—it's necessary.

In their leadership, Reds can also be bossy. They often expect subordinates to remember their place in the pecking order and respond accordingly. They are often hard to work for or live with because they order others around with little regard for established schedules, family commitments, or professional concerns. If they are challenged they often become aggressive due to their intimidating nature and arrogant attitude. Whether they maintain a position of leader or follower, Reds are often inclined to make their point aggressively to whoever crosses their path. They are not shamed by public awareness of their demanding behavior. Without much tact, they relentlessly pursue elements in their life that need attention, whether it be a misplaced hotel reservation or a child's unacceptable report card. Aggression makes a point without concern for other individual feelings. Unhealthy Reds are typically aggressive.

ASSERTIVE AND DETERMINED

On the other hand, positive assertion flows as easily to the healthy Red personality as water falls from a duck's back. They need no coaxing to establish their position in any situation. "Knowing" that they are right helps convince Reds of their position while intimidating the other parties. Business groups are *always* enhanced by the presence of healthy Reds. Reds speak their minds directly and honestly, regardless of the effect it will have on their popularity.

They are very strong-willed and determined. Reds take firm stands and expect others to follow. Others often do follow when Reds present themselves and their ideas with clean motives. However, this same strength of determination can also be experienced as a limitation when Reds are disagreeable or argumentative.

DISAGREEABLE

Disagreeable is a word that comes to mind when pondering Red limitations. Whether it is for the sake of maintaining the fine art of debate or a driving need to convert the world to their beliefs, Reds can be quite opinionated and stubborn on most topics, ranging from how to pay a bill (by cash, check, or credit card) to meeting deadlines ("I don't care if I don't need it by Wednesday. You still need to complete it because I told you to!").

A logical complement to their disagreeable nature and their logical minds is that Reds enjoy the merits of verbal arguments. They seem comfortable with this style of verbal expression. It requires very little for a Red to confront another person. They are so comfortable, in fact, that they rarely even recognize the conflict they've created.

Reds are not natural conversationalists. They are natural lecturers. The ability to listen and empathize are often limited traits in the Red personality. These limitations cause many Reds to experience loneliness, although they rarely admit that they are lonely. They often blame their loneliness on others (e.g., "my husband left me in this mess without a friend in the world"—spoken by a Red woman ten years after their divorce. Or, "If people were only more educated or intelligent they could appreciate me").

RESOURCEFUL AND SELF-RELIANT

Reds, because of their resourcefulness and self-reliance, often challenge those in authority and successfully control their own destiny. If I were ever caught in an emergency or distressing situation, I would most prefer to be in the company of a Red personality. They eat, sleep, and breathe action. No situation will get the best of them until they have exhausted every possibility for remedy. They simply don't give up easily. They are rarely intimidated or threatened by life's obstacles. They have a great competitive sense, and their opponents (whether it be an earthquake or a mother-in-law) will not find an easy victory.

RELENTLESS AND IMPATIENT

If you need an agent, a fund-raising chairperson, or a political ally, advertise for the Red personality characteristics. Nobody promotes like a Red. I have already alluded to their bold, assertive, and competitive nature. They are also pragmatic. Rather than concerning themselves with the frills, they get at the heart of problems and quickly demand a resolution.

The Red personality
moves forcefully through life.

Reds throw themselves into causes. If they feel you have something worthwhile to offer, they will gladly do what they can to assist you. Reds are relentless in their commitment to causes they believe in. They are as comfortable promoting others as themselves when they are committed to a concept. When converted to a concept, Reds know no equal. They are difficult to convince but equally difficult to restrain once converted. Upon discovering a child's dancing talents, Red parents drive long distances and provide financial assistance to see their child succeed. (In fact, this book would most likely never have been published had it not been for the assistance of three close Red friends. Two gave me the confidence to write, with their numerous suggestions, time, and support. The other met me for early morning breakfasts, demanding to read a new chapter every time we met. When I left a message to cancel our first breakfast, my friend called me at eleven the night before our scheduled breakfast and asked if I was canceling because I hadn't completed my "homework." She was right. I was sliding and needed her encouragement.)

Reds usually pursue whatever they want (whether it is healthy or unhealthy) until they have it. They want everyone to respond whenever and however they deem appropriate. They struggle with impatience. They can't wait for others to "grow up" and behave the way Reds know they ought to behave. Red infants demand to be held *immediately* upon request (crying). Red salespeople not only demand that you listen but also require you to answer silly questions ("Now really, Mrs. Meriweather, wouldn't you rather be driving a new Cadillac rather than the old one your friends have seen you driving for years?"). Red parents often demand respect rather than concerning themselves with earning it. Red employers can't tolerate indecisiveness or poor productivity. One of the gravest errors in Reds' leadership style is impatience. They typically step in too quickly, and often too harshly as well.

Bob is a powerful CEO. He wastes little time getting to the point and searching for the bottom line. He has no patience with people who "waste" his time with all the details. His Blue controller, John, needs to constantly cover all the bases of the company and insists on sending lengthy memos to Bob regarding material Bob has no desire to read.

Bob told me he was tired of John's irritating memos and was going to tell him to stop writing them with the expectation of discussing them at a future date. I reminded him of the Color Code and how from John's Blue perspective it was most important to have Bob's appreciation of his hard work and support in decisions he was making to feel secure. Bob agreed to allow John to continue with the memos, but requested that John highlight the three paragraphs he felt were the most significant, as if Bob had only three minutes in his day to review the memo. To date, that compromise has kept them on the same winning team for years.

Often the most critical stumbling block for Reds
in identifying themselves is denial.

CALCULATING AND MANIPULATIVE

Reds are often calculating and manipulative in order to control lives and produce results. Reds don't casually toss their lives in the air and hope for a favorable wind. They create their own wind and attempt to force life to blow in their direction.

I have seen the lives of close friends temporarily destroyed by the shrewd manipulation of an unhealthy Red personality. As a young professional, I worked for a drug-prevention program where the boss was just such a Red. Many of my colleagues were former drug users and had confided in our boss many of the events, feelings, and fears they were struggling with in their pursuit of a drug-free life. He hired these individuals knowing their personal histories and then used this knowledge to back them down when they inquired about raises, promotions, or other work-related expectations that he disliked.

Comments like *"Now* I understand why your father threw you out of the house. Were you this defiant when *he* asked small favors of you?" or, "You still expect something else to make you happy—first drugs and now more money" were common in staff or individual meetings with this director.

LACK INTIMACY ORIENTATION

Without question, the greatest deterrent to a Red's success in experiencing a quality lifestyle lies in their inability to be intimate with other people. They are so determined and productive that their lack of intimacy is often ignored or denied as a significant concern. Unless corrected, it does eventually relegate Reds to a supervisory "caretaker of humanity" role, as opposed to an involved "member of the human team."

As businesspeople, they can often be simultaneously brilliant and brutal. Unfortunately, this calculating mind reduces true intimacy to an impractical notion as well as to a highly unlikely possibility. One Red patient eventually lost the woman of his dreams because he kept postponing their marriage in order to get the right timing for the best tax break. Intimacy requires equality, and a competitive Red with a calculating mind doesn't often find equality to be a worthy ambition.

Reds probably watch more television and put in more overtime at work than any other personality. Unfortunately, this also diverts them from ever having to face the issue of intimacy in relationships. They rarely have hobbies (as do Blues and Whites) or friends (as do Yellows). They are lost without their career or family. On a recent river rafting trip, a Red could hardly wait three hours to find a phone so he could call his wife and see how she was doing. It sounds very romantic, but the reality was that he had not been away from her in ten years of marriage and, despite being with close friends, he felt lost and uncomfortable without her at his side. Truth is, he is rarely *with* her even when he is at home. Rather, he is constantly working on a book or writing an article. He rarely just sits with her. But he *needs* her. And needing his affection, she plays along with his "attentive" phone calls, acting as if his sun rises and sets with her.

Reds are often the first to remind you they are eager to leave home and be out on their own at eighteen years of age. They are also the first to come home (whether physically or emotionally) and seek the comfort of a loving and caring family. Some Reds will milk every last ounce of sympathy from any illness (especially Red men). Other Reds hide their pain and discomfort. These behaviors are dishonest and selfish. They do not lead to genuine intimacy. Rather, they most often leave a Red individual skeptical and lonely.

This emptiness often creates a very angry individual who *feels* very deeply his or her powerlessness to demand quality relationships. One forty-year-old patient told me he had never learned to love. He realized it through our sessions working with his son. One session he wept, "I finally woke up at forty and realized I did not know the slightest thing about living and loving." This anger comes from the frustration of Reds wanting to *control* rather than *share* their destiny, and with Reds it lies at the very base of their insecurities. They want a loving relationship but find they are powerless to control the process. As a result, many abandon their wants for a more controlled lifestyle.

It's lonely at the top,
but you eat better.

RED LIMITATIONS

Reds are a myriad of dynamic limitations. They are not subtle and undefined. Reds are actually easily detected and understood. They can be difficult to live and work with unless they get their own way. Reds are often taxing and demanding. They will argue "at the drop of a hat." Their selfish nature is a constant reminder to other personalities that Reds will always consider themselves number one. They are often insensitive and arrogant, which creates distance and distrust. Intimacy is, perhaps, their least developed skill. As a result of their critical and disagreeable nature, they argue from logic and are capable of manipulating with constant mind calculation. Highly verbal individuals, Reds often criticize and intimidate others. They are particularly guilty of denial ("Who, me?"). They are often surprised to find out that others may see them in a negative light, but they see finding fault with others to be an essential part of their daily routine. Their tactless and stubborn behavior tends to expose a frustrated individual who blooms in positions of power and control, yet shrinks from social life when leadership opportunities run dry. Always processing a new thought, these often brilliant individuals must be constantly aware of their limitations in order to avoid cutting themselves off from experiencing a quality life.

RED STRENGTHS

Healthy Reds are the lifeblood of humanity. They are the movers and shakers of society. They are known for their dominating nature. They are the powerful leaders and responsible delegators. Red personalities can be an asset to any organization. They enjoy competition and challenges. They call easily upon their inner core for self-motivation and direction.

They focus precisely when setting goals and tenaciously assert their rights (and the rights of any organization, person, or cause they value). They value productivity and success, and willingly pay the price for both. They enjoy organizational teamwork as well as individualism. Reds promote most aspects of life with self-confidence and tenacity. They are constant reminders of the power derived from rational thinking and assertive communication. They are the standard we use to measure our intellectual prowess. They model those leadership skills we seek to emulate. Reds represent the fire used by early theorists in the nature theory. Their lights continue to burn brightly as a beacon of strength and productivity, warming and reassuring us with their resourceful and protective nature.

"For Reds, winning isn't everything,
it's the only thing."

RED STRENGTHS

AS AN INDIVIDUAL

- excels with logical thinking
- committed to a productive lifestyle
- dynamic and direct
- thrives on independence
- natural leader
- highly resourceful (strong survivor)
- creative in crises

AS A COMMUNICATOR

- operates in a very logical, sensible manner
- direct and honest with opinions
- communicates thoughts well verbally
- directs the conversation in a productive, pragmatic way
- tells others where they stand in a relationship

AS A GOAL SETTER

- natural goal setter—sets goals comfortably and confidently
- maintains strong sense of perspective (sees the whole picture)
- highly disciplined
- highly productive with follow-through
- makes decisions quickly and easily
- strong goal orientation (wants to move up the ladder)

AS A CAREER PERSON

- thrives in leadership positions
- comfortable with power (as long as he or she has it)
- excellent organizer
- delegates superbly
- quick to make decisions and handles responsibilities well
- self-motivated
- thrives on competition
- dynamic and assertive
- highly task-oriented and efficient

- confident of ability to achieve
- trusts own business instincts—difficult to discourage

AS A PARENT

- excellent decision maker
- unquestioned as leader in home
- assumes responsibility for protecting family
- excellent provider
- quick with good advice and direction
- promotes group cohesiveness or comfortable being alone
- promotes children's activities

AS A CHILD

- communicates what he or she is thinking
- highly verbal
- strong sense of independence
- willing to risk and try new experiences
- takes charge of situation when parents are gone
- capable of bouncing back in negative environment
- maintains the power to turn a poor situation around
- believes in self—maintains high self-esteem

AS A FRIEND

- direct and quick with suggestions
- great in emergencies or disasters
- promotes group activities
- engages in conflict comfortably and directly
- productive in solving dilemmas

AS A COMMITTED COMPANION

- highly protective of companion
- loyal to the relationship
- promotes interesting experiences
- takes primary responsibility for financial needs
- reliable and dependable
- initiates interaction and activities

CAREERS MOST LIKELY TO ATTRACT REDS

Administrator	Lawyer	Building contractor
Police officer	Medical doctor	Sales
Military officer	Tax accountant	Marketing
Politician	Realtor	Clergy (minister)
Entrepreneur	Professional critic	School superintendent

Note: Reds are most naturally driven up the career ladder of success.

Of course, all personality types can be found in every occupation because of the numerous variables in every career.

PERSONALITIES WHO APPEAR TO BE REDS

HILLARY CLINTON: Tenacious and confident in her own abilities, she publicly ignores the continued allegations of her husband's infidelities. Her motto seems to be, "Just get me to the White House, Bill, where I can *do* something meaningful, then we can talk."

THE REVEREND BILLY GRAHAM: When he first went to Russia to preach about God, someone reminded him that they were all Communists (and thus atheists) over there. To this, he stood proud and said, "Not when I'm done, they won't be," and confidently took them his message of Christianity.

MADONNA: What haven't we seen already? And yet she continues to self-promote with a passion that cannot be ignored.

RED NATIONS

China
Japan
Germany

RED LIMITATIONS

AS AN INDIVIDUAL

- generally seeks to serve self (what's in it for me?)
- promotes turmoil and conflict when a personal goal is to be gained

- out of touch with own feelings
- rationalizes and denies own failings
- always right
- cannot relax and feel comfortable unless producing something
- often arrogant and defiant of authority
- inconsiderate of other's feelings (selfish)
- won't admit inadequacies for fear of losing power and control

AS A COMMUNICATOR

- unemotional and detached from feelings
- insensitive and tactless
- unappreciative of detail and beauty
- bored with "idle chatter"
- little emotional perspective makes for poor insight into others
- intuition is jaded by personal insecurities and judgments
- harsh and judgmental
- lacks ability to share self intimately
- poor listener

AS A GOAL SETTER

- impatient with self in completing goals
- too rigid with expectations of his or her destiny
- lives life on paper rather than with people
- encourages quantity rather than quality
- angers easily if goals aren't achieved or are blocked
- blames others for personal misfortunes

AS A CAREER PERSON

- seeks power in order to control others
- refuses to relax—drives self and others
- dislikes being told what to do
- may be insensitive to others in order to get ahead in business
- makes decisions too quickly
- doesn't often think the problem through or consult others for advice
- less concerned with people than task completion
- requires others' loyalty and obedience
- authoritarian and uncompromising
- critical of others and slow to give compliments
- often too competitive to enjoy the competition

AS A PARENT

- expects high performance without offering assistance
- wants strict obedience
- requires loyalty from family at all costs
- unfeeling and insensitive to children's fears and concerns
- requires the final say on important decisions
- detached from children—doesn't share self emotionally
- does not tolerate deviations from set expectations
- establishes harsh and limiting boundaries
- poor listener
- impatient with play and other nonessential trivia
- lacks insight into children's emotional needs
- difficult to please—remains unimpressed
- strong sense of right and wrong—badgers child when perceived as wrong

AS A CHILD

- expends high energy manipulating parents to get own way
- often defiant
- resists control—feels he or she knows more than parents
- critical of parents
- fights constantly with siblings for control and power
- subconsciously hides insecurities and emotional needs
- aloof and distant from family
- highly independent or requires others to entertain him or her
- demanding—parents can never do enough right
- finds it difficult to give sincere compliments
- dramatic and overreactive to pain
- expects to be catered to, especially when sick
- poor listener

AS A FRIEND

- insensitive and unemotional
- doesn't like to admit the need for friendships
- remains detached from sharing self completely
- enters friendships asking, "What's in it for me?"
- listens only when convenient
- maintains mostly rational friendships

- tries to control group activities
- expects friends to do things his or her way
- impatient with others
- negative, critical, and judgmental of others
- feels it is more important to be right than agreeable
- blunt or rude when angered
- boring
- expects to be entertained while waiting for action to begin
- stubborn
- denies any personal inadequacies or responsibility

AS A COMMITTED COMPANION

- primarily concerned with self-gratification
- gives priority to work over personal relationships
- demanding and arrogant
- hides insecurities
- critical of companion for imperfections
- lacks sensitivity
- often unaware of intimacy and rejects its priority in a relationship
- poor listener

How to Develop a Positive Connection with Reds

Do:

1. Present issues logically
2. Demand their attention and respect
3. Do your homework!
4. Be direct, brief, and specific in conversation
5. Be productive and efficient
6. Offer them leadership opportunities
7. Verbalize your feelings
8. Support their decisive nature
9. Promote their intelligent reasoning where appropriate
10. Be prepared with facts and figures
11. Respect their need to make their own decisions their own way

Don't:

1. Embarrass them in front of others
2. Argue from an emotional perspective
3. Always use authoritarian approach
4. Use physical punishment
5. Be slow and indecisive
6. Expect a personal and intimate relationship
7. Attack them personally
8. Take their arguments personally
9. Wait for them to solicit your opinion
10. Demand constant social interaction (allow for alone time)

Recommended Time-Management Tips for Reds

1. Connect with others emotionally and socially. It motivates them to be more forthright and cooperative in helping you accomplish your agenda.
2. Praise and promote the positive in others, helping them focus on shared priorities. Negative or critical attitudes and behaviors can create fear, driving people to the crisis, reaction, or escape quadrants.
3. Relax. Rome wasn't built in a day. Being overly demanding of yourself and others doesn't breed confidence or quality.
4. Set goals for yourself that you can achieve with your strong discipline. Set different goals and accept different styles when dealing with groups.
5. Avoid blaming others for failing to meet commitments, which is often a natural reaction for Reds in a crisis.
6. Think your problems through and seek others' advice when organizing your life. Reds can make hasty decisions and ignore the needs or perceptions of others who are affected.
7. Realize that you can't do it all. Be open to suggestions. Brainstorming ideas and solutions with others will save you time and improve others' morale.
8. Be careful about imposing your demands on others' time. You don't want them to feel invalidated in meeting their own agendas.

"Your gene pool could use a little chlorine."

Chapter Six

BLUES:
THE DO-GOODERS

*Life cannot bestow on anyone
a more gratifying reward
than the sincere appreciation
and trust of a Blue friend,
employer, or family member.*

EMOTIONAL AND ADMIRED

The Blues are often the most admired of all the personalities. They represent so many of the virtues we aspire to, such as honesty, empathy, self-sacrifice, loyalty, sincerity, and self-discipline. They seem to come by these virtues naturally, which creates an image of righteousness and respect. They resemble a lighted beacon of goodness and truth—a standard of excellence for the rest of us to aim for. Blues appreciate creativity, committed relationships, and disciplined achievement. With these combined assets, a strong and purposeful individual inevitably evolves. They are deeply committed, fiercely loyal, and well-behaved members of society. They are highly opinionated and tough competitors for any personality to face because they generally base all opinions on emotion and moral principle. Although Blues can be logical, they are more likely to respond to an emotional plea.

For Blues, life is emotionally a double-edged sword. On the positive side they are giving and sensitive. On the negative end they can be unforgiving and too sensitive. In fact, they can be so sensitive that they stop giving altogether. A common statement by my Blue patients is: "My emotions have ruled me all my life." Perhaps their true vulnerable point is their unbridled emotions. They want so badly to feel loved. They seek understanding from others while often refusing to understand themselves. Blues ride a powerful roller coaster of emotions. Sensitive to all kinds of trivial matters, they constantly find themselves vulnerable to emotional trauma.

Depression is frequently experienced by Blues. Allowing their hearts to rule their minds, they often think and behave irrationally. The following example comes from the journal notes of a Blue patient. It is an extreme case of the "moody Blues." However, it clearly expresses the frustration most Blues experience with accepting others' behavior when it doesn't meet their high standards and often unrealistic expectations. One evening she was reflecting on her recently dissolved marriage and wrote the following entry in her journal:

Happy Anniversary to me. I hate Jason [my husband]. I hate myself. I hate everyone, especially I hate living. I am so angry and bitter it feels like I cannot go on living because it is too uncomfortable. There is no joy—no hope. I feel only bitterness and hatred and anger at life, even at God because things are so awful. I don't even like people who want to help or support me. I wish I could just go away from everyone and everything. Nothing would be better, of course.

There is just no way around this portion of life that I can see. Perhaps if I would humble myself and pray for some relief I might get it, but I'm too mad for that even. I'm mad at God! I'm mad at Jesus! I'm mad at my parents! I'm mad at my kids! I'm mad at myself! And I *hate* Jason! I would like to see harm come to him I think. But then I'd be mad because he doesn't even have life insurance. They'd probably make me pay for his funeral too.

I just hate everything. I wish I would die, but I can't and that makes me mad too. I'm mad that life is so rotten and there's no way out. So I'll just be mad for a while longer because I don't see any viable options. But I want to be clear about communicating this: LIFE SUCKS AND I HATE ALL OF IT!!!!!

I'm so tired of being "RESPONSIBLE" for everything—even the kids. I wish someone would put me in a mental institution so I could be taken care of and have no responsibility. Then I wouldn't have to take care of my kids or anyone—or worry about Jason's bills. I hate him! I hate everything! Life seems so unfair. I don't want any of this. I don't want to grow or progress or get stronger.

I want to be left alone for a while by everyone—God included! I don't want anyone to expect anything from me because I'm tired of being capable. I'm tired of people saying how great I'm doing. I'm tired of the whole bullcrap situation. In fact, I'm even tired of writing this depressing garbage, so goodbye.

When my patient shared this with me, she no longer felt the anger displayed in her journal notes. Instead, she felt rather foolish, at times laughing while she shared her writings with me. Three days later she called me and said, "I can't believe this. I feel exactly the way I felt when I wrote those notes. What's wrong with me? I feel like I'm losing my mind!" Actually, she had never found her mind (logical thinking). She was being victimized by an undisciplined heart.

Blues see the world through positive and healthy emotional eyes as well. They care deeply for those elements of living that tug at their hearts. Weddings, parades, and birthdays are great cause for celebration, but Blues even see beyond the events and take time to reflect on the lives of those involved. They think of their own weddings and what it means to be in love. They consider all the hours it takes to prepare the costumes and mechanics of a parade as it passes by. Blues wonder how their aging grandmother feels on her seventieth birthday, and are mesmerized by a three-year-old blowing out candles on a cake. They "make" time for sharing the important moments of life.

COMMITTED AND LOYAL

Life is a sequence of commitments for Blues. Committing to relationships is perhaps their greatest strength. They enjoy companionship, and willingly sacrifice personal gain in order to share intimate relationships. Blues give freely of themselves in valued relationships.

Because of their willingness to commit to relationships, Blues enter into deep friendships that often last a lifetime. They are highly dependable, and consider a verbal promise to be as binding as any written contract. They pride themselves on maintaining long-term relationships. This admirable trait of loyalty gives credibility to the concept that Blues usually enjoy far richer relationships than any other personality type.

Blues are completely loyal to people. Blues remain committed through the good times and the bad. When one realizes the depth of their commitment, it is easy to understand why fair or foul weather has little impact on a Blue's loyalty. An excellent example of this commitment is the life of one of my Blue patients, Jenny. She had never gotten along with her mother while growing up. In fact, she struggled simply to maintain a civil relationship in the face of her mother's constant attempts to sabotage her. Her mother repeatedly humiliated her by calling her names and mocking her for her lack of popularity with boys through the dating years. Despite the obvious favoritism her mother had displayed for Jenny's older brothers and sisters, Jenny was the only one of the children willing to undertake the tremendous responsibility of caring for her invalid mother during the final painful days of her life.

Our paths crossed when Jenny sought psychological help in order to sustain the courage necessary to face this woman she had so often struggled with through the years. Jenny stayed close to her mother's bedside, despite her mother's repeated abuse and lack of appreciation, until she died. Would other personalities have been able to commit so completely?

PERFECTIONISTIC

Blues are usually perfectionists. Blues are highly critical of themselves and others. They have such unrealistic expectations that they can never satisfy themselves nor expect others to meet their level of excellence. This is one reason they are difficult employers and parents. I call my Blue daughter "Little Miss Hard-to-Please." They really do want things done right. Unfortunately, right is defined as whatever they want done and however *they* want it done.

> *Blues are the most controlling personality.*
> *They are fiercely connected to the lives they live*
> *and often appear to be emotionally unstoppable,*
> *as though on a mission from God.*

Blues are typically skeptical about their own creative talents. They are such perfectionists that they often hide their skills and abilities because they fear they aren't good enough. It's most unfortunate because Blues are so talented and perhaps the most creative of all the colors. However, Blues are highly insecure, and often fear the possibility of rejection if they display their enviable creativity and talents.

HIGHLY DEMANDING

Blues often struggle with effective verbal communication, and consequently others often have no idea what Blues' real expectations are, nor how to proceed in meeting them. Even knowing their expectations is not always helpful, because meeting their unrealistic expectations would take more energy than others are willing to give. I'm referring specifically to a parent's expectation of straight A's on a report card, spotless rooms, chores done promptly and properly every day. I wonder if Blues don't represent 80 percent of the parents who scream at their children. We would all scream if we had their perfectionistic expectations. They confuse priorities and fail to realize that a more rational approach to expectations would be healthier and far more productive.

Blue employers demand that their employees make a commitment of time and talent to the company. A report worth doing at all is worth doing well. They expect excellence even on projects that probably shouldn't require it. For example, they often stress the quality of a project as more important than the relationship (e.g., cleaning the house becomes a priority over a child's feeling loved, or an employer is more concerned with being on time than how well an employee treats the customers). (And right now the Blues are thinking, "And what's wrong with that? Why shouldn't I have both?") They don't say what they want but magically believe that everyone thinks the way they do and will produce the results they do.

Blues often don't delegate well. They stand over others like a mother hen in order to avoid error. This protection is construed by Blues to mean nurturing. It is actually distrust. They believe that by maintaining a strong emotional tie with each employee they are being supportive and promoting effective employee relations. Then, they ask, why do so many employees feel they are being strangled or spied on? It's so difficult to convince Blues that their intentions are not clear and their expectations are so demanding that subordinates often wish they would go back to their own offices and leave everyone else alone. However, employees don't often tell their Blue boss this because the boss is overly sensitive and usually means well, so no one wants to hurt his or her feelings. Instead of honest, direct communications, Blues typically get dishonest patronizing from employees.

SELF-DISCIPLINED AND STABLE

A Blue must have written the slogan "If a job's worth doing, it's worth doing well." Self-discipline comes from deep within the Blues' personality core. Throwing themselves into a project often brings out the best in Blues. They seek opportunities to develop their many talents.

This perpetual exercising of self-discipline brings stability and order to their lives. Many people learn to depend on Blues because of their steady and predictable natures. They provide us with a sense of security. They thrive in environments where security is valued and nourished. With proper support and cooperation, they will bring creative gifts of the highest possible caliber. Their gifts always come from the heart.

SELF-SACRIFICING AND NURTURING

With rare exceptions, Blues think of others before themselves, and bring love to the lives of those they touch. They love to serve. Doing for others gives them tremendous satisfaction. Being productive is important, but producing for people they care about seems to make the contribution mean much more to them. *They always seek purpose in their lives.* They want the sense of having lived for something more than simply earning a wage or changing a diaper.

UNFORGIVING AND RESENTFUL

Ironically, Blues *give* more than any personality but *forgive* the least. I have encountered many Blues who have yet to forgive their parents for damages done during childhood. It is quite easy to find Blues in an audience. I simply ask for a show of hands from those who can remember all the bad things their kindergarten teacher did to them. Blues always remember. Reds don't remember; they have already taken care of the teacher by putting tacks on her chair. Yellows thought it was funny and enjoyed the attention whether it was good or bad. And Whites aren't sure whether they went to kindergarten, so what's to remember?

One of Blues' most self-destructive weaknesses is grudge-holding. It often goes hand in hand with their excellent memory. One sixty-seven-year-old patient resented her White husband for numerous reasons over a span of fifty years of married life. She was so angry at him once that she secretly took her wedding dress down from her closet and donated it to a charitable organization. Needless to say, her motives were less than charitable. Blues can become so obsessed with "getting even" that they don't instantly see how the lust for begrudgery can be so intense that even self-defeating behavior feels preferable to letting things go unredressed.

This woman was so committed to hurting her husband that she neglected to realize that giving away a wedding dress is far less significant to men than women! The truth is he never noticed. So she kept telling him how much it should have hurt him when, in fact, she only hurt herself. Years later, when their granddaughter wanted to be married in grandmother's wedding dress, you can imagine her immense pain when she realized that she had, in the end, only hurt herself. Furthermore, she kept her husband's limited self-esteem in negative check by constantly undermining him. She exemplifies the Blues' need to get even and their struggle with letting go of resentment.

WORRIED AND GUILTY

Blues also seem to worry about everything. All this excess worry makes it possible to handle only so much excitement in one day. I remember one patient who "thought" she had a major decision to make. Her decision was between leaving for the East Coast on June 11th for two weeks to visit family, or going to an all-expenses-paid three-day church convention with her husband, which ended June 7th. That left her only three days to repack and get ready for her trip back East. But she always enjoyed being with her husband at the church conventions. She didn't know whether to stay home and be ready for her trip to the East or to go to the convention. She was also afraid that her kids would tear the house apart while she was gone (we're talking about twenty-five-year-old twins). Blues do not appreciate being rushed through life, regardless of the quality of events they are being rushed to enjoy. Worry about others, rather than productively engaging in activities of their own, can be a serious problem for Blues.

A thirty-year-old woman experienced worry whenever she drove on the freeway. If a car changed lanes behind her while she was driving in the middle lane, she immediately cross-examined herself by asking, "Am I driving too fast? Too slow? Are my brake lights disturbing other drivers?"

Worry and guilt generally mark the path to most Blues' homes. They can be "guilted" into almost anything. They often neglect to see that their true motives in many circumstances are based on guilt. For wrongs they think they've done, Blues will chastise themselves seemingly forever.

Larry is a talented CEO whose business career is highlighted by tremendous success. He is blessed with a savvy one cannot learn in academic institutions. Still he is known to pace the floors at night, plagued by second-guessing himself and worrying about decisions he can't do anything about. Despite his uncanny intuition and solid experience, he cannot trust himself and let go once decisions have been made. Instead, he ruminates about possible "worst case scenarios" and whether or not he has carefully considered all the correct options.

APPROPRIATE AND SINCERE

Blues value culture and appropriate behavior. They understand the value of manners and propriety in society. Blues deem it their personal responsibility to serve as the moral watchdogs for society. They are comfortably obedient to laws and authority. Blues think society requires structure and discipline in order to function properly. They always seek to preserve the dignity and quality of human life.

No other strength labels the Blues as uniquely as their sincerity. One of life's great experiences is to earn and experience their trust. Life cannot bestow on anyone a more gratifying reward than the sincere appreciation and trust of a Blue friend, employer, or family member.

PURPOSEFUL AND DEDICATED

Blues have a strong work ethic, and often find their lives cluttered with "necessary responsibilities" that leave them little or no time for spontaneous play. Play is often seen as frivolous and unproductive. It's not uncommon to see a Blue mother productively knitting or reading at a park while her children climb, swing, run, and devour their free time with no concern for anything but momentary pleasure. Blues envy the peace of mind and carefree attitude Yellows glide through life with. They often cry "unfair" and wish either the other personalities would enjoy life less, or at least reward the Blues for their dedication to the more noble concept of purposeful work. Unfortunately, neither wish is likely to come true.

> *Blues deem it their personal responsibility*
> *to serve as the moral watchdogs for society.*

MOODY AND COMPLEX

Another telltale sign of Blues is their mood swings. They never wake up happy or sad. They have to think about it first. If they are happy or sad during the day, it is because they choose to be. They can't seem simply to accept an emotion without taking full responsibility for selecting it.

Blues are highly complex individuals with many extremes. They have such powerful strengths and debilitating limitations. They are sensitive, tense, caring, critical, giving, and unforgiving at the same time. Their focus is on emotional rather than rational connections. Despite this, they are often guilty of emotional rigidity. In other words, they get stuck in emotional ruts. They lose perspective and find themselves misunderstood. Unable to express their feelings effectively, the Blues struggle to pump more energy into frustrating relationships to experience the intimacy that is essential for them in order to feel their life has purpose. Sometimes the energy they pump is healthy, and sometimes it is destructive. The complexity of the Blue personality frustrates Blues as much as it does the other personalities who have to interact with them. Perhaps this explains why Blues are so critical of themselves as well as of others.

SELF-RIGHTEOUS AND INSECURE

Each personality color has its own share of insecurity. However, no personality displays it as publicly as Blues. Blues have a powerful personality. They feel driven to participate in life. They voice their opinions, albeit sometimes only within the safe walls of their homes. They have strong values and belief systems. However, they are torn by guilt feelings, the unrealistic expectations caused by their perfectionistic attitude and skepticism. They are often caught between wanting to be involved and fearing their ability to be successful.

This insecurity is made more complicated by their unique self-righteous attitude. Perhaps no statement describes this attitude better than the bumper sticker slogan "Those of us who think they know everything [referring to the Reds] annoy those of us who really do." Unlike the vocal, arrogant Reds, Blues silently remind themselves how unfortunate it is that others must remain so ignorant. There is a certain smugness connected with Blues. They piously view the world with a suspicious eye. This tends to give Blues a pessimistic nature. They wish others would care enough to adopt the Blues' attitude of perfection. They are frustrated with the realization that many people prefer to accept life rather than to modify it. Self-righteousness does not breed intimacy. Rather, it promotes emotional distance and deception.

BLUE LIMITATIONS

Probably the greatest enemy of Blues is themselves. Their self-righteous attitudes are merely cover for deep insecurity. They are often too emotional and judgmental to enjoy intimacy. They continually depress themselves and others with unrealistic expectations of perfection. Lacking trust, they find themselves skeptical and suspicious of others. Blues often find themselves bitter, resentful, and unforgiving of those who have crossed them in life. Overwhelming guilt and worry continue to drive them inward, seeking solace from the only one who truly understands them—themselves. Blues are hard to please and tense about schedules. They are moody and find leadership a difficult dilemma. Blues aren't generally playful or spontaneous. In anger, they are the personality most likely to believe "Life's a bitch and then you die." They often fail to see the positive side to life. Blues become angry when others find them to be irrational and emotionally rigid in relationships. Blues exemplify Pogo's famous line, "We have met the enemy and he is us."

BLUE STRENGTHS

Like the earth that sustained and nurtured our earliest ancestors, Blues are also steady, ordered, and enduring. They offer culture, beauty, and emotional security. Blues love with a passion. They see intimate relationships and creative accomplishments rather than material possessions as the finer things in life. They bring culture and decency to home and society. They appreciate uplifting experiences, and feel most comfortable in creative and productive environments. They want a sense of purpose in their lives, and willingly sacrifice personal luxuries for more meaningful accomplishments.

They are highly committed individuals. Loyalty to people and sincerity in relationships (at home and work) are their trademarks. They believe in all causes that bring a higher quality to the human experience. They listen with endearing empathy and speak with emotional zeal. Blues truly value their connections to people and enjoy the accomplishments of others. With perfection as their guide, they strive to be the best they can be. They expect the same in their fellow beings. Obediently, they accept the need for authority, and put their energy into supporting law and order. They are essentially the glue that binds society together. Blues give us positive examples in the way they organize their lives, giving preference to personal relationships and quality achievements. They add that special touch of excellence as they freely commit their hearts and souls to the betterment of us all in our shared journey through life.

BLUE STRENGTHS

AS AN INDIVIDUAL

- sees life as a serious endeavor
- appreciates beauty and detail
- has a strong aesthetic sense
- stable and dependable (plowhorse versus racehorse)
- sincere and emotionally deep
- analytically oriented (concerned with why one behaves as he/she does)
- high achiever
- deep sense of purpose

AS A COMMUNICATOR

- able to enjoy sensitive and deep conversation
- strong skills in empathizing with others
- remembers feelings and thoughts shared in conversation
- willing to give conversations time to run their course
- prefers small groups

AS A GOAL SETTER

- highly disciplined
- receptive to other suggestions
- strong goal orientation
- plans well and follows through superbly

AS A CAREER PERSON

- excellent behind-the-scenes worker
- respectful of employer because of employer's position
- enjoys detail and schedules
- receptive of creative thinking in others
- gives more of self than required or expected

AS A PARENT

- encourages academics and/or trade development in children
- excellent trainer of skills (e.g., manners, study habits)
- very observant
- empathic and sensitive
- sincerely loyal to children
- excellent in long-term commitments
- keeps home clean and cozy
- sincerely seeks to understand children's behavior
- self-sacrificing

AS A CHILD

- proper and behaved
- easily disciplined verbally
- concerned about being a good family member
- sensitive and concerned about other family members
- loyal to parents and siblings regardless of quality of relationship
- seeks learning opportunities

AS A FRIEND

- loyal forever once friendship is established
- genuine concern for other person's well-being
- remembers special holidays and promotes celebrations
- encouraging in times of trouble
- willing to commit time to the relationship

AS A COMMITTED COMPANION

- gives the relationship priority over other activities
- values intimacy and places high priority on it

- considers spouse first in decision making
- responsible for making ongoing contribution to relationship
- enjoys sharing intimacy and places high priority on it

CAREERS MOST LIKELY TO ATTRACT BLUES

Teacher	Banker	Nurse
Homemaker	Clergy/Minister	Engineer
Psychotherapist	Accountant	Librarian
Computer programmer	Politician	Journalist
Musician	Architect	Carpenter

Note: Blues are most capable of adapting in the career world.

PERSONALITIES WHO APPEAR TO BE BLUES

ABRAHAM LINCOLN: Renowned for his trademark of fairness, he always sought the most noble path that would benefit all parties, if possible. He sought truth as a guiding principle in his personal and professional relationships.

PRINCESS DIANA: Always dressed appropriately, she carried herself with dignity and class. Emotions ruled her life, and she rendered herself vulnerable to the general public, continually gaining sympathy and support for herself and her causes.

WALT DISNEY: A creative genius, he loved the process more than the bottom line and relished design and details.

BLUE NATIONS

United States
England
Denmark

"If you love someone, set them free.
If they come back, they're yours;
if not, hunt them down and kill them!"

BLUE LIMITATIONS

AS AN INDIVIDUAL

- highly emotional
- smug and self-righteous
- controlling and/or envious of others' success when too easily obtained
- strong perfecting and performance orientation
- verbally self-abusive

AS A COMMUNICATOR

- has intensely held opinions on many issues
- tends to lecture and overdiscuss issues
- rigid with principles and unwilling to negotiate
- fears risking self in conversation
- argues primarily from emotional perspective
- strong expectations for others to be sensitive and deep
- expects others to read his or her mind and know his or her feelings

AS A GOAL SETTER

- sets unrealistically high goals
- easily discouraged when unsuccessful in accomplishments
- easily frustrated by lack of team cooperation
- expects others to understand his or her goals and make them a priority

AS A CAREER PERSON

- feels others are not capable of doing things as well as he or she
- craves security in career
- feels inadequate with natural talents and creativity
- shies away from public exposure and performance
- establishes high and often unrealistic expectations for self and others
- tends to overplan and overprepare
- critical of others' work and of self
- overextends self

AS A PARENT

- blames children for being unappreciative of parenting efforts
- can be moody and unpredictable
- easily irritated by mistakes and shortcomings of others
- usually loves with strings attached
- tends to give heavy doses of guilt to children
- lacks ability to relax
- requires a purpose in order to play
- controlling and overprotective of children
- too precise and exact with expectations
- feels a clean home is a high priority
- accepts guilt feelings too easily and readily
- not spontaneous with activities
- frustrates children with unrealistic expectations
- strong sense of right and wrong—badgers children if convinced they may be wrong

AS A CHILD

- easily frustrated
- feels guilty over minor concerns
- moody and emotional (cries instead of facing issues rationally)
- feelings are easily hurt
- martyr-like and complains about life
- self-esteem is dependent on outside influences
- has difficulty relaxing and often feels uncomfortable
- withholds affection if angered (pouts)
- waits for parent to initiate ideas and then criticizes unacceptable suggestions

AS A FRIEND

- highly insecure about other's acceptance and approval
- feels rejected easily
- when depressed or depressive, feels it is friend's job to understand
- can be revengeful and bitter if crossed or scarred emotionally
- critical of friends' principles or activities if not similar
- expects friends to maintain strong loyalty
- wishes friends would communicate more often
- rarely playful and spontaneous

- blames others for his or her unhappiness ("if only you were more . . .")
- demands affection and intimacy
- demands time and attention of partner
- highly manipulative in seeking support or understanding
- suspicious of others' motives (distrustful)
- unforgiving of past misunderstandings and wrongdoings
- clings to companion too much
- withholds feelings when frightened he or she may be rejected

How to Develop a Positive Connection with Blues

Do:

1. Emphasize their security in the relationship
2. Be sensitive and soft-spoken in your approach
3. Be sincere and genuine
4. Behave appropriately and well mannered
5. Limit their risk level
6. Promote their creativity
7. Appreciate them
8. Allow ample time for them to gather their thoughts before expressing themselves
9. Be loyal
10. Do thorough analysis before making presentations

Don't:

1. Make them feel guilty
2. Be rude or abrupt
3. Promote too much change
4. Expect spontaneity
5. Abandon them
6. Expect them to bounce back easily or quickly from depression
7. Demand perfection (they already expect too much from themselves)
8. Push them too quickly into making decisions

9. Expect them to forgive quickly when crossed
10. Demand immediate action or quick verbal bantering

Recommended Time-Management Tips for Blues

1. Think rationally rather than reactively when pressured. Emotionalism can create chaos and unnecessary distress.
2. Clearly state your limits when others impose deadlines on you.
3. Settle for less. Perfectionism often narrows your focus, causing you to ignore other important aspects of your life.
4. Don't set unrealistic expectations for yourself or others to the extent that everyone feels overwhelmed. Simply see goals as road markers rather than criteria for success.
5. Don't personalize your interactions with other people. Blues often suffer from feeling let down by others or from quitting because they let others down. Concentrate on the task at hand rather than becoming emotionally discouraged or critical.
6. See time management as a compromise rather than "all or nothing." If you fail to meet a deadline, learn to punt. It will free you to be more creative and less self-critical.
7. Realize that there are limits to what you can control. You cannot control other people.
8. Set a ten-minute time limit to worry about any topic in the day. When your time is up, so is your worrying. Get on with living in the present moment and doing what you can do rather than focusing on what is out of your control.

"Leave me alone, I'm having a crisis."

Chapter Seven

WHITES: THE PEACEKEEPERS

*Whites offer us all
a model for gentle
human dignity.*

PEACEFUL AND DIPLOMATIC

Whites most completely represent the peacemaker. They sincerely believe in the value of diplomacy, and diligently seek to promote cooperation at all cost.

How many times have we all said, "Will everybody just settle down? All I want right now is some PEACE!" At that moment, if we could simply transform everyone into a White personality, our wish for peace would become reality. Every parent prays for a child with a White personality. Every teacher deserves at least one student with a White personality in each class. Everybody is better off for knowing one intimately. Whites offer us all a model for gentle human dignity. They quietly move through life with an easy, unruffled style. Whites appreciate the cooperative nature of mankind, and keep working to achieve a peaceful coexistence among all living things.

Whites are usually difficult to know. They operate on a self-serving power orientation, but so subtly that it often leaves one wondering whether Whites are the manipulated or the manipulator. Whites are often lost, inviting others to rescue and protect them in life. Caught in their own neediness, Whites often find it difficult to grow. They remain victims, often silently traumatized by their anger, rather than honestly acknowledging their feelings. Whites can be very timid and shy, which keeps them from living life to the fullest. They may depend on others to make their life happen.

INSECURE AND NONASSERTIVE

Whites can be difficult to read. Whites appear to approach life so simply that one may misinterpret them and believe them to be at peace when their real feelings may actually be fear, timidity, laziness, or personal inadequacy. They are such good-natured individuals that people generally prefer not to ruffle Whites' feathers or make waves around them. People typically ignore Whites' limitations and acknowledge their strengths. This is particularly difficult for those who are intimately involved with Whites (parents, spouses, children, teachers, friends). The urge to protect Whites by ignoring their deficiencies and their limitations ultimately sabotages the need for them to stand up for themselves, even though such behavior is contrary to their innate nature.

A deeply regrettable incident recounted by a twenty-year-old female patient illuminates the White self-doubt and unwillingness to confront others. My patient experienced sexual intercourse for the first time at the age of sixteen in the backseat of a car. Immediately following intercourse, her drunk date threw up. He was suddenly furious. She was concerned about the mess in his car and his angry feelings, so she comforted him by saying, "That's okay. I'll help clean it up." Without the slightest concern for her feelings, he remarked, "I'm not worried about that. I'm worried about my girlfriend finding out I've been drinking again." Had they not just experienced an "intimate" sexual encounter? Wasn't she special to him? She continued this absurdity without confrontation by staying involved with him for another year before she could finally let go.

Whites can be very passive. They can follow you through life without assuming any leadership of their own. They often make others the core of their existence, neglecting to develop their own sense of purpose and direction. Some Whites become so attached to one individual that they refuse to develop outside interests or make any commitments that would separate them from their relationship.

A couple in their thirties were dating seriously when the woman (Red) decided to take a weekend cruise with a girlfriend. Her boyfriend (White) was terribly hurt and insecure. She finally got tired of his whining and told him she was going with her girlfriend and could never consider marrying him if he didn't get his own life together without always waiting for her to include him in her plans. She was thrilled when he announced that he was going to visit a good friend in Montana the same weekend she went on the cruise. However, after careful consideration of what motivated his behavior, it became apparent that he was simply satisfying her request for independence in order not to jeopardize their potential marriage plans. Subsequently, she insisted that he be the one to initiate his independent plan the next time, rather than simply reacting to hers.

DOUBTFUL AND DEPENDENT

Whites doubt themselves so much that they constantly demand proof of acceptance. "Prove to me," they say, "that you accept me. Stay with me always and be there for me, for I am inadequate and you are strong." The price is high when one tries to accept, protect, and rescue a clingy White. It is much like holding a man by his wrists when he is falling from a cliff. The longer you hold on, the heavier he becomes. Yet he feels he is safer in your grasp than trusting himself and assisting in the rescue by climbing back up. The nobility of the rescue soon loses its shine, and the rescuer becomes the victim. If you "care," you feel obligated to hold on for life, to give up a life of your own in order to save his. If you let go, society rebukes you for giving up and selfishly seeking your own rewards elsewhere. Such dilemmas are commonly experienced by clinging Whites and those they encounter in life.

In order to encourage this unhealthy, although seemingly secure type of relationship, Whites seek to please others. Whites often get the support of others through service. This service typically comes with strings attached. Usually the strings come in the form of protection, security, control, support, and direction.

Jeff had been the perfect child (Whites usually are) and later resisted rocking the boat for any reason when his parents retired. Knowing this, Jeff's parents repeatedly controlled his choices despite the fact that he had been married once, held a very responsible job, and maintained a desirable lifestyle. Then Jeff, who is Caucasian, wanted very much to marry an Asian woman. His mother flatly refused to entertain the idea, and his father supported his "traumatized" wife. Jeff felt abandoned. He had been a wonderful, caring son. When his only brother had turned his back on their parents because of their meddling, Jeff had remained loyal. Now he felt torn in half. He was devoted and loyal both to his parents and his girl-friend. Notice that I didn't mention loyal to himself. He had not yet developed loyalty to himself. He didn't count, yet. He experienced his value and self-worth through others. Now he needed to find himself and challenge his secure relationship with his parents if he was ever to know self-respect. Through months of therapy and inner struggling, he freed himself of his parents and pursued a life based on his own values and beliefs. Jeff eventually married his fiancée. Jeff will never feel as welcomed or as "loved" by his parents as he did before, but he now recognizes that pleasing himself appropriately is far more gratifying than living his life to please others.

TOLERANT AND PATIENT

Unless other personalities push Whites into a combative stance, they can tolerate an enormous amount of pain. Whites are tolerant of dis-agreeable behavior regardless of the personal discomfort they may feel. One mother (White) watched her young teenaged son leave home on two separate occasions "just because he felt like it." He simply wanted to live somewhere else. This mother was deeply con-cerned and maintained positive communication despite her son's inappropriate and selfish behavior.

I recently asked 100 university students to identify the trait they felt was most important for a successful parent to develop. Independently, 95 percent of them ranked *patience* as the most significant virtue for suc-cessful parenting. I was amazed at this overwhelming response from these young adults who had only recently been children, and who, for the most part, were not yet parents. What about love, discipline, and leadership? Why hadn't they given the edge to communication or some other attribute? The students offered me a valuable insight into par-enting and the White personality. They said that "patience indicates a trust in human dignity—a belief that people can make the right choices in life when given the free agency to act for themselves." What a pow-erful statement! I have appreciated the White personality with new depth since that educational experience.

Whites most completely
represent the peacemaker.

IMPRESSIONABLE

Whites are quite impressionable. They observe everything and keep a watchful eye on the human condition. This can make a negative childhood very traumatic for Whites. One patient tearfully told me of her last encounter with her father when she was only five years old. He had a fight with her mother and was leaving their yard. She asked if she could go with him. She knew her parents were fighting but never considered he was leaving for good. She thought he was going to the store, and she wanted to be with him. He said she couldn't come, and he left. She went inside and saw her mother sobbing, and realized this was more serious than the other times. After this devastating experience, my patient never developed trust or the capacity for sharing her feelings freely with anyone. She still calls her father on special occasions, but nothing has erased the pain she experienced that day as a five-year-old watching her daddy leave and later realizing he'd never come home again.

WITHHOLDS FEELINGS

Whites don't trust freely. They usually hold their true feelings very close to the heart, safely tucked away from others who may not approve of or value them. One intellectually brilliant man offered to tutor his Harvard medical school roommates free of charge. He later realized that it was his way of expressing his warm feelings toward them without having to discuss them openly. He regrets now that he never shared himself. He shared his knowledge because he was secure in that. Looking back, he realizes that he might have been able to establish good friendships if he had been able to trust others with his inner feelings and thoughts.

BLENDABLE AND KIND

The gentle nature of Whites typically shines through regardless of their level of trust. They remain kind and agreeable with almost everyone they meet. Whites are so blendable. A sure sign of a White personality is the individual who genuinely feels like a rainbow of colors. Whites can find themselves in all personalities because they are so capable of blending in.

UNPRODUCTIVE DREAMERS

Whites often remain unproductive dreamers. They have tremendous plans and can often imagine themselves to be elsewhere, but their dreams remain just that—dreams, unless they can focus and make them concrete. These flaws leave Whites and those intimately connected with them unsettled and disappointed. Whites are the least effective of all the personalities at implementing changes. (Yellows run a close second.)

I remember one White accountant who could never decide what he really wanted to do professionally. Several firms he worked for had folded, and each time, even with the realization that his current job would be terminated, he had remained until the end rather than seeking other employment. His wife was terribly distressed by his ambivalence and yet remained highly supportive. Finally, he shared how his real dream in life was to own a small food franchise. He had the necessary business skills, and his wife had terrific people skills. Years passed and nothing ever came of the man's dream. His wife remained supportive and successfully pursued her own career. However, he was never able to commit to his dream of owning his own business.

UNMOTIVATED

This lack of direction breeds a lack of motivation. Until Whites establish goals and commit to accomplishing those goals, they are highly unmotivated. One White friend of mine would experience moments of brilliance when he would "see the light" and commit to a particular goal. Within a short time span, as with a shooting star, this brilliance and excitement would be explained away and lost until another momentary flash of encouragement arrived. Setting and accomplishing his goals didn't come easily. However, goals are the only hope for unmotivated Whites. Until they are able to establish direction in their lives, Whites often remain unsettled and discouraged.

> *If you ever want to witness quiet human majesty,*
> *simply observe a healthy White personality*
> *bless another's life with random acts of kindness.*
> *But you must watch closely, because*
> *they will never announce their own heroics.*

ACCEPTING

Whites are conceivably capable of being the best friends to all personalities. They find accepting others rather simple. They have such tolerant expectations of others that people value their companionship and seek their nonjudgmental relationships. Whites enjoy doing almost anything with anyone, anywhere. They can enjoy a wide variety of people and experiences, and consequently often find themselves in unusual relationships or life situations.

BORING AND LAZY

Whites miss many potentially wonderful moments in life because they look to others rather than to themselves for excitement and relevance in life. Perhaps the word that Whites least like to accept responsibility for is *boring*. Yet Whites can be just that—boring. Perhaps the example that best depicts this dependency is the following typical directionless relationship between two Whites.

Two Whites dated for years before deciding to marry. Their courtship consisted primarily of shared television viewing and quiet moments together. They married, and after five years they decided they were wrong for each other. Neither was happy or finding life particularly fulfilling. During the next five years this couple remained married but separate in their dreams and aspirations. He pursued a college degree and she moved to another city to become a police officer. Neither committed to sharing decision making. Neither made the decision to leave. After seven more wasted years of living apart but not choosing truly separate lives, they divorced. Why did it take so long? Both admitted they couldn't agree on who should file the papers!

Whites are vulnerable to wasting time. They may give it away to boredom, laziness, or dull reluctance to change. I have seen wives leave husbands, husbands leave wives, employees leave employers, kids and parents leave each other, friendships dissolve, and a myriad of other potentially wonderful relationships end primarily because of boredom. The worst part is that the person leaving often feels very guilty because the grounds for separation aren't dramatic ones such as infidelity, distrust, or abuse. Life with a boring White can be devastating and draining.

Lazy (just try and get one moving in the early morning) and reluctant, the White personality often moves sluggishly through life. They are in no hurry to experience life. They feel certain life will wait for them. Their motto could be "Everything comes to he who waits." Everything (good and bad) does come to he who waits. However, what he gets when it finally comes may be a far cry from what he would have chosen.

TIMID AND EMOTIONALLY UNSURE

Whites remind me of the cowardly lion in *The Wizard of Oz*. They can be a frightened group of individuals. This should not imply that they are necessarily afraid of physical danger, but rather emotional trauma. One young woman feared rejection so much that she developed seizures. She was taunted by the kids in elementary school, and when she could no longer handle it, she developed a method for diverting the attention from her emotional insecurities to a physical handicap (seizures). This eventually resulted in coddling by adults and peer avoidance. Unfortunately, adult adulation wasn't her need, and peer avoidance had almost the same effect as taunting when other kids ran off to slumber parties and ate lunch together at school.

GENTLE AND EVEN-TEMPERED

The White child is truly a gift from heaven. They are so simple. They are usually the easiest babies to care for. There is a unique gentleness to these children that promotes family harmony. They are the children who travel through life with an even temper. New experiences can traumatize a White child. However, they typically enjoy a peaceful, casual existence.

AIMLESS AND MISGUIDED

Sometimes Whites, because of their aimless and misguided nature, approach life too casually. Particularly frustrating for the rest of us is the energy we must expend to make up for them: White children forgetting lunches; White friends neglecting to pick up the children for baseball practice; White husbands unable to select a career direction; and White siblings not willing to develop their own friendships. Whites rarely realize how selfish their limitations are. By presenting themselves as kind but helpless souls, they often seem to ignore the pressure their inadequacy places on everyone else.

How enjoyable can life be when you have to constantly remind someone to brush his teeth, call the hotel for reservations, what time school or work begins, etc., etc., etc. Whites often respond to these reminders with a casual (albeit disdaining) remark such as "Why do you have to get so huffy about everything?" "Whose life is it anyway?" "Go on and mind your own business and leave me alone." The frustration mounts for the other personalities who have much greater expectations for Whites than Whites have for themselves. Whites are notorious for requiring assistance in planning and processing life. They are less known for accepting, and in fact are capable of resisting, the very assistance they require.

INDECISIVE

Whites rarely seek leadership positions. They are uncomfortable making decisions that may be wrong, and avoid responsibilities that require decision making. They are more comfortable as a follower or in a less involved role, leaving group decision making to others. Whites would rather just accept others' decisions than assert themselves with their own opinions. One patient asked his wife, "Honey, on this test of Dr. Hartman's, it wants to know if I'm decisive. Do you think I am or not?" We all shared a good laugh, recognizing that he never realized what he was asking until she said, "Honey, somehow I think you just answered your own question better than I could ever hope to!"

SILENT AND STUBBORN

Whites can be very strong and stubborn. One of my White patients hated high school. He despised homework and all the demands of education. He was particularly bright but unwilling to engage in conflict with either parents or teachers. How does one satisfy everyone (including oneself) when there is no agreement on what must be done? This was his dilemma. He hated homework, and they demanded that it be done. For one solid semester in eighth grade, this young man, Michael, did every homework assignment and never turned one of them in to his teachers. Every night his parents would ask him if he had done his homework, and he would answer yes. When his grades slipped dramatically and they requested to see his work, he promptly showed them. By the end of the semester, his parents thought they were going crazy. Were his teachers out to get their son? They had seen his work, but the teachers kept telling them that he had not completed it. This case depicts the silent, strong, stubborn nature of Whites.

> *"All things eventually come*
> *to he who patiently waits."*
> —Revised White Chinese Proverb

Whites prefer to give the silent treatment because they are uncomfortable with confrontation. It is very difficult to live with people who silently resent your behavior. Whites seem to take advantage of others' natural curiosity by refusing to discuss their feelings openly, forcing other personalities to struggle to understand them. Whites often feel very deeply, but it is very difficult for them to express their feelings to others. One White father took an intolerable amount of abuse from his Red stepson for years in order to maintain peace in the home. His wife refused to allow him to discipline the child. He simply suffered in silence. Finally, after multiple problems including molestation, school failures, etc., the mother allowed her husband to take a more active role in disciplining his stepson. He had never released his true anger for all the disruptions this child had brought to his life. With his wife's approval, he massively overcompensated, going on the offensive and physically striking his stepson whenever he could find justification.

WHITE LIMITATIONS

Whites often seem boring and uninvolved. They are often unwilling to set goals. They frequently refuse to pay the price of involvement because they may fear the inevitable consequences of confrontation or rejection. This fear keeps them from experiencing intimacy. Their indecision limits their accomplishments. In order to feel secure, Whites pay great attention to the needs of others and strive at all costs to please those they encounter in life. They express themselves reluctantly, preferring to let others believe as they will. Meanwhile, the

Whites go about their lives as they choose, avoiding conflict and confrontations. Whites silently accept whatever comes their way. What they don't value, they stubbornly discard in time. They often do not allow those desirable experiences that require the effort of risk, leadership, and honest expression into their lives.

WHITE STRENGTHS

On the positive side, **Whites are the satisfied ones.** They are contented and agreeable individuals who easily accommodate others through life. **They complement every personality regardless of differences in style.** Their gentle nature and diplomacy wins them many loyal friends. Their agreeable and peaceful dispositions make them an asset to any family, friendship, or business that is fortunate enough to include them. Whites are typically moderate people without the extremes of other personalities. Like the water they represent, they flow over and around life's difficulties, rather than demanding that obstacles in their path be moved. Their leadership is solid and fair. They tolerate differences and encourage camaraderie with all team members. The chameleon is their mascot and reflects their ability to adapt and blend with everyone. They enjoy the enviable strength of balance. They are receptive to every personality and willingly learn from all of them. Whites are most effective at putting life's crises in proper perspective. Satisfied and even-tempered, they ask little of life. They often enjoy the protection of stronger personalities. Patient and tolerant, they have much to give. And give they do, with gentle approval for those fortunate enough to experience their accepting embrace.

AS AN INDIVIDUAL

- quiet, reflective, and peaceful
- sincere and genuine lifestyle
- appears to accept life comfortably
- patient with self and others
- enjoys life's simplicity
- compatible with others
- kind to animals and people
- blends into all situations

AS A COMMUNICATOR

- receptive to others' input
- negotiator and mediator on issues
- listens superbly
- strong empathy skills

AS A GOAL SETTER

- receptive to suggestions
- appreciates exposure to many possibilities
- recognizes the value of goal setting
- trusts self to succeed in many different environments

AS A CAREER PERSON

- accommodates others easily
- handles bureaucratic environments well
- negotiates well
- calm under pressure
- prefers slower pace and "think" time
- sometimes puts self in dangerous occupations for excitement
- nonconformist

AS A PARENT

- flows well with crises
- takes time to enjoy each child
- agreeable with difficult children
- respected by children for gentle manner and style
- slow to react with anger
- supportive and considerate
- accepts companion's decision—demonstrates unity
- patient with deviant and inappropriate behavior
- accepts differences superbly

"I finally got it together,
but forgot where to put it."

Color Code

profile listed behaviors

red - power
blue - intimacy
white peace
yellow fun

behaviors are determined by needs & wants

needs & wants are determined by motives

motives are our innermost reasons
why we think & behave as we to
driving force behind our personalities

motives are the principal means of
identifying a personality color

motives, needs & wants are neutral —
p. 50

AS A CHILD

- very agreeable to established traditions and boundaries
- nondemanding
- willing to accommodate siblings and parents
- plays well by self
- accepts life with drama

AS A FRIEND

- patient and enduring through good and bad times
- tolerant of unkind behavior
- supportive and accepting
- listens with empathy
- relaxed in most situations
- likes most people
- liked by most people
- compatible with different personalities
- enjoys observing others
- nondemanding of friendship

AS A COMMITTED COMPANION

- tolerant of others' tardiness
- can entertain self easily
- appreciates leadership qualities in others
- loyal and committed to relationship
- willing to accept beliefs and values of companion

CAREERS MOST LIKELY TO ATTRACT WHITES

Forest ranger	Recreation leader	Veterinarian
Dentist	Researcher	Lawyer
Bureaucrat	Homemaker	Engineer
Computer programmer	Police officer	F.B.I. agent
Military service	Preschool teacher	Truck driver

Note: Whites and Yellows are usually the least motivated to succeed in the career world.

PERSONALITIES WHO APPEAR TO BE WHITES

ALBERT EINSTEIN: A genius and highly observant, he let his thinking do his talking. Personally withdrawn, he was most comfortable in the world of ideas and intellectual exchange. He preferred quietly doing the research for his remarkable theories behind the scenes, rather than heralding their importance to the public.

MICHAEL JACKSON: Multitalented professionally and yet personally self-effacing, he listens well but verbalizes very little. Prefers quiet, limited personal connections.

JIMMY CARTER: Better thought of as a world diplomat than a savvy political force, he exudes kindness and quiet dignity. He never displays zealous egotism, but walks softly and carries a big stick.

WHITE NATIONS

Finland
Switzerland
Canada

WHITE LIMITATIONS

AS AN INDIVIDUAL

- boring because detached
- takes passive approach to life
- unresponsive or not openly excited about experiences
- has problems becoming intimate
- bashful and unsure of self
- easily manipulated into changing plans
- ambivalent about direction and goals to pursue
- often lazy and unwilling to take responsibility for self
- resists making commitments

AS A COMMUNICATOR

- fearful of confrontation
- unable to respond quickly in conversation
- dishonest with feelings—often agrees only to please others

- hesitant to engage others in conversation
- doesn't contribute openly
- accepts others' decisions without seeking best solution
- gives very little energy to conversation unless forced to
- refuses to take a stand on issues
- prefers to observe others interact

AS A GOAL SETTER

- takes a "wait and see" attitude to life experiences
- waits for a sign or for someone else to make decisions for them
- lacks consistency in goal setting
- sees goals as demanding and therefore restrictive
- waits for others to set his or her goals and then criticizes the goals set for him or her

AS A CAREER PERSON

- low profile
- low energy
- directionless—requires leadership from others
- resents strong direction and leadership from others
- works at a slow pace
- resists power dominance of other personalities
- difficult to motivate and inspire
- fears change and risk taking
- willing to stay in same monotonous job
- easily manipulated by others when unmotivated or unconcerned

AS A PARENT

- refuses to engage in conflict with spouse about children
- doesn't initiate activities and interaction with children
- poor disciplinarian
- works obsessively to maintain peace
- poor leadership and delegation with children
- easily abused by children when promoting unpopular ideas
- easily controlled or ignored by spouse or children

AS A CHILD

- resents being pressured to do things
- doesn't contribute much to conversations
- contributes quietly to family activities
- waits for parent to initiate ideas and then criticizes unacceptable suggestions
- prefers the comforts of home to the demands of the world
- indifferent to family dilemmas
- uninvolved in family action
- doesn't complete tasks

AS A FRIEND

- lacks creativity to make suggestions
- easily led by others' opinions
- won't express honest perception if controversial
- passive
- requires extra protection and a lot of support
- easily hurt and defeated

AS A COMMITTED COMPANION

- prefers the other person to lead
- boring and indecisive
- too accommodating
- won't make suggestions for activities
- willing to let life and love pass him or her by
- may experience difficulty initiating relationships
- feels too inadequate to take a stand and voice opinions
- not emotional about intimate relationships

How to Develop a Positive Connection with Whites

Do:

1. Be kind
2. Be logical, clear, and firm about the content you present
3. Provide a structure (boundaries) for them to operate in
4. Be patient and gentle

5. Introduce options and ideas for their involvement
6. Be simple and open
7. Acknowledge and accept their individuality
8. Be casual, informal, and relaxed in presentation style
9. Look for nonverbal clues to their feelings
10. Listen quietly

Don't:

1. Be cruel or insensitive
2. Expect them to need much social interaction
3. Force immediate verbal expression; accept written communication
4. Be domineering or too intense
5. Demand conformity to unrealistic expectations/behaviors
6. Overwhelm them with too much at once
7. Force confrontation
8. Speak too fast
9. Take away all their daydreams
10. Demand leadership

Recommended Time-Management Tips for Whites

1. State verbally how you feel and what you perceive about yourself, current tasks, and others' behavior. Whites are vulnerable to wasting energy because they can't accurately identify how they feel and present it confidently to others.
2. Empower yourself by addressing issues rather than avoiding them.
3. Conflict can be enriching. Share your ideas and seek others' input, rather than taking their feedback personally. See them as enlightening and broadening your horizons. Time management in a vacuum can be limiting and dangerous.
4. Seek a sense of urgency. Whites can miss living passionate lives by refusing to get excited about projects and people. Don't let time pass you by.
5. Set proactive agendas, rather than merely reacting to agendas others set for you. Proactive attitudes will challenge your natural tendency to being passive-aggressive.
6. Don't be overly defensive when others seem demanding. Focus on *what* is being said rather than *how* it's being said.

7. Risk a little. Set goals that require effort and build confidence rather than taking a "wait and see" attitude.
8. Make the effort to control daydreams that rob you of valuable time to get legitimate work done.

*"I used to be apathetic,
but now I just don't care."*

Chapter Eight

YELLOWS:
THE FUN LOVERS

*Happy is as happy does. Yellow people love themselves
because they know exactly what they love to do
and always find the time and resources to do it.*

HAPPY AND FUN

Riding on the primary motive of fun, Yellows reflect the spirit of the
wind and the life-giving miracle of fresh air. They are as essential to
society as breathing is to the human existence. Yellows love life. They
are spirited, exciting, and have an innate ability to be happy. They
have a mental attitude that allows them to appreciate what they have,
rather than being miserable about what they lack. Fate often appears
to smile on them, and they are considered to be very lucky.

SELF-CENTERED AND UNCOMMITTED

Also because of the primary motive of fun, Yellows exemplify the ultimate lightweight personality. Yellows bound through life well focused
on themselves. They frequently fail to develop the depth necessary to
contribute substantially to society. Yellows struggle to understand
why anyone would rather earn their keep than take the easy road
through life. Perhaps their most serious limitation is their inability to
commit. Because of their enthusiasm, Yellows start more projects
than any other group but successfully complete the fewest, due to
their lack of commitment. (Typical of Yellows, one patient com-
plained that she had started 394 diets in one year.)

Commitment requires constant dedication, something that unduly taxes a Yellow's capacity for endurance. They usually cannot concentrate long enough to convince others that their intentions are genuine and trustworthy. One young man was unable to commit to marriage and repeatedly broke engagements and women's hearts. He was completely overwhelmed by the thought of a lifelong commitment. He enjoyed the romance but feared the expectations of a committed relationship. Eventually, he fell deeply in love and, once again, felt motivated to consider the possibility of marriage. However, his uncertainty overcame him, and he called his father for advice. He respected his father and listened to his wise counsel. His father knew his son's fear of commitment was creating his difficulty, but he also knew the young man had a fine character. The father simply reminded him that divorce was always an option and, if necessary, he could always exercise that option in the future.

This wise father offered his Yellow son an escape route that allowed him to marry. He provided the essential ingredient in every Yellow's life—an escape, an out, a chance to run away, if necessary. His wisdom and effective parenting brought his son to the altar. As a result, my very Blue wife and I happily celebrated our twenty-second wedding anniversary this year.

It is equally difficult for a Yellow to commit to personal development. Getting to know oneself is difficult for everyone. Yellows often give up before they really tackle problems in their psychological makeup. Commitment to painful soul searching usually ends up way at the bottom of their list of priorities. Yellows are unwilling to pay the price of true self-confidence, which is a lifetime of commitment to those experiences, people, and values one cherishes. Yellows go with the flow as long as it keeps flowing and is flashy. They love excitement and willingly forgo commitment, with its discomfort, in order to feel momentary pleasure.

IRRESPONSIBLE

While society has come up with some wonderful adjectives to describe Yellows (some of which I can't even put in this book), the word that most accurately describes the negative essence of the Yellow personality is *irresponsible*. Remember that wonderful song, "Call me unreliable . . . call me undependable"? Save yourself some time and simply call them Yellow.

Yellows have a most difficult time accepting responsibility for themselves. Somehow they truly believe it is someone else's responsibility to take care of them. It doesn't matter who—just someone else. After all, Yellows believe that no one is having the fun they are having, so what could others possibly be doing that is more important than concerning themselves with the needs of the Yellows? Perhaps the greatest concern with Yellows is their loss of playtime in life. Their rebellious natures can be cute while they are still young, but society has little tolerance for adult slackers. There is perhaps nothing more tragic than an aging Yellow without character. Their faces bear the heavy lines from year-round tans. Their personal belongings are often minimal because they have never concerned themselves with caring for possessions properly. They have few intimate friends. Yellows often take the easy path, which is across soft dirt that buckles under the burdensome emptiness and dependency of the Yellow's life.

Their irresponsible nature and inability to commit often makes taming Yellows seem an impossible dream. They are typically so charismatic that others fail to see their limitations. Only after a period of time do they see Yellows for what they often are—beautiful, prancing sprinters who rarely go the distance. After committing time and energy to such a performer, the owner becomes disenchanted and often feels anger and regret at having believed in his or her capacity to change this "Yellow" sprinter into a reliable runner who will go the distance in a relationship.

Yellows do not feel comfortable with the pressures that often come with being responsible. One patient told her Yellow husband, "If I weren't around, you would probably be lighting candles every night rather than remembering to pay your electric bill." After talking with them for a short time, I was certain that she was right. He had neglected to pay the last three months' mortgage payment of $825, so they decided to sell their home (which afforded them a tremendous tax advantage) and now rent a small apartment, half the size of their home, for $700 a month and zero tax advantage. He further justified this costly business decision by saying, "All I need is a place with a little land for my dog and so that my wife can have a horse. Other than that I just want to travel. In fact, if I had my way, we would load up the van right now and go live in Mexico for a while."

We discussed his Blue wife's need for a secure environment and more stability for raising children. He told me he had already matured, because when he first met her all he did was cash his paycheck each week, deposit it in his back pocket, and enjoy life until he reached in his back pocket and found all the money was gone. Then he would just sit around the house or bum off his buddies until he earned his next paycheck. As with most Yellows, life is for today, and saving money is for those who don't know how to live today. Yellows have a very hard time putting off until tomorrow what can be done today as long as it is fun. They philosophize that working is for people who don't know how to party. Those readers familiar with the Aesop fable about the grasshopper who lived only for the moment can appreciate the extreme lack of perspective many Yellows (like the grasshopper) have for living beyond the moment.

Blaming others is a classic pattern for irresponsible Yellows. I was working with one young man (Mike) who wept when we discussed his Red father and the nonexistent relationship they had. After two sessions, Mike was much less rebellious and making substantial progress, until one day he confessed that he had stolen his father's bank card and withdrawn over $850 over the last three months. Once he began, he didn't know how to stop or tell anyone. At last he had been discovered and would have to face his father, whom he despised. With his mother attentively listening in my office, the young man spent fifteen minutes explaining why he could never tell his father because his father wouldn't understand. I knew Mike always excused his delinquent behavior in school and home by blaming his father. Now he had stolen his father's money and had spent it all frivolously on himself, and still he wanted his mother and me to excuse him because his father was (in his eyes) a terrible man. For years Mike hadn't wanted to change himself, so he simply blamed his truancies, failing grades, lack of friends, and, now, *stealing,* on the inadequacies of his father.

One Yellow patient in her midtwenties spent her life telling everyone how boring and old-fashioned her parents were. She justified her negative attitude by reminding others how unsuccessful her parents were financially and that they didn't communicate well with each other. She found hundreds of reasons why she would rather die than live their lifestyle. Therapy continued off and on for about a year before she finally began to see that rather than responsibly focusing on her personal growth, she had spent an enormous amount of energy criticizing her "frumpy old parents who knew nothing about living." She began to recognize that she had actually produced very little in her own life. She had completed only three credits of college. She had never sustained a meaningful relationship with a man. She had been unable to lose any weight for the period of one year. Her friends were exactly like her. She was in debt up to her ears with no sign of change. She had not held a job for longer than five months. It all came crashing in on her like a tidal wave when I reminded her that she had discontinued therapy, in part because of the financial strain, and that her "frumpy old parents who knew nothing about living" had approached me and offered to help pay for my services if I felt it would help her. She had maligned them her entire life. Yet they knew enough about real living to offer assistance to their daughter without any strings attached.

She finally broke down and expressed her self-hatred. She did not want a boring life like her parents, but she realized that she had been totally ineffective in building a more positive one for herself. While attacking them, she had produced nothing. She acknowledged that she loved herself only when she performed and produced, yet she was so undisciplined and irresponsible that she had known only repeated failure. She had great talents and numerous interests but, as yet, had been unwilling to acknowledge them and then commit to anything long enough to experience the joy that comes from responsible effort.

Too many married Yellows excuse having affairs by blaming the insensitivity of their spouses. "If she or he were more willing to enjoy sex with me, then I wouldn't have to do this." Of course, they fail to recognize that often the reason their spouses don't enjoy sex may be their own lack of commitment or other shortcomings of theirs. Instead, Yellows find places to put their blame and move on through life, carelessly avoiding any responsibility for having to look at or change themselves. This irresponsible nature could be remedied much more easily if Yellows had a sense of conscience or guilt, but neither accompanies Yellows very far on their journey through life. Believing that rules are relevant only when they serve the needs of the individual, Yellows may too freely abandon tradition in favor of personal gratification, ignoring long-term consequences.

Yellows love life.

ENTHUSIASTIC AND CAREFREE

Yellows seek enchanting opportunities and find life laced with silver linings. They rarely become bogged down with details or "emotional baggage," which for them means controlling friends, poor work conditions, and other undesirable and demanding circumstances. Yellows are as vulnerable to these experiences as any personality, but they have a strong yearning for freedom and subconsciously recognize baggage and instinctively move away from its influence.

117

Yellows represent enthusiasm and share this excitement with everyone they meet. They are terrific at social involvements and have a way of making a party out of everyday living. They remind us of our youth and the joy that comes from innocent hopes and optimistic dreams.

PLAYFUL AND EXCITING

Yellows generally enjoy life regardless of what they are doing. Even when working hard, Yellows appear to be having a good time. Their lives are lived with the confidence that the best is yet to come. They have a zest for living that is contagious. A Blue individual called a Yellow friend long distance after five years of silence and said, "I've missed the life we shared as friends in college. You always seemed to make life happen for me. I often reflect back on our friendship and remember all the excitement you always stirred up. I miss you because you breathed life into me." The Yellow friend had no idea that he had been the instigator of all the fun. He naively assumed that everyone's primary goal in life was to have a good time. He also thought most people experienced life as freely and as comfortably as he did. Later in life, he learned that his was the unique and enviable style that Yellows cultivate wherever they go. They seem to know how to make life fun regardless of their circumstances.

No personality plays the way Yellows do. They are so spontaneous that they are always ready for whatever fun opportunities come their way. They often find themselves sporting T-shirts with slogans such as "Are we having fun yet?" and "It's OK to PLAY." They do not need to be productive in their play. The activity of play is, in itself, valuable enough to warrant a Yellow's attention.

Yellows love surprises. They love to celebrate everything imaginable. They find holidays and special moments refreshing and, barring a memory lapse (which they are noted for), they will make the most of every opportunity to have fun.

SUPERFICIAL

Ski resorts, beaches, amusement parks, and other magical environments are filled with Yellows seeking the good life. One of my first professional experiences was working with young people in Park City, Utah, at that time a sleepy little town with one elementary school and a secondary school. The families were primarily of the low to middle socioeconomic class. In fact, some of the kids' parents were coal miners left over from the "good old days." Imagine the task I faced in trying to convince these young people that, in the long run, a life of stability and commitment was far preferable to the momentary pleasures of playing on the ski slopes all season, drinking too much, taking too many drugs, and having casual sex. The full-time ski enthusiasts were gorgeous, trim, smiling, and carefree imitators of happiness. The parents of these young people made popcorn at night and sweated over how to come up with next month's mortgage. The young people were torn between the playful, carefree world many Yellows espouse and the real world in which they were told personal responsibility and concern for others provides a foundation for a rewarding life.

> *Yellows are the people connectors*
> *and the social glue of society.*

Yellows enjoy the company of others but often find themselves unwilling to commit beyond the pleasures of momentary good times. Yellows resist activities or people requiring endurance, which keeps them from perhaps the greatest goal of all—high self-esteem based on earned productivity and the kind of deep intimacy experienced only in long-term, committed relationships.

DISORGANIZED AND INCOMPLETE

Yellows would like to change not themselves but, rather, the world around them—life circumstances. In fact, they enjoy change. However, *what* they change is usually unimportant, and *when* they change is often counterproductive. One Yellow friend lamented that every time he had a big project coming due, he would clean his garage instead. Rather than focus on the essential project, he wasted hours focusing on irrelevant puttering. Equally frustrating to him was his inability to organize effectively. He even left his garage in a constant state of disruption rather than creating order. When he would finally tackle the essential project, he would be forced to toss it together instead of having time to prepare a quality presentation. He felt incomplete, as if he were almost cheating himself and others of the best quality performance that he was capable of.

Yellows learn early in life to cut corners. They often claim credit for accomplishments they haven't actually fully achieved. They simply tell half-truths, or feel it isn't that big a deal whether they are what they say as long as it doesn't hurt anyone.

Life has a way of providing consequences for our behaviors. You reap what you sow. Many Yellows are very talented and would love the applause of others. Yet they are unwilling to put in the time and effort to earn the praise they seek.

IMPULSIVE AND UNDISCIPLINED

Yellows often display flighty and undisciplined dispositions. They are terribly restless and find sticking with any task quite boring. Yellows often experience numerous job changes—not because the jobs are uninteresting but because the Yellows generally become bored. Yellows believe life should be experienced in the fast lane if it's going to be experienced at all.

Yellows are impulsive and restless. One can never be sure what to expect from these unpredictable individuals. Here today, gone to Maui! They are quick to change but often do so unproductively. It is hard to hang on to these flighty Yellows who constantly seek the free and easy life. They know how to have a good time and wish everyone else would work to make that possible for them.

One Yellow man purchased a new video camera and let it sit in the box for a week before a friend happened to drop by and notice it. His friend had the best time figuring out where to connect things and how to use the zoom lens. The camera owner was momentarily intrigued until his friend recommended that he read the instruction book himself so he could use the camera effectively. Weeks later, after the Yellow's wife had pressed him repeatedly to remember to bring the camera to various events, he realized he couldn't continue to play stupid, so he announced that the camera didn't work right anymore. It was brilliant manipulation. He knew his Blue wife wouldn't be able to accept a broken camera sitting around the house after they had paid so much money for it. He also knew that she wouldn't return the camera until she had tried to fix it herself. Within a matter of two hours, she had mastered the camera, and she became the official photographer for the rest of their marriage. Yellows prefer not to be bothered with the details of life. They simply want the praise for what they do accomplish and the credit for whatever commitments they miraculously maintain in their lives.

Yellows are very interested in preserving wildlife. In other words, they are always ready to throw a party. Daily routine quickly becomes monotonous, and Yellows slip away into new and different environments. They hate exercise unless they can socialize at the same time or watch themselves in a mirror. Yellows find amazing excuses for not disciplining themselves. Once their excuses fail them, and society imposes restrictions on them, be prepared for sullen, angry behavior.

Anger is never experienced when one is powerful. Anger is expressed when one feels powerless. Yellows often express anger when life becomes difficult and unfair. They feel instant frustration when problems aren't easily solved. Few Yellows, therefore, ever become chief executive officers or powerful leaders. (President Ronald Reagan was the exception, and Nancy was no Yellow!) They are not interested in power, and even if they were, the dedication required to stay with a challenging problem long enough to solve it would quickly discourage them. Trying to fix things when they lack the necessary skill infuriates Yellows. Daily activities like driving on busy freeways, balancing checkbooks, putting oil in the car, looking up numbers in a telephone directory, etc., can upset Yellows so easily that they often lose their concentration and begin rummaging through their minds for ways to escape the insanity others call "responsible living."

CHARISMATIC AND POPULAR

Yellows find it easy to relate to people of all ages. They make friends with all the kids on their block. They charm elderly people in stores and babies in strollers with their entertaining style. Their joyful natures brighten the dispositions of many of those whom they encounter.

Yellows often appear to be very attractive because of their personality. The reason so many Yellows appear attractive is that they are skilled at choosing a style that emphasizes their best physical and social qualities. They have the most engaging style of any of the personalities. The adjective commonly used for Yellows is *charismatic*. They parent charismatically. They conduct business charismatically. They converse charismatically. Often considered the Pied Pipers of humanity, Yellows can easily move groups of people to tears and/or laughter.

Yellows love to entertain and be entertained. They often stage productions in the garage for neighborhood children, run for student body office in school, and choose careers in which they have a great deal of exposure to people. They give freely of themselves. Perhaps because they crave their own freedom so dearly, Yellows do not seek to control others. They live without many expectations and give without concern for what they might receive.

"Don't sweat the small stuff . . .
and it's all small stuff!"

They are often the life of the party in social settings. Yellows find laughter and interpersonal relationships easy. They sincerely like people and typically find themselves surrounded by friends. They are very popular in most environments without ever having to seek social acceptance. Their trusting nature draws others to them. Yellows are typically very open, which makes their friendship easy to understand and maintain. Yellows are usually carefree. Other personalities seek out Yellow friends for their positive and cheerful manner.

NAIVE AND TRUSTING

No other personality experiences life with as much naive trust as do Yellows. They don't think things through prior to speaking or doing.

Yellows often find themselves victims of their own naivete. They are easily fooled and easy prey for more sophisticated and calculating personalities. They trust easily and yet often build high walls to prevent intimacy once sufficient emotional scarring has occurred.

One young man was promised a bonus for every client he drew into his law firm. He was highly engaging and had a knack for creating clientele for his firm. He trusted his senior partners. However, instead of receiving a bonus, he was chastised for not racking up the same number of billable hours as his colleagues, who were unable to create clientele but were more capable of servicing the clients he brought to the firm. He was the rainmaker but was unrewarded for his gifts. Eventually, he left the firm to work for himself when he discovered how much money he had made for the senior partners by bringing in clientele to the firm without the fair compensation they had earlier agreed upon.

Yellows are not particularly bothered by commitments such as appointments being broken, but broken emotional commitments can be devastating. If Yellows have been bitterly hurt, they may get stuck in superficial relationships. This is particularly unfortunate because, deep inside, Yellows are driven by intimacy. They are denying themselves one of their greatest needs because of imagined or real broken promises in their lives. It is not uncommon to see misguided, superficial Yellows floating through life as if they preferred their freedom to intimacy, but such behavior typically comes from earlier scars or distrust. Since Blues are known for their sincerity and loyalty, this may, at least in part, explain why Yellows often seek their companionship.

FLIPPANT CHATTERBOX

Yellows are often nicknamed "chatterbox" because they can find *anything* interesting enough to talk about. This is helpful on dates but can be quite stressful for colleagues and family members. When their idle chatter is combined with rude and loud behavior, Yellows are considered obnoxious. This label always offends them because they can't comprehend why anyone wouldn't find them as delightful and entertaining as they find themselves.

One distressed mother feared she would gag her four-year-old child if something didn't change soon. She was so tired of nonstop conversation that she admittedly stopped listening simply to save her own sanity. (Personally, I think she was also concerned for the child's physical well-being.) She liked her quiet time, and every time she simply sat down to gather her thoughts, her daughter pounced on her lap and tried to cheer her up. The mother actually hid from her child at times throughout the day so that she might enjoy some peace.

The conversational approach to life is also frustrating when you want to be serious, and Yellows don't want to, can't, or won't be. "Just once," a desperate husband lamented, "could my wife listen and feel my pain without making a joke out of everything? Not everything belongs in the Sunday funnies. I can't begin to tell you the number of times I have held my feelings inside because I knew she would make light of something I felt more serious about." So goes the irritation of trying to communicate deeply with a lighthearted Yellow.

Unless they are corrected, Yellows often take a flippant, rude, and self-centered approach to the rest of the family. They are often socially adept and poke fun at other family members who lack the necessary social skills to defend themselves. They are notorious for interrupting whether you are busy or not. Nothing is sacred to the Yellows, and they are equally certain that nothing is sacred to others. Whether you are on the telephone or reading, Yellows will find a way of distracting you until you acknowledge their needs. This often infuriates those who accompany Yellows through life. When you add up all the small irritations, Yellows can be quite disconcerting to encounter. They are loud show-offs willing to embarrass anyone for a good-natured laugh. They interrupt without hesitation, feeling that nothing is so important that it can't wait for them. They talk constantly as if words were the music of life. They regard themselves as cute and entertaining. Quick-witted and quick-tongued, Yellows can toss sarcastic bombs with an expertise rivaled only by Reds. Their vanity and self-centeredness can become intolerable after a lengthy period of time. They can be a frustrating force to deal with in the social realm.

YELLOW LIMITATIONS

Yellows have little regard for the property of others. They are sloppy and messy individuals who keep themselves clean and polished while their homes often suffer from neglect. They want to look particularly good to the world, and when social praise is a consideration, they are quick to comply with society's standards. Otherwise, housekeeping may require too much effort.

They are disorganized in their environments and personal thoughts. Rather than focusing on real issues and important events, Yellows putter with minor concerns and irrelevant activity. They have a difficult time committing to anything that takes priority over play-time, and consequently often find themselves in superficial and empty relationships as well as being somewhat superficial and empty themselves once they are in a relationship.

YELLOW STRENGTHS

Despite their struggle with self-discipline and commitment, Yellows are eager to experience all facets of life. They naively call for the spotlight to be focused on them as though they were always center stage. Yellows are our constant reminder that you are as young as you feel. They remain youthful in their attitudes toward new ideas, change, relationships, occupations, and the future. Yellows carry that child-like quality of hope that inspires others to appreciate and value themselves as well as the wonderful world in which they live. Yellows promote the good in others and willingly ignore their limitations. Yellows are more inclined to like themselves for what they are rather than what they do. They are the people connectors and the social glue of society. Yellows express themselves candidly and genuinely. They give playful attention to living and inspire others to do the same. They freely offer their opinions as well as themselves, often spreading a contagious spirit of friendship wherever they go. Once your life has been intimately touched by a Yellow, you will more fully appreciate the incredible joy achievable by the human soul and the optimistic hope attainable within the human heart.

YELLOW STRENGTHS

AS AN INDIVIDUAL

- highly optimistic (rarely depressed)
- likes self and accepts others easily
- loves to volunteer for opportunities
- sees life as an experience to be enjoyed
- flashy (racehorse rather than plowhorse)
- adventurous and daring

AS A COMMUNICATOR

- thinks quickly on his or her feet and can express this spontaneously
- enjoys and promotes being physical (hugs, touching)
- easy to converse with
- comfortable with people
- able to express self directly in conflict
- energized by large groups
- superb at superficial conversation

AS A GOAL SETTER

- appreciates and lives for the present
- gives priority to playtime
- very flexible
- accepts guidance from others
- disciplined if he or she finds the task fun and challenging
- demands action rather than study

AS A CAREER PERSON

- people-oriented
- friendly
- able to take risks
- high energy
- inspires colleagues and subordinates to cooperate and excel
- charismatic and enjoyable to work with
- breaks up monotony of work world
- likes to tackle short-term projects with visible results
- enjoys dressing up and also comfortable with casual attire
- supports dreams and intuitive thinking

AS A PARENT

- highly entertaining
- promotes fun family activities
- excellent short-term leader
- finds touching children natural and comfortable
- flows easily with negative expcriences
- turns crisis into comedy
- nonjudgmental about children's friends
- children enjoy their company and seek them out
- concern themselves with the broad picture rather than the details

AS A CHILD

- fun to have around
- playful and entertaining
- enjoys new experiences
- accepting of differences
- loves to socialize (brings friends home)
- easy to talk to
- strong visual learner
- loves physical contact (hugging, kissing)
- pliable—willing to bend in order to please
- curious and inquisitive

AS A FRIEND

- exciting and fun to be with (never dull or boring)
- often places friends before family
- forgiving of self and others
- lively and entertaining
- vulnerable, innocent, and trusting
- endearing
- willing to free up schedule in order to play

AS A COMMITTED COMPANION

- brings excitement to spouse
- promotes romance with a creative flair
- enjoys unusual experiences
- not burdened with emotional baggage
- has few expectations of others
- agreeable to change
- accepts others' suggestions

CAREERS MOST LIKELY TO ATTRACT YELLOWS

Firefighter	Beautician	Secretary
International consultant	Entertainer	Receptionist
Travel agent	Tour guide	Sales
Recreation leader	Circus performer	Retail
Lifeguard	Insurance agent	Clergy/Minister

Note: Yellows are generally least capable of consistently committing to the requirements for financial success or the career world.

PERSONALITIES WHO APPEAR TO BE YELLOWS

BILL CLINTON: President Clinton has magically survived a myriad of assaults on his personal character and professional competence, but he never runs for cover. His winning smile and positive manner help people trust him. He is intellectually bright and verbally quick, making him difficult to pin down or ever catch off-guard.

RONALD REAGAN: One of America's most adored presidents, Ronald Reagan's trademark was optimism and charisma. He spoke with con-

viction and always exuded an inviting warmth. He carried himself
with a carefree confidence that put others at ease around him.

ELVIS PRESLEY: Dynamic and rebellious. His vulnerability and trusting
nature were charming and disarming. He was personable and gener-
ous. He lived for the moment, and his naivete and emotionalism
caused irrational decisions to prematurely end his scattered brilliance
as a performer. As with all good Yellows, people are still hoping to find
him alive so the party can continue.

YELLOW NATIONS

Mexico
Australia
Brazil

"I get enough exercise just pushing my luck."

YELLOW LIMITATIONS

AS AN INDIVIDUAL

- needs to look good socially (high priority)
- irresponsible and unreliable
- self-centered and egotistical
- flighty and uncommitted
- lots of talk with little action
- superficial and mostly interested in a good time
- unwilling to experience pain in order to produce quality
- undisciplined
- loud and obnoxious in public places
- exaggerates successes and omits unpleasant truths
- unable to confront or face issues

AS A COMMUNICATOR

- often speaks before thinking
- unsympathetic about depression in others

- makes insensitive jokes about serious and sensitive issues
- lightminded and superficial
- often repetitious
- interrupts others freely
- overly dramatic in expressing self (often uses superlatives)
- often talks too much about everything and nothing
- poor listener
- forgets what others have said

AS A GOAL SETTER

- terribly undisciplined in committing to goals
- prefers to play today rather than plan for tomorrow
- feels no need to prepare for the future
- restless and finds it difficult to stick with long-term goals
- more interested in appearing onstage than writing the script
- disorganized and scattered in too many directions

AS A CAREER PERSON

- requires that all activities be fun
- can handle stress only for short periods of time
- poor concentration for any length of time
- unwilling to dedicate self to a cause without vacations
- resents authority and defiant to leaders
- sloppy and unpredictable
- needs a lot of interaction with people
- takes few things seriously

AS A PARENT

- self-centered and more concerned about self than children's needs
- more interested in enjoying children than teaching them
- can be sarcastic with children
- unwilling to spend a lot of time and energy on children's behalf
- inconsistent with discipline
- irresponsible and too permissive with children
- bad role model for positive work habits
- lacks discipline for housecleaning or providing stable income

AS A CHILD

- sassy and demanding
- defiant of authority
- forgetful of assignments and parental expectations
- more concerned with friends than family
- teases siblings constantly
- insensitive to parents' responsibilities or needs
- prefers to take the easy road whenever possible
- shows little concern for family problems and responsibilities
- unconcerned with financial issues

AS A FRIEND

- spends most of time discussing own life
- shows up at his or her convenience
- undependable in a crisis
- unwilling to commit to long-term needs of distressed friends
- pursues own life regardless of friends' situations or needs
- uncomfortable in painful or distressing environments
- makes new friends easily and without guilt, often at the expense of old friends

AS A COMMITTED COMPANION

- uncommitted and flighty in long-term relationships
- undependable and inconsiderate of the needs of others
- prefers to enter a relationship knowing there is an escape
- unwilling to hang in there during the difficult times
- quick-tempered in unpleasant circumstances requiring patience
- unwilling to invest time in personal growth to improve relationships
- capable of ignoring the feelings of others and focusing on self

How to Develop a Positive Relationship with Yellows

Do:

1. Be positive and proactive with them in your life
2. Adore and praise them legitimately
3. Touch them physically

4. Accept their playful teasing
5. Remember they are more sensitive than they appear
6. Value their social interaction skills and people connections
7. Remember they hold feelings deeply
8. Promote creative and fun activities for and with them
9. Enjoy their charismatic innocence
10. Allow them opportunity for verbal expression

Don't:

1. Be too serious or sober in criticism
2. Push them too intensely
3. Ignore them
4. Forget they have "down" time also
5. Demand perfection
6. Expect them to dwell on problems
7. Give them too much rope, or they may hang themselves
8. Classify them as just lightweight social butterflies
9. Attack their sensitivity or be unforgiving
10. Totally control their schedules or consume their time

Recommended Time-Management Tips for Yellows

1. Realize that "busyness" is not necessarily the same as purposeful action. Reflect on what is important and give it legitimate attention.
2. Set specific goals each day and prioritize them. Start working on your A1 goal first. Don't go to your A2 priority until you complete your A1. Do them in order.
3. Focus on "what's necessary" rather than "what's fun." Quality requires both. Don't let others take on the responsibility of handling your "necessary" tasks.
4. Set achievable "time bits" where you focus on a specific task for a specific amount of time and create a fun reward for sticking to it. Break up the monotony.
5. Commit to the bigger picture. Create a long-term plan of substance and seek specific activities you can complete to make it a reality.
6. Balance undemanding creativity with focused commitments. You'll feed both your need for unstructured play and your need for accomplishment.

7. Do a little planning up front so you "get it right" the first time. You'll save yourself tremendous time.
8. Face the issues rather than spending time on trivia.
9. Listen well so you don't have to interrupt others for information already presented.

"Hard work may not kill me, but why take a chance?"

Chapter Nine

SECONDARY COLORS

Few people exhibit only the behaviors of one color.
While everyone has only one core,
our personalities are often influenced
by our secondary colors.

There are three specific reasons why people readily embrace the Color Code:

1. It is simple to understand.
2. It is easy to apply.
3. It is accurate.

A psychological theory is only as good as its ability to accurately identify and predict human behavior. Using the driving core motive as the foundation for my work assures an accuracy that a premise based solely on observed behavior cannot hope to offer. The driving core motive in everyone's personality is the critical element that will not only facilitate personal development but will grant others a personal view into everyone they encounter.

I have lectured to hundreds of thousands of people. I have worked intimately as a personal coach with thousands of individuals. Ever since developing *The Color Code,* I have always found the driving core motive in each person with whom I've had contact. Admittedly, I've been slow to discover it at times and initially wrong at other times. But I have always found their true core motive, and we both knew it was accurate when we finally discovered it. By the way, when you find your innate core motive, it feels like "coming home" to a safe and comfortable place—a place free of pretense and demands. It simply feels right.

Some people identify themselves correctly from the first time they hear or read my theory. Others struggle finding themselves for various reasons. Ironically, as the author of this theory, I was initially wrong identifying myself. At first I pegged myself as a Red. Actually, nothing could be further from the truth. When I took the Hartman Personality Profile from a childhood perspective, I was 43 Yellow, 1 White, and 1 Red. Statistically, there appears to be no Red or any secondary color at all.

However, when I review the profile, it becomes readily clear that my secondary preferences are overwhelmingly Red, as opposed to Blue or White. In other words, when I had to struggle to make a decision on any given question, it was almost exclusively between the Yellow and the Red option. This brings in the exciting variable of how our secondary color influences our personalities.

My clinical research indicates that there are four main reasons that best explain why some people struggle to correctly identify their core driving personality motive. They are:

1. An individual is reared in a strong autocratic family where express attitudes and behaviors were determined solely by one or both parents (or any significant familial figure).
2. Unresolved and/or untreated sexual abuse.
3. Theological and/or cultural biases.
4. An individual is born with a closely blended personality.

This chapter focuses primarily on the fourth reason: An individual is born with a closely blended personality. However, allow me to give a brief clarification of why and how the first three reasons play such a critical role in confusing people about who they innately are:

Reason #1 An individual is reared in a strong autocratic family where express attitudes and behaviors were determined solely by one or both parents (or any significant familial figure).

Actually this is my story. My mother (whom I absolutely adore) is so Red that she is just one step shy of Attila the Hun! She ran our home of seven children with tremendous confidence and authority. In fact, in writing *The Color Code,* I researched my own brothers and sisters and was astounded to find a Red brother who so pales next to our Red mother that I almost missed correctly identifying him. (And, trust me, he is no lightweight, either.) Mom was so committed to us and loved every minute of being home to rear us (a rather unique attitude in today's world), but no one ever crossed her and lived. We knew early in life that survival depended on working *with* her rather than *against* her. Consequently, she completely directed all of our lives, and I embraced numerous Red (as opposed to Yellow) qualities because she deemed them to have the most value just by her role model. Fortunately, she never demeaned my Yellow gifts. She actually rather enjoyed them. But they always (and only) found value in conjunction with Red behavior such as responsibility and accountability.

> *When you find your innate core motive,*
> *it feels like "coming home"*
> *to a safe and comfortable place—*
> *a place free of pretense and demands.*
> *It simply feels right.*

Far too many people will never know themselves because their parents (or a significant familial figure) set the course everyone was to embrace. Sadly, I have encountered thousands of people who remain angry at mothers for controlling them and robbing them of the personal preferences they would have chosen given their innate personality.

Reason #2   Unresolved and/or untreated sexual abuse.

Free agency is the cornerstone of the human experience. Perhaps nothing has caused me greater emotional pain than to work with people who were sexually betrayed early in life by someone they trusted (and clearly should have been able to trust!). I don't know of any indiscretion that is more destructive to the human soul than sexual abuse. It's terribly invasive and demeaning. It steals hope and innocence and actually leaves deep scars, self-doubt, and a propensity to make poor choices with regard to the men or women with whom they are intimate.

So much has already been written on this topic. I merely want to add my voice of experience that sexual abuse can be a terrifying and powerful force in deadening the human soul—thus seriously derailing one's accurate perception of oneself. If you have been a victim of sexual abuse, consider who you really are inside as opposed to what attitude and/or behavior you may have embraced to protect yourself or vent your anger for having lost your innocence so young.

Reason #3   Theological and/or cultural biases.

Myth: Men are logical and women are emotional! This false statement continues to permeate our society, convincing Red and White women they really aren't thinking logically, and Blue and Yellow men that they really don't feel those emotions they have. Nonsense. But how often do we hear biased comments like "big boys don't cry" and "women just cry to manipulate you"? We are so afraid to face the truth of who we are that we often make rash and self-serving comments at the expense of others so we can feel better about ourselves. Do yourself a favor and get beyond rigid theological and/or cultural biases in order to embrace everyone's true personality identity.

Of course, people learn quickly how to get on in this world. If someone gets a consistent message that they are wrong to behave a certain way because a religion and/or society so dictates, they usually defer personal preference to survival and acceptance of group norms. Some individuals have deferred so much throughout their lives that they are either terribly angry about everything, or they no longer even resemble who they were at birth. If you want to talk about human tragedies, that's the real human tragedy—to be robbed of your very being!

> *Blues with strong Red secondary*
> *experience the most difficult internal struggles.*
> *They are also typically*
> *the most resourceful of personalities.*

So much more could be written about each of these reasons that block individuals from being fully human and feeling fully alive. However, the focus of this book is on innate personalities as opposed to outside influences. While other factors do impact us, they are not the primary influence in determining our personalities. That distinguished role will forever be played by our driving core motive. This is why it is so critical to correctly identify who we innately are.

More than any other secondary factor, secondary colors are most prominent in determining our unique personality. Secondary colors refer to personality strengths and limitations that belong to a personality not of our own core, but represented in our attitudes and/or behaviors. For example, you may be an assertive Red with tremendous compassion (Mother Teresa comes to mind). Compassion does not innately belong to the Red personality, and yet a person with a Red personality may enjoy its gift (whether innate or learned). In this example, assertiveness would be considered primary or natural to the core personality, while compassion would be considered to be a secondary color influence. Compassion, of course, is a positive trait. There are as many negative traits capable of providing negative secondary influences as well. For example, consider working for a sincere Blue personality who is selfish. The sincerity is primary, but it becomes seriously tainted by the secondary trait of selfishness.

I have discovered that we are far more forgiving of others when they act according to their natural, innate core personalities. We expect Reds to lead and Whites to be kind. However, when people stray from their innate comfort zone, others become uncomfortable, especially when someone displays limitations unlike their innate personality (for example, if a Yellow becomes reclusive or a Blue becomes bossy). If you had never heard about the Color Code, you would still have an intuition and expectation for how others will behave. When they act incongruently and go beyond the lines we have established as acceptable for them, conflict or avoidance usually occurs.

These same expectations can get in the way of personal development as well. So often when a selfish, emotionally guarded Red begins to stretch and take the charactered path (which means to develop personality strengths outside one's core personality), others react negatively. Based on their history with the individual, they refuse to accept the change. We like people to stay in the boxes we have come to know them by. Any deviation from what we have determined to be acceptable is uncomfortable for us, and thus we immediately react to preserve the status quo, whether it is positive or negative. This also explains why personal change is so difficult and why so many of us abandon ourselves and the charactered journey before we've completed our work.

Secondary colors are those traits, whether positive or negative, that directly influence our primary core color to our benefit or detriment. After completing the Hartman Personality Profile, you will have an excellent awareness of your primary core and secondary colors. However, what the profile does not tell you is whether your secondary color is positive or negative. The Hartman Character Profile will provide you with those answers. That's why it is so crucial for us to correctly identify our core personality before focusing on secondary color influences. Once we have correctly laid the foundation of our core personality, we can begin the inviting task of uniquely filling out our personality with secondary color blends.

There are pluses and minuses to having strong secondary color(s) in our personality. One plus is that having the strengths of a secondary color can balance you. You can draw on gifts of other personalities more comfortably than people who display no secondary influences. You are also more adept at understanding other personalities, because there may be parts of you that think as others do. The most common reason that people don't get along with others comes from a lack of understanding of why others think and act as they do. Having a secondary color helps us cross that bridge of understanding.

The minuses of having a strong secondary color(s) can best be explained in two parts. When you have strengths in two colors, you may find yourself in a constant internal battle as to which innate strength to follow in any given situation. People with strong Red and Blue tendencies suffer the most from this because both personalities are so controlling. When your secondary color is Yellow or White, there tends to be less conflict because those colors offer a more passive and accepting agenda.

The conflict is even more pronounced, however, when you have innate positive traits in one color and innate negative traits in another. Talk about sending dual messages! Take, for example, a strong blend of Red and Blue (and there are many of you!). The strengths and limitations of these two personalities are dramatically incongruent. Reds can be self-ish, while Blues are generally more thoughtful. Blues can be self-critical, while Reds prefer to criticize others. When a person with a Blue core personality operates in the negative Red zone, they send mixed messages and get limited results. Before the Color Code they never understood why this happened. Remember, we accept people in their natural core personality, so when they start acting out, especially in the negatives of their secondary color, we become confused and, for self-preservation, we either distance ourselves or attack. The Blue individual who innately seeks intimacy and knows he or she cares deeply for you will become confused when his or her Red negative behaviors are displayed. The Blue may know that he or she cares deeply, but the behavior is bossy, demeaning, or calculated, and it definitely does not feel safe or inviting. Blues must rid themselves of their negative Red traits or suffer a lifetime of sending and receiving mixed messages.

It is far more important to free yourself of the limitations of your secondary color than your primary color. People are far more forgiving of our limitations within our primary personality than of secondary color flaws. More importantly for us, perhaps, is that displaying the limitations of a secondary color does more damage in preventing us from experiencing our driving core motive than displaying our core limitations will.

Let me give you a personal example. I am a Yellow who is driven by the core motive of fun. I travel often for business and have learned that being assertive (Red) gets problems with airlines and hotels addressed and resolved much more efficiently than my innate nature of simply going with the flow (Yellow). However, I have discovered that when I begin expecting others to perform at a higher level, and thus become more critical in my evaluation of them, I become less happy and positive and therefore have less fun. It can be very challenging to balance developing the gifts of other personalities while remaining true to your own innate core motive.

Motives become the important factor in determining whether it is best to embrace a particular attitude or behavior at any given time. If one's motive is clean, it becomes mandatory for good mental health to act on it. However, if one's motive is dirty (i.e., based on fear or ignorance), it is equally critical that one *not* act on it. We must always check on motives for clarity when selecting attitudes and/or behaviors. Whatever traits we don't have control over will control us. If we allow ourselves to behave according to how we feel, we will soon find that our excuses of "that's just how I am" will forge a lifetime of self-betrayal and produce anxiety for others. We must always be aware of our motives and how they drive our attitudes and behaviors.

> People with strong Yellow and White blends
> enjoy the best "people skills."
> If you can't enjoy them, consider yourself
> the one with the problem.

Secondary colors can skew our personalities so that we no longer act according to who we innately know ourselves to be. I have worked with Reds who have strong secondary Blue traits, and they appear to be White. Rather than accenting the strengths of their Red and their Blue gifts, they abandon the battle and act White. Of course, this leaves no real winners. We don't get their Red or Blue strengths, and they don't experience their core motive of power with Blue accents of compassion and quality. Never let your secondary color drain you of your innate core motive or strengths. The value of our secondary color can be fully experienced only when we remain true to our innate core personality motive.

Secondary colors explain the many nuances of people despite being limited to only four optional driving core motives. Have you ever considered how few variables there are that make up the human face? Variables include eyes, ears, nose, chin, mouth, hair. Not that many really! And yet do you know any faces that look exactly alike? Of all the millions of people who share this planet Earth at any given moment, isn't it rather amazing that none look exactly alike given the relatively limited number of physical attributes that create our physical identity? This same phenomenon exists with our personalities as well. While there are only four core motives, there are numerous variables that create unique and diverse personalities such that no two individuals are ever the same. The gift that *The Color Code* offers is an honest foundation of core motives from which we can understand and further develop our own unique personalities.

Part Three

❈❈❈

RELATIONSHIPS:
THE COLOR CONNECTIONS

INTRODUCTION

Reds and Blues spend their lifetimes
trying to control others.
Whites and Yellows spend their lifetimes
refusing to be controlled.

UNDERSTANDING THE COLOR CONNECTIONS

The next three chapters will specifically focus on what each personality can expect when interacting with another personality. Personality plays a critical role in every aspect of our business and personal lives. **This year 85 percent of the employees who lose their jobs will lose them because of personality conflicts. Only 15 percent will lose their jobs because they lack technical expertise.**

Whenever a child is born, the parents and grandparents check for ten fingers and ten toes. They focus on the physically obvious qualities that will pale by comparison in importance to the innate core personality the child has. It may be a matter of only a few days or, in other cases, many years before the full impact of the personality of a newborn child or a recently hired employee is realized.

Equally intriguing will be the interaction between the newborn child or recently hired employee and the already existing personalities in the family or the company. Some are soothing, while others always stir the pot. Some are accommodating, while others seem to bring multiple agendas with them. Some arrive with a fairly healthy personality already in place, while others struggle an entire lifetime to make sense of themselves.

And how could anyone get married without first knowing the personality of the one with whom they plan to spend a lifetime? Initially, I considered printing on the front cover: "Don't marry anyone until you've read this book!" While any color can successfully marry any other color, *The Color Code* will identify specific benefits and consequences of each and every union.

Similarly, the Hartman Personality and Character profiles are used by numerous businesses as tools for interviewing prospective employees and providing semiannual work reviews. Countless hours and dollars are wasted every year by neglecting to screen applicants properly, putting people in the wrong jobs, and failing to properly motivate and reward employees based on their personalities.

Employees see companies differently based on their personalities. I recently asked employees of a corporation to assess the temperature of their company. In reviewing their responses, the most significant factor in determining their answers was their personality color. Even when they gave the same responses on leadership, their reasons for the responses varied with their colors. A Red secretary said, "We have no procedures in place. I've even offered to write the procedure manual, but our president said I have more important things to do with my time, like he knows anyway." The Blue project manager said, "I thought I would feel more connected to upper management. They haven't even introduced me to the owner. How can I be loyal to a business where I am ignored?" The White accountant said, "Well, communication has been a problem in every company I've ever worked for." He went on to explain in very vague, nonthreatening language how it can be difficult to lead people with such opposing views. The Yellow sales representative said, "I think it's great how everyone tries here. We just need to appreciate what a great opportunity working at this company offers us."

If you interact with other people, personally or professionally, these next three chapters are for you. Study them to identify the natural connections and roadblocks you will most likely experience in the interaction of different personalities. In the end, the quality of your life comes down to the relationship you develop. Successful lives are always illustrated by successful relationships. Learn how to make your personality work for you in the various relationships you currently experience.

Chapter Ten

THE RED CONNECTIONS

*Red-Red relationships are typically
the most dynamic of all the color connections.*

RED-RED RELATIONSHIPS

"FIREWORKS"

RED RULES OF LIFE (AND THERE ARE ONLY TWO)

Rule 1: Reds are ALWAYS right.
Rule 2: If (and that's a huge "if") Reds are wrong, see Rule 1.

Red-Red relationships are typically the most dynamic of all the color connections. Both people are direct, decisive, and determined. They are such intense people that everything about their relationship is generally bold and high profile.

One close friend told me about her childhood with two very Red parents. Her father came home one evening from working in the fields and became so angry when dinner wasn't ready that he took the uncooked beans from the stove and threw them out in the backyard. This infuriated his wife, who quickly responded by taking his rifle from the kitchen and tossing it out by the beans. They took turns tossing things from the kitchen until it was almost empty and their backyard a cluttered mess. Then they both looked at each other, laughed, and went out to eat at a restaurant, leaving their children to fend for themselves.

This powerful combination can be highly productive. Reds are task-oriented and find little need to concentrate on intimacy or compassion toward each other. Both typically enjoy the leadership role, and because there is usually room for only one king of the jungle, they tend not to attract each other for long-term commitments. Reds are more likely to seek companions with a softer, more compassionate color. Healthy Red relationships often exist and flourish as friendships, in careers, or even between parents and children. However, Red-Red combinations are not generally well represented in marital relationships.

Mutual respect is the key element of a Red-Red relationship. Because of their intense strength, they must learn to respect one another. Respect affords a Red the opportunity of accepting the other's point of view. When they value each other's perspectives, they are more likely to alter some of their decisions in order to share mutual dreams. Otherwise, Red-Red relationships merely reflect two separate people living their own lives with little evidence of a shared lifestyle.

When Reds refuse to share decision making or to accept each other's perceptions, they suffer an intolerable stalemate in their relationship. How do two people get anywhere when both of them are absolutely certain that they know the best way to get there, and neither will budge? This dilemma is not uncommon with two Reds in any given relationship. Most Red children are certain that *they* know a better way to raise children than their parents. They are right, and nothing the parent can say or do seems to convince them otherwise. Most Red parents are certain that *they* know the only way to raise children, and nothing the child can say or do seems to convince them otherwise.

Reds demand to control their own lives as well as the lives of anyone who will allow it (including other Reds). Because both Reds in any relationship want control, it often becomes a matter of who has the greater power. Typically, Red parents have control over their Red children, and Red employers have an edge over Red employees. I was raised in a large family with a very powerful Red mother who clearly dominated our lives. In developing the color theory, I was initially unable to assess the personalities of my own brothers and sisters. My mother was so powerful that we *all* acquiesced to her. (In our later years, we nicknamed her the "Little General," referring to her dominant manner.) Her dominance so far exceeded the natural power of her children that I initially neglected to see any Red personalities among my brothers and sisters. They were dominated by a more powerful Red and unable to reflect their innate personalities until they left home and developed families of their own. Crossing a Red in his or her own territory is like trying to tell a New York cab driver that he doesn't know how to drive. Good luck!!

Despite the typical domination of Red parents, society is replete with numerous examples of Red children who assert themselves with their Red parents. Relatively few of the Red youths I have known have survived the teenage years without vowing to leave home before they were eighteen. One Red sixteen-year-old client, Linda, was in direct conflict almost daily with her Red stepfather, Rick. She struggled to comply with his "unreasonable" curfews and numerous parental expectations in order to accommodate her White mother. Her dad's rules seemed impossible to accept. Earning her way in the world seemed far more appealing than continuing to subject herself to his control. She resisted any authority or control. She resented school, so she refused to study. She detested having to grow up.

One day I asked her, "Linda, since you are so unhappy, have you ever thought of leaving home and moving out on your own?" Her eyes seemed to pierce mine with the dullest and yet most defiant stare. Coldly, and convincingly, she said, "I have contemplated that a thousand times." By her tone of voice, I knew she wasn't exaggerating.

She ran way from home two weeks later. She preferred to sleep on a couch at a friend's, work for minimum wage, and put up with an employer's demands rather than prolong what seemed lifetime servitude to her Red stepfather. Note: She returned home within a month with a greater appreciation for her parents. However, she still struggles with parental leadership and authority.

Reds do not like or value anyone who dictates their destiny. Yet they are quite comfortable dictating the destiny of others. (Of course they are. If you had all the answers, wouldn't you feel compelled to design and dictate others' futures for them?) The price they pay for this power orientation and lack of mutual respect is high. Intimacy rarely flourishes with the constant battle cries of debate. Positive energy is often deflected to defend one's position. Sharing feelings becomes a secondary consideration because vulnerability is seen as unproductive in a defensive and combative atmosphere. When two Reds are certain that they are right, and refuse to respect one another, the result can be similar to the pounding of a jackhammer against cement.

HIGHLY MOTIVATED

Most relationships involving a Red revolve around the Red personality. Reds are so bold and dominant. When they feel strongly about having a family reunion, a family reunion is held whether others plan to attend or not. Two healthy Reds carry their own motivations within themselves. They push each other with strong expectations and become a highly organized front.

One Red parent and Red child were so motivated to work out their differences that they set a record in my office for short-term therapy. Selfish as Reds tend to be, these two patients had one goal—to escape my office. I never saw two individuals learn diplomacy and acceptance more rapidly than this pair. Their motivation actually promoted good relations within the home until genuine attitudinal changes could follow and further ensure positive parent-child relations.

LACK OF EMOTIONAL BAGGAGE

Reds benefit greatly from how little emotional baggage they allow in their lives. Reds don't require many emotional support systems in order for them to perform well. They are thrilled to share a task with another Red because neither needs to remember to acknowledge the other with "warm fuzzies" and/or repeated statements of appreciation. "Just get it done and forget the feeling!" they shout.

In the early 1950s, a highly successful American Jewish businessman conducted a major business transaction with an individual in Germany. Both were very Red and highly competent in their fields. Upon entering the German's office, the Jewish businessman was stunned to see Fascist memorabilia depicting this man's obvious sympathy for Nazi Germany. World War II had only recently ended, and the fresh memories of the Nazis' brutal extermination of millions of Jews brought a terrible anger within the American Jewish businessman. He was actually sickened to be with this individual whom he instantly hated. However, business was business, and his purpose in being there was to conduct a business meeting. He pulled himself together and successfully completed their transaction, forgetting the painful memorabilia that initially had brought him tremendous personal trauma. Despite his continued anger, he successfully maintained a productive business relationship with this man.

Reds are rarely discouraged. They don't typically drain each other with emotional blackmail—e.g., "Either you spend time with me, or I won't go to your mother's house for dinner." They are generally independent and enjoy their self-sufficient natures. They don't expend a lot of energy trying to make the other feel loved. They are more concerned with productivity and accomplishment.

SHARED VALUES OF PRODUCTIVITY

Reds often push each other to be productive. They enjoy knowing each is highly responsible and will come through on whatever assignments they have agreed to complete. Reds enjoy a shared value of time. They are fast paced and determined. They enjoy working together and accomplishing a great deal thanks to their strong task-orientation.

One Red author was writing a book with a Blue friend. His Blue friend polished every page to perfection. The Red author was furious each week with his friend's lack of productivity. He completed all his sections of the book but was held up by his Blue friend, who was simply unable to produce. "I only regret not writing it by myself or with another Red," he said. He readily agreed that his Blue friend's writing was brilliant, but feared the book would never get published if his friend didn't cut the perfection stuff and just produce. Reds appreciate productivity and are likely to work best with those who share similar beliefs—even if what they produce together falls short of perfection.

PRODUCTIVE GOAL SETTING

One Red married couple was terribly successful in accomplishing goals. They were proud that they both loved goal setting, and willingly gave it high priority in their relationship. The woman commented, "We go to Las Vegas or some fun place alone every six months and evaluate our successes and failures. Then we establish a new set of goals for the next six months. I can't tell you how exciting it is to lie in bed with your spouse and feel more challenged than you do with your business colleagues. I often feel like we are cooperatively competing with each other to see who can most creatively produce the most exciting and successful life."

EXTREME COMPETITION

While cooperative competition is highly productive, Red-Red relationships are equally susceptible to extreme competition, which produces negative interaction. This color combination probably travels farther and accomplishes more than most relationships. The question is the quality (rather than quantity) of their trips. Red-Red relationships most probably will arrive first at the top of the mountain. (They are highly task oriented and value completion of any activity.) However, while they are at the top of the mountain, the others may well be farther down the path enjoying a wildflower or an exquisite sunset the Reds missed in their hurry to complete the hike. Reds often arrive at life's end with few moments that really captured their hearts. More often their walls are lined with numerous trophies and conquests. They remind me of the couple who travel in Europe in order to come home and tell everyone where they went. The "going" appears to be less appealing than the "having been." They often live in the future with a sense of triumph for having completed a determined goal. Many Red parents comment on how pleased they are with how well their children turned out, while other personalities reminisce about moments they shared as a family in the growing years. Red-Red relationships often miss the pure enjoyment of the activity they are mutually engaged in, or, perhaps, they simply enjoy it differently from the way other personalities do.

Because of their competitive natures, Red-Red relationships seem to be more prone to obsessive-compulsive behavior than other personality combinations. One Red married couple reflects the common trend in the working world of Reds. They have put off having children for ten years in order to build a successful business. Their entire world revolves around their business. Their social engagements are always connected with helping the business. Evenings spent alone generally focus on business-related conversation. Reading material is typically work oriented. They are financially secure and yet have great difficulty slowing down because of their obsession with the business.

Overeating and dieting are common obsessions with Red couples, as well. Community or church work are noted commitments Reds make in life. They can become compulsive about completing tasks or promoting causes, and hardly notice whether other relationship intimacies (or lack thereof) even exist. Whatever the obsession or compulsion, Red-Red relationships are most assuredly productive. Reds will surge ahead whether the cause is worthy or not. As long as they feel gratified by the relationship, Reds will bulldoze through any obstacles to meet the needs of the relationship.

Competition can be very healthy, when done in the spirit of cooperation. It is difficult for two Reds to maintain a proper perspective on their competitiveness because they tend to see things in terms of winning or losing, with little gray area in between. Red-Red relationships prefer to win and dedicate themselves to that end, but if they must lose, they will often cause others to lose as well.

They are highly competitive and willingly pay whatever price is necessary in order to come out on top of any experience they deem valuable enough to pursue. This style of relationship necessitates a highly communicative interaction. Reds display a remarkable ability and willingness to confront one another. They are equally inclined to express hostility and aggression toward each other.

COMMUNICATION

Red companions tend to be highly critical of each other in a relationship. They are also prone to unite and mock others outside of the relationship. I remember one family with a set of Red twin boys who ridiculed each other mercilessly, and yet they could unite and turn on their parents or other siblings in a flash. They were often negative and dominated most family activities with their critical natures.

Reds generally come to relationships equipped with powerful verbal skills. They are quick with the tongue and can banter with the best of them. When you put two angry Reds together, it is similar to two speeding jets crashing in midair. No one ever truly wins. It is a loss for both. On numerous occasions, I have had to stand up and wave my hands during a therapy session with two Reds just to stop their verbal assaults. Some would spend the entire time attacking each other if there wasn't a referee. Neither wants to give the other one the satisfaction of "winning," so they keep at the same issues long after the issues should be laid to rest.

Reds do not usually listen well. Typically, Reds are very impatient listeners. When they do hear, they selectively hear only those parts of the conversation they agree with or accept. If Reds are not careful, they will set themselves up for living separate, rigid lives because they are unwilling to accept what others have to say. Reds are often poor listeners because they need to be right. They refuse to hear what others say if they perceive that it may force them to accept and admit their own mistakes or limitations and change their behavior.

This unwillingness to listen is demonstrated in the following example of a Red married couple. One night they were playing around and he began biting her (nibbling at first, harder later on). For five years she had repeatedly asked him to stop biting her. He refused to listen and repeatedly said that it was fun and playful. He never really believed she was serious.

This night he was biting her and it really hurt. She told him to stop and he simply laughed, ignoring her requests. She became so angry that she finally carried through on a threat she had been making for years and popped him in the mouth as hard as she could. He couldn't believe it. She couldn't either, but now there was no turning back for either of them. They went after each other physically until their three children were frantic with fear. Imagine the scene. The young children together tried to pull their parents apart. The husband yanked the phone from the wall so no one could call for help and continued to assault his wife and now the kids. Finally his wife forced him out of the house and locked the doors. He spent the night in his car and would hardly speak the next day when she finally let him back in the house.

For years she had asked that he stop biting her. For years he had refused to hear. When we discussed it in my office the following day, he could not see how his inability to listen had played a major role in the conflict. If he had simply heard her requests to stop biting, which had been made over a five-year period, this incident would never have taken place. Unfortunately, he could only see how *she* had over-reacted ("I didn't bite her *that* hard") and unfairly locked him out of his own house. Reds find it difficult to listen without trying to win conversations. They are notorious for wanting the last word rather than hearing the last feeling.

Reds can be very insensitive in conversation. They are more concerned with presenting perceived facts than generating kind feeling. I still laugh when I think back to a comment a Red mother made at a family gathering. Picture all five of her adult male children and their spouses seated at a dinner table. Grandchildren were running around outside. A beautiful dinner had been prepared, and the room was full of enthusiastic conversation. Toward the end of the dinner, the subject of one brother's depression came up. The Red mother boldly stated, "I don't understand what his problem is. I have five boys and they were all perfect when they left my home. I guess it all started in their marriages." The Red daughters-in-law were furious. The gauntlet had been thrown down, and simple discussion would not suffice. Needless to say, a most enjoyable family dinner was quickly, and rather abruptly, ended. Problem resolution and mutual understanding is rarely experienced in Red-Red relationships, because the conversations often lack intimacy. Neither listens nor accepts responsibility.

One of the most positive aspects of a Red-Red communication is their willingness to confront each other on almost all issues at any time. No tiptoeing or walking on eggshells is necessary here. Reds have little regard (and less respect) for dishonest diplomacy. If you have something to say in a relationship, Reds feel it should be said. If the other person has a problem with that, Reds feel the other person has the problem. Reds willingly take the initiative in confronting each other directly, and thus enjoy a rare strength in the communication process. I have often known two Reds to end up laughing at themselves following heated arguments that would have silenced other personalities for days. Remember the two who threw everything out of the kitchen? They have a refreshing ability to look at issues rather than always focusing on the personal side of conflict.

LACK OF WARMTH

Warmth is not a word often used to describe Red-Red relationships. They are so intense, critical, and tactless that they do not exude or cultivate a lot of gentleness or provide much accommodation in their interpersonal relations. Most Reds have difficulty sharing positive feelings. Unfortunately, they have little difficulty sharing negative feelings. Of all the personalities, Reds are probably most comfortable with the feeling of anger. They express it often, along with many other critical and negative emotions. However, they are often slow to respond with positive, supportive comments.

ACTIVE

Reds are particularly active people. As a twosome they will generate a lot of energy and involvement. They often find they have to schedule with their two calendars to maintain good communication. Rather than assuming a secondary position of support they both head off in whatever directions feel personally fulfilling. This requires a high degree of tolerance and constant feedback from one to the other. One Red couple lists every appointment on the chalkboard by the telephone. Unfortunately, when one feels her activity is more important for both to attend than their previously listed activity, she simply crosses out the first entry and displays her own. Imagine the interesting communication that promotes!

Red-Red relationships can have so many powerful characteristics (positive and negative) that it behooves all Reds to develop their assets and alter their liabilities. The positive values in many Red-Red relationships include mutual respect, high motivation, lack of emotional baggage, high productivity, effective goal setting, willingness to confront issues and each other, and strong activity orientation. The liabilities include lack of intimacy, power struggles focusing on "winning" and "being right," unwillingness to compromise, extreme competition, insensitive communication, and lack of warmth.

No other combination of personalities
must work as hard to be successfully compatible
as Reds and Blues.

RED-BLUE RELATIONSHIPS

"BLOOD, SWEAT, AND TEARS"

No other combination of personalities must work as hard to be successfully compatible as Reds and Blues. Both want to be in control.
They are equally strong and determined individuals. However, their
motives, needs, wants, and behaviors are mostly opposite. Theirs is a
difficult union, and yet the strong sense of commitment and loyalty
they share substantially increases their chances for success. They each
assume responsibility for various roles and must respect the other's
leadership in his or her role.

OVERVIEW

Red Personality	Blue Personality
MOTIVE	
Power	Intimacy
NEEDS	
to be right	to be understood
to be respected	to be appreciated
to look good to others	to be good for self
(technically)	(morally)
approval of a limited few	general acceptance
WANTS	
challenging adventure	security
leadership	autonomy
to please self	to please others
to hide insecurities (tightly)	to reveal insecurities (openly)
BEHAVIOR STYLE	
highly complex	highly complex
high productivity	strong perfectionism

RELATIONSHIPS: THE COLOR CONNECTIONS

Red Personality	Blue Personality
controlling of others	controlling of self and others
enjoys a high profile	prefers a low profile
welcomes change	prefers stability
logical (unemotional)	emotional (irrational)
insensitive	too sensitive
delegator	doer
manipulative	manipulative
impatient	impatient but long suffering
direct communication (with facts)	direct communication (with feelings)
innovative	creative
intense	intense
demanding	demanding
unforgiving but moves on	unforgiving and resentful
confrontational	confrontational
strong verbal	strong nonverbal
possessive	possessive
tactless	tactful
rebellious	acquiescent
responsible	responsible
achiever	achiever
gives advice and expects compliance	gives advice and expects compliance
does not seek advice	seeks advice from knowledgeable people
intimidating	intimidating
critical of others	critical of self and others
arrogant	self-righteous
gives others guilt	gives others and self guilt
conflict-oriented if necessary to get own way	willing to deal with conflict for principles

Red Personality	Blue Personality
proactive	pessimistic
poor listener	caring listener
difficult to share feelings with	complex and deep when sharing feelings
doesn't love easily but strong commitment	loves deeply and is disappointed by those who can't love (maintains strong commitment)
defies rules	complies with rules
lies to save face	lies to spare others embarrassment

RED-BLUE INTERPERSONAL RELATIONSHIPS
(In-depth Presentation)

POWER   versus   **INTIMACY**

The greatest struggle for Reds and Blues may well be based in their differing motives. Reds are motivated by power, and Blues are motivated by intimacy. Neither offers the other what he or she wants without first demanding that his or her own needs be met as well. The following conversation reflects their unique perspectives.

Red: Do what I say, and we'll get along just fine.
Blue: Tell me you appreciate me, and I'll walk to the ends of the earth for you.

Typical frustration between Blues and Reds involves perceptions of intimacy.

A national sales manager (Red) for a training company requests telephone calls from each of his thirty trainers to inform him about the results of seminars they conducted. Results to him mean numbers, referrals, and bottom line. One of his top trainers is Blue. Results to him mean successful life changes and connection with his audience, as well as the bottom line.

Prior to Blue's knowing the Color Code, their weekly phone calls went like this: Blue trainer calls Red sales manager. Red sales manager is unavailable and prefers message to be left on his voice mail. Blue wants to talk about the seminar directly, so he leaves a message to call him back. Frustrated Red sales manager calls back *because he needs the numbers* that Blue trainer refused to divulge without sharing stories of people connections from the seminars. They play phone tag three times and finally connect. This dialogue follows:

Blue trainer: Had thirty-seven people at the seminar. Two people gave me referral cards for other companies to contact. But the best part was this guy who comes up to me afterwards and tells me how the seminar has saved his job. He understands how to apply time-management principles better at home as well. He also wanted me to know—
Red sales manager: Thanks, Tom. I got the numbers and I gotta go!

Both hang up frustrated. The Red sales manager hates having to hear from Tom each week, but he's one of his top trainers. Tom is frustrated every time the sales manager stops him from sharing what really matters to him from the seminar.

After Tom learned the Color Code, their dialogue went like this:

Blue trainer: (calls Red sales manager and gets voice mail) Hi. This is Tom. Had thirty-seven people in Dallas. Got two referrals and faxed them to Cindy for follow-up. Bye for now.
Red sales manager: (smiles listening to voice mail, transfers the numbers to his report, and calls Tom regularly to check on how he is doing because he wants him to feel connected since he's a top trainer.)

Note: Blue learned to speak Red's language. Red gets his numbers, and Blue doesn't take Red's lack of interest personally. Blue is currently entertaining offers at other companies where he feels more connection. Red offered increase in salary. Blue accepted more money and is still looking.

A Blue Wife commenting on her Red husband:

He never really loved me. Twenty-five years ago we went on our honeymoon and ended up staying with his sister who I had never even met. We slept on their living room couch. He would leave me with his sister while he went hunting and fishing with his buddies every day. One day I became physically ill with food poisoning and when he finally came home that night at eleven P.M., all he said was, "I heard you were sick. Are you better now?" He had a great honeymoon with his buddies, and at the time I thought maybe he needed that after all the

157

hoopla with the wedding. I remember being down by the lake one day and watching a couple walking hand in hand. I wept for two hours over it. I've always built my world around him. He has never done the same for me.

One sixty-year-old Blue woman finally relinquished her struggle for intimacy with her Red husband and became a volunteer for Traveler's Aid at the airport. She realized that he was a wonderful man. She didn't want a divorce, so she redirected her needs for intimacy to other people. It isn't the same as receiving her husband's affection, but it is much healthier than continuing the battle for the intimacy he neither understands nor apparently values.

CHALLENGING	versus	SECURITY
ADVENTURE		

Red: C'mon, let's live a little. After all, we only go around once. We've made money before, and we can do it again. Nothing is going to happen and if it does, we'll figure out a solution. We always have before.

Blue: I don't feel good about making lots of changes right now. We should wait until things settle down before we try something else. You're so old. You can't start a new business at this late date. What will I do if you die and leave me with all these bills?

PLEASES SELF	versus	PLEASES OTHERS

Reds are basically selfish, while Blues enjoy being self-sacrificing. If a family were making banana splits, and there was a limited supply of ice cream, the Red would try to talk one of the others into having something else so he would get the banana split. The Blue would find something else to eat and give the full banana split portions to the others.

TO HIDE INSECURITIES	versus	TO REVEAL INSECURITIES
(tightly)		(openly)

Red: You can't go around just trusting everyone you see. It doesn't matter how I feel anyway. What really matters is the issue at hand. Why do you always end up talking about feelings and garbage no one can do anything about anyway?

Blue: I just want to feel close to you. I need you to know how special and important you are to me. Can't we ever forget business and talk about us? We used to dream about our future together and feel close. I'm scared we won't make it in our marriage. I don't feel like a good parent anymore. And I know I haven't been a good spouse to you either.

Red: You are making mountains out of molehills. Of course I love you. Now let's stop talking about things we can't resolve. You knew who I was when you married me, so what's the big deal?

Blue: I just want to spend more time with you and get to know you better. I want you to know me and understand my feelings.

Blue husband concerning Red wife:

I have come to the conclusion that she either is totally void of feelings or totally insecure and afraid that whoever gets inside her head won't like her when they really find out who she is in there.

Red wife's inward thoughts:

Showing my feelings is a sign of weakness. I am not weak, and therefore I will never show any feelings. Besides, people might use them against me later on.

or

What is the big deal with feelings? You should know how I feel. I must love you. I married you, didn't I?

HIGH PRODUCTIVITY	versus	STRONG PERFECTIONISM

Red: If a job's worth doing, let's stop talking and get it done.
Blue: If a job's worth doing at all, it's worth doing right.

Reds want to complete the task, while Blues want the task to be completed perfectly. This is most frustrating in a Red-Blue relationship, because both people are highly committed to productivity, but they rarely agree on the quality of the finished product or the necessary schedules. Particularly noticeable times of conflict are packing for vacations, having friends over for dinner, or completing a project at work.

Red: (driven by productivity) I feel like my reputation is at stake for every deadline I miss.
Blue: (driven by perfectionism) I feel like my name is on every article of clothing I sew.

LOGICAL (unemotional)   versus   EMOTIONAL (irrational)

Dialogue between Red employer and Blue employee:

Red: Why you do what you do is totally unimportant to me. Just perform.

Blue: Why would I perform for someone who doesn't care about why I do what I do?

Red: How I feel about you has nothing to do with how well you should perform.

Blue: How you feel about me has everything to do with how well I perform.

Red: Look, just do your job well and everything will be fine.

Blue: Look, just appreciate me and tell me how well I'm doing my job and everything will be just fine.

One couple were distressed when the Red wife wouldn't intercede in arguments between the Blue father and Blue daughter. "If you loved me," he would say, "you would stand up for me. For no other reason than the fact that I'm the parent, you should defend me." The Red wife was furious that he would try to force her to referee between her two emotional "children." Reds quickly tire of others' emotional baggage and their need to be loved and told so all the time.

Blues usually feel emotionally betrayed by Reds. One Blue wife tearfully said after twenty-five years of marriage to a Red husband, "Last night I had the best evening of our entire marriage. . . . My eight-year-old daughter and I went out shopping and to the movies."

Reds typically feel traumatized by Blues taking everything personally. Reds appear insensitive (and often are), but they speak their minds directly and mean no malicious harm with their directness.

"Just remember that if I fire you, your work is unacceptable. Otherwise, carry on and know I am pleased," says the Red employer. The Blue appreciates hearing daily about the quality of her work and the reassuring sense of security on the job. Reds tire quickly of all the emotional needs of Blues. The less the Blues get reassured, the greater their need for it becomes.

INSENSITIVE   versus   TOO SENSITIVE

An evening out:

Blue: Do you think what I'm wearing will be appropriate for the party tonight?

Red: Don't ask me again whether I like the dress you're wearing. It's fine. If I didn't like it, I'd ask you to wear something else.

Philosophical differences:

Blue: Life's a bitch and then you die.
Red: If you continue to bitch, you're going to die.

Twenty years later:

Blue: I was three months pregnant with our third child. I felt fat and ugly and you still forced me to have sex with you.
Red: This is ridiculous. That was twenty years ago. Are you still whining about that?
Blue: I've never forgiven you for forcing yourself on me when I felt so ugly and fat.
Red: Just because you were three months pregnant and felt ugly and fat didn't necessarily mean my sex drive ceased to exist.

IMPATIENT	versus	IMPATIENT BUT LONG SUFFERING

Blue parent to child:

I want you to clean your room right now. We are not going to live like pigs. I clean the house every day so we can have a nice environment, and you need to help too. It seems like nobody works around here but me, and I'm sick and tired of doing it all. If you can't get your room cleaned, then don't ask me to do anything for you.

Note: Other personalities call this the "Blue lecture." It usually lasts anywhere from five minutes to an hour, depending on the degree of the Blue's need to be understood.

Red parent to child:

If you expect to be breathing in five minutes, your room had better be clean.

INTENSE

Everything is a big deal in Red-Blue relationships. They care deeply and commit strongly to life. Neither is willing to take a backseat. Both have terrific concentration. Reds exude a more powerful verbal intensity, while Blues use a gritty nonverbal intensity. Reds are usually verbally dynamic, while Blues are nonverbally dynamic. Both personalities are intense and focused.

UNFORGIVING BUT MOVES ON	versus	UNFORGIVING AND RESENTFUL

Blues remember *everything* that ever happened in a relationship. They feel the same joy or anger that they felt twenty years before. They scar deeply and do not forgive easily. They withhold affection and genuine intimacy because of their resentment. In their hearts, Reds don't forgive any more than Blues. Intellectually, their heads simply help them move on and cope more efficiently with life. Speaking of her upcoming thirty-year-anniversary cruise to Alaska with her Red husband, one Blue wife resentfully remarked, "We never had a real honeymoon. So it's about time he showed me a good time. We'll have a great second honeymoon whether he likes it or not!"

POSSESSIVE

Both are prone to jealously and control. Both love with strings attached. "What's in it for me?" is a common concern they share. Both need to know they are number one in the relationship. Reds are more possessive of things, while Blues are more possessive of people.

REBELLIOUS	versus	ACQUIESCENT

Driving in a car to work:

Blue: The speed limit is fifty-five miles per hour and that is precisely what I intend to go.

Red: Rules were made for people. People weren't made for rules!

Blue: People made the rules and people should follow the rules the people they elect make. Besides, it saves lives.

Red: *Your* driving will never save lives. I have an important meeting to get to on time.

Blue: If no one obeyed the law, think of the chaos we would have.

Red: If people would just use their brains and think a little when they drive we wouldn't need these ridiculous laws. I don't need them because I'm a thinking driver.

In a work setting:

I remember a working relationship I once shared with two men (one Red and one Blue). The Blue would constantly question whether our supervisor would approve the decision we were making, and the Red would constantly suggest we do it first and ask questions later. The Blue personality saw the Red as too rebellious, and the Red personality saw the Blue as too acquiescent. Together they were a terrific balance to the team. Blues tend to see the barbed wire on top of the fence. Reds see the holes underneath.

RESPONSIBLE

Both personalities are highly dependable. They take commitment seriously and act accordingly. Neither tolerates irresponsibility well. Both are highly principled. Reds are fiercely loyal to causes, while Blues are fiercely loyal to people.

ACHIEVER

Both are regarded as tremendous taskmasters. They work hard throughout their lives to succeed. Both give work a high priority. Play is always secondary to Reds and Blues. Reds often achieve best through others, and Blues achieve best through themselves. Both do best when allowed to operate within the limits they set for themselves. They are always stretching themselves professionally, but often for different reasons.

INTIMIDATING

Reds and Blues share the dubious honor of being perceived as intimidating. Each intimidates the other. Blues are so good at what they do that they intimidate Reds. Reds are so logical and verbal that they intimidate Blues. Both recognize their unique skill level and can be highly cooperative or terribly destructive. Choosing to win by intimidation is hardly a recommended style for successful relationships. Reds and Blues are often unaware of how they intimidate each other. Consequently, each blames the other for poor communication. Neither is particularly sympathetic to the other's personality. Both remain somewhat aloof and feel justified in their intimidating style.

| CRITICAL OF OTHERS | versus | CRITICAL OF SELF AND OTHERS |

When an issue arises, Reds will generally find the fault to lie with others, while Blues tend to look for the fault within themselves. Reds do a lot of introspection, but rarely in public. Blues are more willing to comment on their own inadequacies as well as on those of others. Both personalities are highly critical and blame-oriented. Neither is comfortable with mistakes.

| ARROGANT | versus | SELF-RIGHTEOUS |

Both feel they are right. Both are quick to judge the other. Neither is quick to see his or her own shortcomings despite repeated remarks from others. Reds exude an arrogance that suggests that they know everything and are always right. Blues maintain a daily vigil of moral self-righteousness and piety, which tends to alienate Reds.

| ACTIVE | versus | NEGATIVE |

Deadlocked in disagreement for exasperating periods of time, Reds and Blues tend to see problems rather than solutions. Reds move more easily through the negative than Blues. However, in their movement, they often dump unnecessary negativity on those around them. Gloomy clouds are often noticeable in the Red-Blue companionship. Neither knows how to play well. They usually depend on others to bring out whatever sunshine life has to offer. However, both are also capable of strong productivity and action, which often pushes them through difficult impasses in the relationship.

| DOESN'T LOVE EASILY BUT STRONG COMMITMENT | versus | LOVES DEEPLY AND IS DISAPPOINTED BY THOSE WHO CAN'T LOVE (maintains strong commitment) |

Reds are amazingly loyal to relationships (personal and professional). They appear to be so distant, and yet they are actually very committed to those they accept into their lives. Reds are not terribly demonstrative with others and often seem quite detached from the world in general. Actually, they can be the finest friends. They can be deeply devoted to their families, as well.

Blues share the strong commitment the Reds feel for relationships. Blues love deeply and commit completely to their families, careers, or whatever they deem valuable. Blues are generally devoted to relationships, despite the pain or disappointments the relationships may bring. Reds and Blues value responsible and committed relationships. Regardless of the quality, Blues find terminating relationships very difficult to do.

MAKING THE MOST OF UNCOMPLEMENTARY OPPOSITES

Reds Need Blues:	Blues Need Reds:
To teach them compassion	To teach them honest feedback
To soften their communication	To teach them assertiveness
To point out details	To get the job done
To encourage them	To give them specific direction
To encourage their risk taking	To foster a sense of security
To plan the action	To execute the plan
To confront them directly	To understand them
To listen without taking comments personally	To appreciate them
To approve of their style and direction	To include them in plans
To trust them	To be trustworthy

POTENTIAL CONFLICTS OF UNCOMPLEMENTARY OPPOSITES

Reds	Blues
Power-oriented	Intimacy-oriented
Selfish	Selfless
Wants to look good	Wants to be good
Logical	Emotional
Insensitive	Compassionate
Productive	Creative
Tactless	Beats around the bush
Stubborn	Stubborn
Arrogant	Self-righteous
Direct and self-assured	Indirect and self-conscious

Reds and Whites operate from a logical axis,
while Blues and Yellows come from an emotional base.

*Red-White relationships are
one of the most comfortable combinations
found among the personalities.*

RED-WHITE RELATIONSHIPS

"FIRE AND ICE"

Red-White relationships are one of the most common combinations found among the personalities. They share many traits (i.e., power orientation, being self-serving, and needing respect). Interestingly, even their differences are often more complementary than distracting. For example, Reds like to lead and Whites enjoy following. The Red says, "Me Tarzan." The White replies, "Terrific. Jane sounds good to me!" The Red is impatient, and the White quite patient, which further encourages the relationship. They accommodate themselves to the other's innate limitations and enhance the other's natural strengths.

OVERVIEW

Red Personality	White Personality
MOTIVE	
Power	Peace
NEEDS	
to be right	to be left alone
to be respected	to be respected
to appear knowledgeable	to feel good within self
approval	acceptance
WANTS	
challenging adventure	secure excitement
leadership	protection
to please self	to please self and others
to hide insecurities (tightly)	to withhold insecurities
BEHAVIOR STYLE	
change	stability
high profile	low profile
high complexity	low complexity

Red Personality	White Personality
controlling	seeks neither control nor to be controlled
unemotional	feels deeply, finds expression of feelings difficult
logical	logical
direct communication (with facts)	direct communication (with facts)
delegator	doer
impatient	patient
demanding	nondemanding
tense	relaxed
possessive	nonpossessive (unless threatened)
confrontational	nonconfrontational
strongly verbal	strongly nonverbal
manipulative	subtly manipulative
can't love easily, but strong commitment	loves easily and strong commitment
high productivity	consistent producer
defiant of rules	compliant with rules
tactless	tactful
gives advice and expects compliance	gives advice only when asked
does not seek advice	accepts advice freely
intimidating	intimidated
critical of others	tolerant of others
arrogant	feels inadequate
gives others guilt	feels a lot of guilt
unforgiving but moves on	releases but remembers
innovative	creative
negative	overwhelmed
obsessive-compulsive	dedicated only when interested

Red Personality	White Personality
difficult to share feelings with	easy to talk to, hard to get feelings from
poor listener	excellent listener
blames others	blames self
insensitive	too sensitive
achiever	lazy
lies to save face	lies to avoid repercussion
rebellious	subversive

RED-WHITE INTERPERSONAL RELATIONSHIPS
(In-depth Presentation)

POWER   *versus*   **PEACE**

The different motives of these personalities are effectively illustrated in a scene between a Red wife and a White husband. She was furious with him one morning about a conversation they were having. She wanted to be right in the worst way, and he wouldn't accommodate her. She suddenly jumped up from her chair at the kitchen table where they were having cereal, picked up her bowl of Wheaties, and smashed it to the floor. In order to preserve whatever peace he could at this point, the husband began picking up the broken pieces and putting them into the trash can. Noticing that he was more interested in keeping peace than acquiescing to her superior intellect, she stormed back into the kitchen and poured milk all over the Wheaties on the floor. Then she ordered him to leave the kitchen until the milk and Wheaties had dried on the floor, making them far more difficult to clean up.

She laughed hysterically as she told the story. "Who eventually did clean up the mess?" I asked. "Well, he did, of course," she mocked. I still have visions of this fifty-five-year-old man stooping over a dried mess of cereal and milk and cleaning it up in order to facilitate peace. They both got what they wanted. She felt powerful and he was at peace.

TO BE RESPECTED

Reds and Whites seek respect in different ways. The Reds expect to be accommodated. The Whites expect to be left alone. Both enjoy distinct time frames and work styles, and continually seek methods of protecting their preferences. Because of their own diminished self-esteem, Whites are more vulnerable to feeling a lack of respect than Reds. Whites handle the way Reds show respect better than any other personalities do. They often take Reds with a grain of salt. One White husband told me, "I'm the boss around the house. My wife gave me permission to say that."

| CHALLENGING | versus | SECURE |
| ADVENTURE | | EXCITEMENT |

Reds thrive on adventure. They love the opportunity to risk physical danger. My Red daughter constantly tries to handle faster and scarier rides at amusement parks. From an early age she experienced thrills from adventures. Whites also enjoy excitement but want the assurance of support systems and/or guidelines. Police officers tend to be primarily Red and White personalities. They thrive on the adventure and excitement offered by this occupation.

| LEADERSHIP | versus | PROTECTION |

Remember "Me Tarzan"; "Terrific. Jane sounds good to me"? Both are quite comfortable with the roles of leader and follower in a Red-White relationship. The problem comes if one or the other chooses to switch roles. It typically comes later in life, if at all. A committed couple or parent-child relationship could potentially experience great difficulty with the change.

One White woman let her Red husband give her a list of chores every day for fifteen years, until she decided enough was enough and started ripping up his lists. Despite her change, he couldn't break the habit of list making for six months.

Another individual let her Red husband make all the decisions. She would then quietly determine whether she liked the decisions he made or not. If he hadn't measured up to her standards (big enough house, enough money, successful enough friends), she became disappointed in him. She eventually was able to see how unfair it was to seek his financial protection and social leadership while casting all blame his direction when he performed beneath her standards.

CHANGE   versus   STABILITY

Red adolescents are constantly telling me they would rather be dead than live the boring lifestyle their parents live. Reds are more willing to risk than Whites are. Whites will risk but must first have both feet firmly on the ground. They are less certain of themselves and typically prefer the comforts of safe, familiar surroundings. Whites don't require the constant action Reds do. They offer a comfortable blend for each other.

HIGH PROFILE   versus   LOW PROFILE

Red: I've got things to do, places to go, and people to see.
White: What things, why so many places, and must we see all those
    people?

Whites make excellent traveling companions because they are perfectly contented to go along for the ride. They are easily entertained. They don't like to be onstage the way their Red friends do. Reds are more driven to see it all and experience everything before they're too old.

CONTROLLING   versus   SEEKS NEITHER CONTROL NOR TO BE CONTROLLED

A classic example of this difference can be found in the world political scene. On one side was Germany, representing the Red. They are a forceful nation with a history of invading other countries and controlling governmental policies throughout the world. Right next door to this powerful Red nation lay Switzerland, equally powerful yet a totally different nation that represents the Whites. The Swiss seek neither to control other nations nor to be controlled by them. They make life very difficult for any nation that tries to control them. They are a peace-loving land with a strong sense of pride. Germany is reflective of the Red personality, promoting its philosophies throughout the world with the obvious belief that they are right and what they believe should be espoused by all. Switzerland represents Whites who never start the war, but they are always quietly counting the money when it's over. So it goes with individual relationships as well.

LOGICAL

Both Reds and Whites have the capacity to be very logical. Both can be very shrewd. Reds are often locked into this mode of thinking, while Whites are capable of operating quite successfully on either an emotional or logical level. Their natural capacity to deal well with logic means Red-White relationships can enjoy hearty discussions on a broad number of topics. Strongly related to this is Reds' ability to communicate directly using facts, while Whites can do it using facts and feelings. They also make a good pair because the Reds stimulate the conversations and the Whites clarify and encourage a feeling tone in the conversations.

| DELEGATOR | versus | DOER |

Reds are most comfortable in a delegating role. They give orders well. They allow others to do the jobs once they have delegated them. They encourage individuality. Whites appreciate this freedom. Whites accomplish numerous things that others will never know about. They do not broadcast their activities the way Reds often do. They simply carry out assignments and go about following personal interests in a comfortable, casual way. Neither seems to mind the other's style. They respect their differences and appreciate that neither is receptive to changing for others, so why waste the time or energy trying?

| IMPATIENT | versus | PATIENT |

Whites quietly explain away a Red's temper. It is as if it isn't a big problem for them. They seem to take it in stride, the way a tourist at Yellowstone expects to see Old Faithful erupt on schedule. While they are not pleased with it, Whites appear to be less concerned with Reds' impatience than other personalities are. Whites believe that everything comes to he who waits.

Reds get the job done. Whites quietly assume the role of friend and supporter. Sometimes Reds are unfairly criticized because of their impatient natures. One Blue woman told me how unfair she had been in judging her parents but couldn't resolve her preference for her (White) father over her (Red) mother. "Dad was so poorly equipped for life," she said. "He couldn't hold down a job, and when he finally landed one, he wouldn't leave on vacation for fear it would be gone when he returned. One summer, my mother simply packed us all in the car and took us to Yosemite for a two-week vacation. Despite her obvious concern for our well-being, I hated her then and I still don't enjoy her company today. It seems that she had no spirit or soul to her. It was all performance and obligation—tense performance at that. Somehow, my father taught me to dream and love and feel. When he died, I lost a very patient, understanding friend. I felt abandoned even though I was left in the very capable care of my mother."

DEMANDING   versus   NONDEMANDING

My favorite quote on Reds' perception of Whites' ability to assert themselves came from a powerful Red lawyer who was frustrated with his passive White wife who was trying to assert herself in their marriage. He was particularly upset one day and commented, "Living with her is like living with a person who has read a book on self-assertion with half the pages already ripped out." Reds initially find it difficult to contend with Whites when they become more demanding in the relationship. However, they quickly learn to appreciate the heightened interaction, and the relationship often improves with this change.

Reds are the most verbally demanding of the personalities. Whites are the least verbally demanding. Red parents have strong expectations of their children. Red employers have strong expectations of their employees. White children and employees are often the best equipped to deal with the strong demands of the Reds. Whites simply tend to accept the relationship as it is and don't demand much of the other person.

It is particularly frustrating for Reds that Whites often don't set goals in the relationship. Reds are so goal-oriented that they expect everyone else to be also. Whites are often comfortable floating through life, while Reds want predetermined action plans. Whites do not see the need to set goals, and rarely follow through as tenaciously as the Reds. This can be annoying to both personalities.

STRONGLY   versus   STRONGLY
VERBAL   NONVERBAL

It is great fun to watch the Red and White personalities in a power duel. Reds verbalize their position, while Whites express themselves nonverbally. In the long run, it is a toss-up as to who is actually stronger. It is often difficult to determine the winner. Most intriguing, however, are their *styles* of presentation. Remember the hunter and the hunted? Which one really gets the best of the other? While the chase is still on, it's hard to tell.

One loving White mother watched while her arrogant Red son ditched school, experimented with the drug scene, and ran away from home. She quietly asserted her position regarding his choices. He continued to verbally lash out at life and all those intimately connected with him. Eventually, he chose to turn away from the drug scene and reestablish himself at school and home. I asked him what changed his mind. He said, "Have you ever felt like you were running in a marathon and there was a guy right next to you, competing with you, but giving you constant moral support and always stopping to get you water from the sideline? No matter what I did, I couldn't shake her. She wore me out until I finally decided she knew a better way to run the race of life than I did."

DOES NOT SEEK ADVICE	versus	ACCEPTS ADVICE FREELY

Reds and Whites differ in their approach to advice. Reds do not often seek advice. Whites don't seek advice as much as they accept advice. Because of their quiet ways, Whites appear to be needing advice and protection. Generally speaking, Whites are far more inclined to be receptive to advice than Reds, especially when it is offered in kindness.

CRITICAL OF OTHERS	versus	TOLERANT OF OTHERS

Most Reds are judgmental, while their White companions innately find themselves highly tolerant. Very few things bring Whites to criticize, while Reds find numerous behaviors in others to be unacceptable. Reds often voice their disapproval, which drives others away and can make it difficult to develop an intimate relationship, while Whites invite others to share and willingly support differences of opinion.

One White patient was mortified when her Red boyfriend almost started a fistfight with a man who parked too close to his car. She was embarrassed by his public display of anger and felt his criticism was totally inappropriate. She even threatened to leave the car and walk home if he didn't just get in the car and drive away. He felt justified because the other guy had no business parking so close, and someone had to tell him. (Who better than a Red, right?) She felt it was just one more unnecessary confrontation that wouldn't have taken place without his constantly critical eye.

ARROGANT versus FEELS INADEQUATE

One White woman felt so inadequate and immoral (she had a child out of wedlock) that she married the first man she met who loved her and had a strong character. (She was hoping for his noble character to make up for her lack of morality. She was hoping his love for her would increase her love for herself.) She selfishly married this man and dutifully stayed with him for eighteen years, masking all her true feelings and never looking within herself to uncover the real hatred she felt for her "spineless, immoral self." We met in therapy after she had fallen in love with another man and had an affair, only to discover that she no longer could live with her husband because she didn't love him. (Naturally, she had *never* loved him. She had used him to make her feel better about herself.) She wasn't a "spineless, immoral person" at all. She was a wonderful, capable human being who had made some poor choices. Rather than seeing herself accurately, she found a husband who loved himself and her and would willingly cover all her inadequacies. Three children later, she woke up and saw herself for the wonderful person she truly was, and now the price for originally taking this easier route was a devastated husband, three frustrated children, betrayed extended family and friends; a much higher price than it would have been had she been able to raise her self-image and accept herself and her poor choices earlier.

Reds often distance themselves with their arrogance in this wonderful world of emotions. They often miss true friendship because they cannot be intimate with someone who is better or worse than they are. (Intimacy requires equality.) Arrogance is a shallow defense of a rich treasure that lies hidden in the heart of Reds. Either they discard this shallow, pitiful defense and let themselves know intimacy and vulnerability, or they remain a prisoner for life in their self-constructed cells. At times, I wonder if the passivity of White's patience and acceptance may be the most effective method for eventually enticing the Red's emotions to the surface.

GIVES OTHERS GUILT versus FEELS A LOT OF GUILT

He was one of the kindest men I had ever met in a therapeutic session. He looked so lost and forlorn. He began our session telling me about

174

his precious daughter, Linda, who had repeatedly rattled her crib starting when she was a year old to get her way. She was Red—demanding all the time. Over the years, she rebelled against their standards, got into drugs, ditched school, slept around, and eventually ran away from home.

On one occasion, he and his (Red) teenage son got a call from Linda's therapist's office telling them to forcibly remove her from his office to a treatment center down the coast. They complied. She was furious, and in her rage spat in her (White) father's face as he restrained her in the backseat. He did nothing to retaliate. She turned to her (Red) brother on the other side and prepared to do the same to him. He calmly said, almost hoping to be defied, "Just try it, sweetheart, and you'll never be able to spit again." She was furious, so she turned back at her father and spat at him again.

I asked him why he'd allowed her to behave as she had. He told me he felt so guilty that he couldn't blame her for spitting. I asked him what he had done that made him feel so guilty, and he couldn't come up with anything. Still he felt guilty. She used this on him her whole life. She knew her Red brother wouldn't take it, so she gave it to her guilt-ridden White dad.

At one point she'd shared a bathroom with her brother. She smoked, and he told her never to do so in the bathroom. She ignored him and did anyway. One day he took her ashtray from the bathroom and spread all the ashes out on her sheets and remade the bed. She never smoked in their bathroom again. The father seemed pleased that his son could counter the daughter so effectively, but was unable or unwilling to challenge her in the same way. Given the green light by her father, a most immature Linda continued to blame him for her messed-up life.

OBSESSIVE-COMPULSIVE	versus	DEDICATED ONLY WHEN INTERESTED

Reds usually become passionate about everything with which they connect. They resemble a young teenager who hooks up with every new fad that comes along. Whether it's food, sports, religion, or whatever, Reds are known to take extreme stands. It is hard to deter them. They can overeat with the same vigor that they arise at 6:00 A.M. to hit a little white ball into holes on green grass. Whatever the obsession, they are compulsive about it. Whites are able to commit just as deeply, but feel very little compulsion to tenaciously follow through. They are, however, equally tenacious when they feel the dedication. Former tennis star Bjorn Borg, who appears to be a White personality, reigned as the king of tennis until he lost interest. He didn't even try to regain his desire. He simply quit. Reds are more inclined to reassert themselves and force the desire to accommodate the obsession.

POOR LISTENER   versus   EXCELLENT LISTENER

Reds generally prefer debates to casual conversation. Whites are most comfortable just hearing what others have to say. Reds are so certain they know everything that they don't often deem it necessary to pay full attention to details in conversation. They are more concerned with giving advice and getting results. Feelings are less important than facts. One (Red) father was more interested in the future problems his overweight (White) daughter would have "landing a husband" than the feelings of low self-esteem her weight condition was causing.

People often seek out Whites for their patience and the gentle manner they use to discuss differences. They are willing to give the time that is necessary to fully understand another individual. Whites are truly interested in others' feelings and life situations. They like being included in others' lives, and freely give the time necessary to encourage warm, communicative relationships.

> Never "do unto others as you would have them do unto you"
> unless they're the same personality color as you.
> Always "do unto others as they would have you do unto them."
> Speak their language.

MAKING THE MOST OF COMPLEMENTARY OPPOSITES

Reds Need Whites:	Whites Need Reds:
To calm them in crisis	To motivate them
To listen to them	To inspire and encourage them
To bounce ideas off	To lead them
To feel safe with	To share risks with
To encourage compromise	To organize them
To delegate responsibility	To establish healthy boundaries
To balance them with perspective	To provide vision
To remind them about quality versus quantity	To keep them task-oriented
To communicate logically with	To set goals and objectives

POTENTIAL CONFLICTS OF COMPLEMENTARY OPPOSITES

Reds	Whites
Too demanding	Too accepting
Arrogant	Self-doubting
Bossy	Passive
Too opinionated	Uncommitted
Always right	Easily walked on
Verbally stubborn	Silently stubborn
Often promotes conflict	Promotes peace at all costs
Always telling	Always asking
Tactless and rude	Craves kindness
Workaholic	Lazy

RED-YELLOW RELATIONSHIPS

"FRIENDLY FIRE"

This combination of personalities is a vibrant one. Reds and Yellows enjoy verbal bantering and enjoy freedom from most of the emotional baggage and heavy sentiments experienced by other personalities. They are adventurous and energetic and often amaze and amuse friends with their zest for living and many accomplishments. They often struggle with the self-centeredness of the Yellow and the selfishness of the Red. The obvious commonality is their preference for looking out for number one—themselves.

They are both excited about change and find little need to be concerned with stability. This Red-Yellow combination is the most difficult to sustain among committed, married couples. Each must work to maintain a healthy perspective on the other. They have to mold the playfulness of the Yellow and the productivity of the Red. This personality combination reminds me of a white-water rafting trip—carefree yet productive, filled with adventure, excitement, and passion. However, the Yellow's lack of commitment and Red's demanding nature can prove difficult to combine unless the Red shows great heart and the Yellow develops a responsible nature. On a positive note, they seem to value themselves and feel a commitment to new experiences and challenges in life.

*Without question this blend
has the greatest difficulty staying married.
When healthy, this blend suffers no emotional baggage
and experiences life to the max.*

OVERVIEW

Red Personality	Yellow Personality
MOTIVE	
Power	Fun
NEEDS	
to be right	superficial connections
to be respected	to be praised
to look good to others (academically)	to look good to others (socially)
intellectual acknowledgment	social acceptance
WANTS	
approval by a select few	approval by the masses
challenging adventure	playful adventure
leadership	freedom
to please self	to be noticed
to hide insecurities (tightly)	to hide insecurities (loosely)
BEHAVIOR STYLE	
likes change	demands change
high profile	high profile
high complexity	low complexity
controlling	craves freedom
logical	emotional
direct communication (with facts)	direct communication (with facts and feelings)
delegator	delegator/performer
impatient	good natured
demanding	obnoxious

178

RELATIONSHIPS: THE COLOR CONNECTIONS

Red Personality	Yellow Personality
intense	carefree
possessive	nonpossessive
confrontational	avoids confrontation
strongly verbal	strongly verbal
manipulative	seeks escape
can't love easily, but strong commitment	loves easily, but poor commitment
high productivity	scattered productivity
defiant of rules	defiant of rules
tactless	tactless (uses humor)
gives advice and expects compliance	gives advice, but unconcerned with compliance
does not seek advice	welcomes positive advice from others
intimidating	inviting
critical of others	accepting of others
arrogant	vain
gives others guilt	rarely gives or accepts guilt
unforgiving but moves on	forgiving
innovative	innovative
negative	positive
obsessive-compulsive	lacks discipline
difficult to share feelings with	easy to share feelings with
poor listener	poor listener
blames others	blames others
conflict-oriented	avoids conflict
lies to save face	lies to save face and not disappoint
expects a lot, unappreciative	low expectations, appreciative
consistent	inconsistent
determined	relaxed
focused	scattered

RED-YELLOW INTERPERSONAL RELATIONSHIPS
(In-depth Presentation)

POWER   *versus*   **FUN**

She knew he was powerful when she married him. He had enjoyed a most successful career in the oil business. He showered her with gifts and kept her heart spinning with numerous romantic intimacies. She was like sunshine in his life. Full of warmth, she radiated happiness and excitement. She represented everything he had bypassed for his hard-driving career. She felt he was more committed to her than he had ever been to his career, and she was right. However, she forgot just how committed he had always been, and still was, to himself. One day he invited her to take a leisurely drive in their convertible Rolls-Royce and enjoy a picnic on the beach. She was thrilled with this playful gesture. When he began driving in a different direction, she became somewhat suspicious. Before long, his selfish plan became more evident. They were headed for his mother's. This Red man despised his mother but felt obligated to visit her periodically, and did so only with his colorful Yellow wife, who could carry the conversation. He was still looking out for himself. The fun possibilities of the picnic were quickly discarded for the more selfish motive of satisfying his personal obligations of visiting his mother.

Yellows' disorganization often frustrates the Reds as much as Reds frustrate Yellows with their obsession with power. Taking charge of one's life is a cornerstone of personal power. Yellows usually fail to understand the importance of personal power and responsibility. Reds are adept at dissecting problems and making sense out of their lives. They are direct and enjoy having control over everything they do. Yellows infuriate Reds with their casual concern about financial matters, social obligations, and protocol. They are more interested in sharing time with fascinating people who laugh than with people who are in control of their lives. Reds enjoy control and find no personality more impossible to control than Yellows. Like a bird, Yellows simply take off and land when they feel like it. Reds often resent the frivolity and feel their all-important power threatened by the casual mockery Yellows frequently display for them.

TO BE RESPECTED   *versus*   **TO BE PRAISED**

Reds are far more concerned with being respected, while Yellows are typically willing to abdicate respect or power in favor of attention.

Reds are always looking out for themselves, while Yellows are hoping *others* are looking out for them. The Reds want to produce the movie and earn the money, while the Yellows want to be onscreen and earn the audience's praise.

Reds don't often compliment others well. In fact, they are generally quite uncomfortable with giving and/or receiving compliments. Jobs needing to be done should be done with little fanfare, in a Red's estimation. Yellows couldn't disagree more. They give compliments easily and sincerely. They love to be acknowledged. Perhaps the greatest need Yellows have with regard to interpersonal relationships is that of being praised. They rarely receive it from their Red companions. Numerous unnecessary family arguments actually stem from Red parents neglecting to praise Yellow children. Red employers miss an easy incentive when they neglect to compliment Yellow employees.

Reds only demand respect. For them, respect is more important than praise. Reds ask to be seen as the experts, the leaders, the knowledgeable ones. They will return the favor tenfold. Reds and Yellows have very different needs. Each must learn much from the other if they are to appreciate each other's different styles.

TO LOOK GOOD TO OTHERS (academically)	versus	TO LOOK GOOD TO OTHERS (socially)

Both Reds and Yellows want to look good. Perhaps nothing allies them more than this motive of hiding their inadequacies in order to appear good on the surface. Reds and Yellows struggle with intimacy because they prefer not to risk themselves emotionally in relationships. Reds are more direct in their defensive posture of guarding their feelings. They are not coy or innocent in the refusal to share themselves. Yellows appear innocent and often invite others in with brash openness. However, they also resist true intimacy. Yellows remind me of deer in the forest. They are beautiful to see, but if you come too close they quickly disappear in the foliage that covers and protects them. Yellows instinctively focus the conversation on others. They often find it difficult to talk about their true feelings because they fear the judgment of others. Without a trained eye, people often fall right into the trap and spend an evening or even a lifetime with Yellows discussing intimacies but never actually being intimate at all.

Perhaps the element most lacking in this combination is emotional depth. Neither caters to the needs of others. Both struggle with intimacy. Together, Reds and Yellows have a most difficult time admitting their inadequacies. They must also work very diligently to overlook the other's inadequacies rather than remembering them for later debate and teasing. Yellows are more likely to expose themselves, but neither risks freely at the truly intimate level. Both require patience and trust in order to free themselves of their most closely guarded secret—their insecurity.

APPROVAL

It is not surprising that both of the more verbal personalities seek approval, while the more passive personalities seek acceptance. Yellows and Reds seek approval for completely different reasons. Yellows seek approval to know they are socially desirable. They do not appear to value their own opinion as much as they do the opinion of others. Reds are typically impressed with the social skills of Yellows. Reds want approval for their intellectual prowess. They need to know that others approve of them academically. Yellows find it easy to approve of Reds' intellectual capacity. What they struggle with is the arrogant style Reds often use to present themselves.

CHALLENGING ADVENTURE	versus	PLAYFUL ADVENTURE

No other personality combination can begin to compete with the adventurous spirit of a healthy Red-Yellow team. They are willing to forgo many of life's luxuries in order to travel the world, risk personal danger, and experience new opportunities. They are known to be constantly remodeling, going back to school, traveling, attending plays, etc. They are terrifically spontaneous and active.

HIGH PROFILE

Red and Yellow personalities feel secure within themselves and open to new challenges and opportunities. They like visibility. They don't work behind the scenes of life but prefer to be onstage. Both enjoy people and often find themselves challenging each other for the spotlight. Reds succeed in maintaining their high profile through knowledge, hard work, and leadership skills. Yellows succeed in maintaining theirs through their innate love for people, charismatic style, and positive energy.

CONTROLLING   versus   CRAVES FREEDOM

Picture in your mind a determined Red mother racing after a runaway Yellow toddler who has escaped through the open front door. Reds want to control most people's destiny. Yellows want the right to determine their own destiny. Whenever Yellows feel their freedom is being challenged, they resist. Reds often frustrate themselves trying to channel a Yellow's zest for life. Both are benefited by the other's perceptions of how to live life. Reds offer responsibility. Yellows offer intrigue. They see their roles in relationships very differently. Successful blending requires an acceptance of the other's perspective.

UNEMOTIONAL   versus   EMOTIONAL

Yellows can live without the depth of emotional connection Blues require, but they are often stunned—unprepared for the limited expression Reds display. One Yellow husband shouted at his Red wife, "I would love to see you just once break down and show your real feelings. You are stoic. It's like getting water out of a stone. I give up! I really do! No human can be that *inhuman*!"

Reds are quite accepting of a Yellow's emotional display, even appreciating their emotional excitement. Upon retirement, one Red employee told his Yellow colleague, "Well, I do have to say this about you. You are definitely one-of-a-kind. I have never met anyone as vivacious and emotionally charged as you seem to be about life."

LOGICAL

Perhaps the saving grace in Red-Yellow relationships from a Red's perspective is the Yellow's ability to reason. Reds are so capable with their reasoning power that they rely on the other person's ability to meet them on their turf. Yellows can do that. Both personalities are skilled at debating issues without necessarily resorting to emotional drama. They share strong verbal skills. Reds and Yellows enjoy the pleasure of boldly debating opposite points of view and remaining personally unscathed. Both are rather direct with their communication. Their relationship is unique in their mutual ability to reason.

DELEGATOR versus DELEGATOR/ PERFORMER

No personality delegates across the board the way Reds do. They are masterful in their ability to see the broad picture and select competent individuals to carry through on the details. Yellows share this ability to pass responsibilities on to others. They, too, are most comfortable with delegation, and trust that others will complete the job. Reds have the edge on vision, while Yellows have the edge on trust. Yellows do not struggle with control as Reds do. They entice others to follow their leadership.

In the long run, it is the Reds who generally remain committed and successful in the position of leadership. They are decisive leaders who willingly focus themselves on tasks. Yellows typically prefer to perform somewhere in the organization or on their own. Managing others can seem too demanding and unpleasant compared to hands-on work. For example, a Yellow university professor who became a department chairman suddenly quit after only two years because he missed being close to students and performing in the classroom. Preparing departmental agendas and fighting university policy held more frustration than reward for him.

DEMANDING versus OBNOXIOUS

Yellows are often poor judges of character. They tend to be more concerned about having a good time than the possible negative consequences of running with unhealthy friends. One Yellow sixteen-year-old was acting up and frustrating his dominant Red father so much that the father ultimately demanded that his son change. "Why don't you give up this crazy attitude of yours, and tell your friends you are a businessman now and all you care to worry about is business transactions?" he requested.

With all the diplomacy of a Yellow teenager, the son sarcastically replied, "Yeah, right, Dad! Now I'm a businessman. I only consider business transactions." Turning to me, as if I were one of his peers, he continued, "In the future it will be necessary for you to contact my social secretary to schedule any therapy sessions in order that we not conflict with business. This is necessary in order to prevent any further disappointments for the chairman of the board, my father."

The next evening, he got drunk and fell asleep in his friend's car. The following morning he had to run three miles to be on time to work as a busboy at his father's restaurant. The more demanding the father became, the more obnoxious the son grew. The more obnoxious the son grew, the more demanding the father became.

There is a happy ending to this story. Reds and Yellows share the common need to look good to others. Father and son were able to reach a compromise that enabled them both to save face in the community and with the boy's friends.

INTENSE   versus   CAREFREE

Reds seem to care about everything, while Yellows appear to care about nothing. Reds are very intense (obsessive-compulsive), while Yellows are carefree and often undisciplined. They represent opposing styles. Reds tenaciously attack problems and hang on until they have solutions. Yellows freely release problems, convinced that most things are never truly resolved anyway, so why get upset about something you can't control. Yellows often help others accept that Reds really are wonderful people who just get carried away with their convictions and forget the human element in life. Reds often move others (Yellows included) to action and create a sense of purpose.

Time and again we see how the people skills of the Yellow and the task skills of the Red, given mutual respect, can complement each other.

POSSESSIVE   versus   NONPOSSESSIVE

Reds are typically possessive about material goods and personal relationships. Yellows are the least possessive of the personalities. They love people and feel certain that they will be loved in return. Reds feel love is best displayed by responsible behavior and kept promises. They are typically unsure of others' love for them.

Sometimes the Yellows' lack of possessiveness is construed as a deficiency in caring. Those they encounter who have this perception may get hurt feelings. Yellows tend to feel, "If you love someone, set them free; if they come back, they're yours; if not, they never were." Reds often seem to believe, "If you love someone, set them free; if they don't come back, hunt them down and kill them."

> *Every color can blend successfully with every other color.*
> *However, there are certain "givens" each blend will experience*
> *and should accept up front.*

MAKING THE MOST OF COMPLEMENTARY SIMILARITIES

Reds Need Yellows:

To teach them charisma
To converse with logically
To accept their leadership
To cheerlead for them
To broaden their myopic vision
To socialize them and
    idolize them
To understand their criticism is
    not meant personally

To teach them spontaneity
    and laughter

Yellows Need Reds:

To focus them
To praise them
To notice them
To risk with them
To give them freedom
To allow for their
    spontaneity
To keep them on task
To accept their boundless
    energy
To be positive and say
    "I'm sorry"

POTENTIAL CONFLICTS OF COMPLEMENTARY SIMILARITIES

Reds

Intense
Workaholic
Rude
Hide intimate feelings
Have strong verbal
    argument skills
Seek power
Factual and profound
Want to look good
    (intellectually)
Driven
Negative and critical

Yellows

Lighthearted
Playful
Insensitive
Hide intimate feelings
Have strong verbal
    argument skills
Seek intimacy
Superficial chatterboxes
Want to look good
    (socially)
Lack focused direction
Positive and accepting

Chapter Eleven

THE BLUE CONNECTIONS

Of all the colorful blends
one finds in relationships,
Blue-Blue combinations run the deepest
emotionally and commit the longest.

BLUE-BLUE RELATIONSHIP

"CLOSE AND COMFORTABLE"

Of all the colorful blends one finds in relationships, Blue-Blue combinations run the deepest emotionally and commit the longest. Blues are intimacy-based, and two Blues have twice the commitment. Healthy Blues make the strongest commitment to their spouse in marriage. No other color marries itself as successfully as Blues. Blue-Blue marriages are also the most common same-color marriages.

In the workforce, Blues share perfectionistic tendencies and appreciate other Blues' dedication and commitment to quality work. Blues are loyal to people and respectful of authority. Blues trust Blues. They are reliable and conscientious. There is seldom any power struggle between Blues. The only exceptions to this come with unhealthy Blues who are fearful, hurt, and angry from previous encounters on the job. Bitter power plays and resentful comments often accompany these Blues. Typically, however, Blues focus on their own responsibilities and remain aloof from political maneuvering in the work setting.

This color combination usually enjoys warm, sharing, sensitive relationships. They share many responsible traits important to successful relationships. They are often seen as role models for building meaningful connections with people. Blue-Blue interaction is sincere and committed. They uniquely share the values of integrity and intimacy.

SHARED INTIMACY

Blues value each other. No other color combination comes by intimacy as naturally as Blue-Blue connections. When Blues are dating or married, they do not come to take the other for granted and start seeking personal hobbies that exclude their companion. On the contrary, Blues are more interested in discovering activities they can enjoy together.

Blues understand that intimacy is not just what goes on in the bedroom. They enjoy late-dinner conversations about shared concerns. They appreciate physical touching and romantic glances throughout the day. They sincerely care about loved ones' difficulties as well as triumphs. Blues understand the importance of remembering both special occasions and mundane ones. They are innately thoughtful and take time to demonstrate that they genuinely care.

Shared intimacy is their greatest strength. They feel the quality that comes from giving their relationship top priority. Blue-Blue combinations of all types (spouse, parent/child, siblings, colleagues, friends) value their relationship most, and experience a natural depth other personality combinations must work hard to understand and achieve.

NONCONFRONTATIONAL

A leadership team of a highly successful technical firm was composed of five members. Four members were strong introverted Blue personalities and one was extroverted Red with a big secondary Blue. The Yellow owner of the business was frustrated with their lack of expressed passion and interpersonal communication. Each member was hired as an expert for his or her own specialty and had no desire for team interaction. In fact, they nicknamed the owner the "social engineer" since they could not relate to the value of team building.

They didn't like being exposed or forced to confront one another. They wouldn't challenge another member of the team unless that person was absent. Rather than tell the Yellow owner they didn't want to work with him, some would show up late or not come at all. They resented the owner's positivism and felt he lacked a sense of reality for day-to-day operations, despite the fact that he formerly had run all operations himself. Their emotional immaturity sabotaged any direct interactions with one another that might have created conflict.

At the third meeting the Blue president of the team admitted it was his idea to have the owner come, because the team refused to work together. The predominant Blue group's defensive posture against the Yellow owner diminished significantly when they realized it was one of "their own" who had requested assistance. Creating synergy is difficult with a predominantly Blue team in the workplace. Like cats, they are territorial and prefer to do the work themselves.

LOYALTY

Blues are loyal to each other. They are loyal to law and order. They are loyal to commitments. They are loyal to society's expectations. This shared loyalty makes their relationships very secure. Blue-Blue combinations are loyal to the person in the marriage, family, career, or friendship—not merely loyal to the institution. For example, Blues commit to the happiness and personal development of their spouses rather than to the religious or social obligations that come with wedding vows and a marriage certificate. Blues care about the people in society. They don't just blindly accept and follow law and order or society's expectations. For example, Blues struggle with drunk drivers because Blues hurt for people whose lives are affected by people who drive under the influence of alcohol. Blue-Blue color combinations do remarkably well at keeping loyalty to each other in proper perspective and at consciously committing to making it the significant priority in their life.

STRONG COMMITMENT

Whatever Blues commit to will succeed. They are a powerful team and willingly giving time and effort to accomplishing everything they value. Blue-Blue parents are often seen as too protective because they appear to overdo everything, from homework to curfew. By the time most kids become teenagers, they no longer suggest that their Blue parents simply overdo. They now refer to their behavior as overkill!

Blues are focused and vulnerable to becoming myopic if they focus on each other too much. One fourteen-year-old Yellow was exasperated with his Blue parents because they supported each other so completely that he felt unable even to present his case before they jointly overruled him. Piety and self-righteousness can also overwhelm genuine commitment, if a moralistic approach is pursued. Blue-Blue combinations must be very careful not to feed each other's shared drive to the extent that other colors feel neglected, judged, and/or abused.

On a positive note, Blue-Blue relationships experience a special sense of commitment to each other. Patrick Henry was one of America's more successful founding fathers. His wife became mentally ill at a time many believed he was about to become the next President of the United States. He forsook it all to remain at home and offer his mentally ill wife the security of a loving and devoted husband until she died. Providing dignity for this woman—who might easily have been abandoned by another in order to pursue his moment in life—was the only acceptable alternative to such a sincerely committed Blue character.

APPRECIATION

Who appreciates a painting more than another painter? Blues give so much to everything they do, that they are most appreciated (which Blues crave) by other Blues. You know the phrase "it takes one to know one." So it goes with Blues. They appreciate the quality in other Blues' work. They see the detail and recognize the time it takes to complete various work projects. They know the sacrifices Blues make to complete projects. They appreciate what few others even identify or understand.

PERFECTIONISM

Blue-Blue combinations do everything "above the call of duty." They believe a job worth doing is a job worth doing well. So how do other colors respond to a unified Blue combination? They often mock them as too perfectionistic and irritating when working on a project. However, Blues find other Blues' concern for detail very refreshing. They appreciate their commitment to quality. They usually value their opinion and expertise. Blue-Blue combinations can be found enjoying remodeling a house or taking classes together. They love to learn and improve themselves and their skills.

> *Of all the same color relationships*
> *blends this is the most natural.*
> *However, when one Blue gets down,*
> *the other Blue stabs himself*
> *so they can bleed together.*

CARING COMMUNICATIONS

Blues turn off the television and talk. They enjoy meaningful conversations with one another. They connect emotionally when they communicate. Blues take the time to really listen to each other. They have tremendous empathy for one another and show concern for the other's tragedies as well as triumphs. They are sensitive to each other's moods and will talk into the early morning hours, if necessary, to understand the other's perspective.

PASSIONATE

Blues live for passion. They want to *feel* life rather than merely exist. Blues need to be involved in activities that count for something. They typically consider family and friends as most important. Unlike some personalities who claim to be very family-oriented and then spend their entire lives at the office or playing with friends, Blues typically spend their time and efforts where they claim their priorities lie.

Obligation is significant but less vital than feelings to Blues. The letter of the law is less appealing than the spirit of the law. Blue-Blue combinations provide each other with reason to be passionate. They care deeply and share intimately. They feel a personal sense of worth in simply being together. Their passion may come in the form of hobbies, career, family, friends, or religion. Blue-Blue combinations encourage passion within themselves by fostering a genuine concern for their partners throughout their lives.

OBEDIENT

Blues are the most obedient of all personalities. Blue-Blue relationships do not struggle as most others do with defiance or resentment of authority. They generally accept law and order as important and follow rules without much difficulty. Both feel strongly about moral obligations and appreciate each other's commitment to high standards and rules.

TRUST

Blues are typically suspicious and lack trust in relationships. Not so with the Blue-Blue color combination in committed personal relationships. Perhaps the reason they trust each other so easily is that neither person gives cause for the other to be suspicious. They usually share their feelings and communicate their goals, plans, and daily activities. Therefore, Blues trust each other and feel secure in the relationship.

DEPRESSION

Blues are not much help to each other when either is severely depressed. They don't have the necessary skills or attitude to demand change or cheer each other up. They typically wait out their companion's depression, which is often counterproductive. One Red once said, "Blues are simply a waste of time." He was referring to their long-suffering patience with each other.

PIOUS RIGIDITY

Blues can be very rigid. This deters their ability to be receptive to other people who see life differently or behave according to different standards. Blues can remain so aloof and smug in a relationship that they get out of touch with others around them. This rigidity limits both growth and intimacy with others outside the Blue-Blue connection.

INTENSITY

Blues are precise and determined in their lives. They approach every aspect of their lives with such intensity that both often experience burnout and distress. They feel so deeply for each other that they aren't much help in providing lighter moments of play or relaxation. Neither plays well or relaxes easily. It frequently becomes necessary for them to look outside of the relationship for a more healthy and proper perspective.

QUALITY

Blues are typically very concerned about the quality in their lives. They maintain high standards and expect the same from others. Blue-Blue relationships enjoy a level of quality few other combinations understand. Blues are generally willing to pay the price necessary for personal integrity. Blues often experience strong bonds of trust, sincerity, and intimacy. They pay attention to each other and see others' needs and concerns. I am reminded of my Blue daughter and her Blue uncle Bill who spent a day at Disneyland together. We were celebrating Uncle Bill's birthday, and after a full day at the amusement park, we sat down for pizza. On her own, my Blue daughter produced a special birthday card for her uncle Bill, complete with stickers she secretly bought at Disneyland. She noticed his need, and he appreciated her concern. They experienced a quality exchange. This awareness, combined with personal integrity, offers Blue-Blue color combinations the possibility of experiencing quality relationships.

BLUE-WHITE RELATIONSHIPS

"GENTLE PERSUASION"

There is a saying that opposites attract. This is true for the most part in committed relationships (e.g., Reds with Whites and Blues with Yellows). The major exception to this rule of thumb lies in the common Blue-White relationships. Perhaps the reason for this combination is the mutual sensitivity and compassion they share.

Blues and Whites are both inclined to be concerned with feelings and are low key in their approach to each other. Interestingly, my experience indicates that Blue women may become bored with White husbands, while Blue men remain appreciative of their White companions' accepting ways.

The major complaints Blues express in respect to Whites are that they lack initiative, are stubborn, and don't commit. Whites are more likely to complain that Blues are too controlling, emotional, and unforgiving. Blues comment positively on the peaceful nature, kindness, willingness to listen, tolerance, and patience of Whites. Whites appreciate Blues for their sincerity, leadership, tactful assertion, and loyalty.

The Blue-White relationship is an intriguing combination that willingly goes through life unnoticed. Healthy Blues are generally the spark plugs in these relationships, while charactered Whites offer strong support.

> *Whites can be abusive in relationships*
> *through their passive-aggressive nature.*
> *Many spouses of Whites tell me,*
> *"I'd divorce him but I have no obvious bruises.*
> *I've just been ignored and bored to death."*

OVERVIEW

Blue Personality	White Personality
MOTIVE	
Intimacy	Peace
NEEDS	
to be understood	to be respected
to be appreciated	power and control of self
to be good for self (morally)	to feel good within self
acceptance	acceptance
WANTS	
security	secure excitement
autonomy	protection
to please others	to please self and others
to reveal insecurities (openly)	to hide insecurities
BEHAVIOR STYLE	
high complexity	low complexity
doer (prefers autonomy)	doer (prefers direction)
very controlling	refuses to be controlled
demanding	nondemanding
highly manipulative	subtly manipulative
stability	stability
emotional	logical
irrational (unrealistic expectations)	rational
too sensitive (verbally)	too sensitive (nonverbally)
achiever	balanced
intense	relaxed
impatient	patient
critical of self and others	tolerant of others
blames self and others	blames self
unforgiving and resentful	releases but remembers

Blue Personality	White Personality
negative	overwhelmed
asserts self when necessary	nonassertive
confrontational	craves peace
willing to deal with conflict on principle	avoids conflict
intimidating	intimidated
strongly verbal and nonverbal	strongly nonverbal
possessive	nonpossessive (unless threatened)
compliant with rules	compliant with rules
tactful	tactful
well-behaved	well-behaved
obliging	obliging
emotionally responsible	emotionally irresponsible
gives advice and expects compliance	gives advice only when asked
seeks advice from experts	accepts advice freely
lies to avoid hurting others	lies to avoid conflicts and repercussion
self-righteous	feels inadequate
feels a lot of guilt	holds guilt inside
caring listener	excellent listener
direct communicator (with feelings)	indirect communicator (with feelings)
complex and deep when sharing feelings	easy to talk to; hard to get feelings from
loves deeply and has strong commitment	loves easily and has strong commitment

BLUE-WHITE INTERPERSONAL RELATIONSHIPS
(In-depth Presentation)

INTIMACY   versus   **PEACE**

Blues generally make intimacy the most important component of every relationship. Whites place peace at the top of their list. Blues promote activities and opportunities that foster sharing. It is not uncommon for Blues to suggest taking tennis lessons *together,* walking on the beach *together,* or quiet conversation *together.* Whites appear receptive to the Blues' desires, if for no other reason than to keep the peace. Whites are equally content to pass the time alone or to go places with others. Their need for togetherness is typically met long before Blues' needs are satisfied. Generally, their desire to please others and get along is so important to Whites that they cooperate with their Blue companions.

Whites are capable of quietly sabotaging the intimacy needs of Blues. One Blue woman was furious with her husband's unwillingness to talk much or share in decision making. In desperation, she finally shouted, "I feel like I'm just talking to the wallpaper. Actually, he's not even strong enough to be considered wallpaper. He's more like the stuff inside the wall."

Blues can nag and harass Whites until there is no peace. One White man who loved his fishing trips had finally grown tired of his Blue wife nagging him about his annual fishing trip with the boys. "I don't know why she can't realize," he said, "that after all her shouting is over, I am going to do exactly what I planned to do in the first place. If she would just stop wasting our time by delaying my plans, we would both be better off."

What makes a Blue-White relationship work is the Blue's willingness to accept a White's peaceful style, and the White's willingness to share intimately with a Blue.

TO BE GOOD FOR SELF(morally)	versus	TO FEEL GOOD WITHIN SELF

Blues and Whites both need to feel good inside, but for very different reasons. Blues are driven by a moral conscience, while Whites are more concerned with avoiding distress. Blues willingly take on an issue if a principle is involved. Whites are more inclined to ignore a problem, regardless of the principle, if they perceive discomfort or distress could result from the confrontations. Blues often resent the lack of involvement and moral commitment of White companions. Whites tend to resent the persistent lecturing and moral demands of Blues.

SECURITY	versus	SECURE EXCITEMENT

"All I want is a solid million dollars in the bank, and then I'll be more willing to risk another relationship with a woman," one Blue patient

said. He represents the strong need Blues have for security, whether
financial, emotional, or physical. Whites are also inclined to seek
security. However, they are more concerned with excitement than
Blues. This additional twist entices them to pursue numerous risks
that their Blue companions forgo. Whites are often very quiet about
expressing their need for excitement but often seek situations that
afford them opportunities for secure excitement. Blues are generally
more comfortable in safe and familiar surroundings, such as the security of known friends and family.

AUTONOMY	versus	PROTECTION

"Do Whites ever say anything without being asked?" a Blue father
inquired. "I can't believe how shallow our communication can be at
times. I have to literally ask every possible question to get any
answers. I would certainly appreciate a little cooperation, a little
shared responsibility for the direction of our relationship."

Whites are basically followers. They go with the established direction of most conversations, peer situations, and decisions. Basically,
they flow with life.

Whites generally accept being directed and protected by others.
Their concern is *how* they are directed and protected. They are terribly resistant to demands or hostile control. Whites resent the *style* of
direction much more than the direction itself.

Blues, on the other hand, accept direction out of obligation and
other appropriate expectations of relationships and societal pressures, but they prefer autonomy. Blues are typically not good team
players. They will not accommodate others the way Whites will. They
do not want to lead anyone (including their White companions),
which creates leadership problems for the personality combinations.
Blues are mostly committed to doing a job right, while Whites are
more concerned with simply getting along. Neither personality
prefers to lead, although Blues end up doing so in the majority of
Blue-White relationships.

TO REVEAL INSECURITIES (openly)	versus	TO REVEAL INSECURITIES

One of the reasons this color combination bonds so warmly is the vulnerability both Blues and Whites bring to the relationship. Through-

out their lives, they share information and feelings, which promotes a closeness and trust few other combinations enjoy or understand. One man and woman were so successful in their ability to expose their inner selves to one another, they eventually fell in love because neither of them had ever achieved such openness in other relationships. Despite the fact that both tried dating others, the ability to trust was never the same. Eventually they married, with the foundation of their relationship built on open communication and trust.

Note: Unhealthy Whites are known to appear vulnerable, but they do not verbally share themselves. This presents a particularly frustrating dilemma for Blue companions who seek verbal sharing (including insecurities).

HIGH COMPLEXITY   versus   LOW COMPLEXITY

Typically Blues are perceived to be more difficult to understand. Actually, both have clear needs. The Blues need to be understood and appreciated. The Whites need to feel in control of themselves and be respected. Whites operate on a power base but seek peaceful, accepting relationships. Blues operate on an intimacy base but seek control and understanding. Relationships of Blues and Whites give validity to the saying "Still waters run deep."

DOER   versus   DOER
(prefers autonomy)   (prefers direction)

Whites usually get the job done. They are not particularly concerned with the schedule or exactness of their work. They do quality work and concern themselves mostly with fulfilling the agreement of the contract. They are steady workers who enjoy both doing the job themselves and delegating it to others. They can be lazy and/or overwhelmed when they accept too much work at one time, or they can lack enthusiasm for their endeavors if they have to deal with rigid supervisors or unfulfilling tasks.

Blues prefer doing the job themselves rather than delegating it to others. They love having skilled jobs that require their particular expertise. In fact, one may well find the artisans of our society are most represented by Blues who enjoy the opportunity of creating and implementing their craft on their own. Therefore, they are more inclined to trust themselves, while Whites are better at delegating the responsibility to others.

CONTROLLING   versus   SEEKS NEITHER
(power play)   TO CONTROL NOR TO
                                                BE CONTROLLED

Blues want to know everything that is going on in their companions' lives. Blue employers tend to be suspicious and keep their eyes on everyone's business. Blue parents are curious about all aspects of their child's life. One White young man, a senior in high school, telephoned his mother from work with a simple request for her advice as to the best brand of floor cleanser to use in mopping up the floor at his job. Watch how the Blue mother extends a simple question into an involved conversation:

White son: Mom, what kind of floor cleaner do we use at home?
Blue mother: Are you cleaning the floor?
White: Yes, Mom, now I have to go, but I just need the name of the best cleaner.
Blue: Is anyone else helping you mop the floor?
White: No! Carl is cleaning the food trays.
Blue: Who is Carl? I've never heard you mention him before.
White: Mother! Just tell me the name of a good floor cleaner!
Blue: There is no need to get upset. I was just wondering how you were doing.
White: I'm fine, Mom. Now could you just tell me the name of that floor cleaner, so I can get done and come home?

Regardless of their age or relationship, Blues tend to try to control Whites. One of my favorite examples comes in the form of a note one Blue thirteen-year-old girl left for her forty-two-year-old White mother, just prior to the girl's departure for a European vacation with her father.

Mom, bye! See you July 10th. I love you. Here's a list *I would like* you or Randy to do.
1. Take Rover (dog) for a run *at least* every day.
2. Feed her at night.
3. Feed the fish a couple times a week.
4. Please trim the trees in front and back yards.
Thanks. Please do these for me. Especially the first two because she'll tear up the yard if you don't. Thanks again. It would make me very happy. Bye. I love you.

Love, Michelle

P.S. Oh, and Mom, please don't dust the hallway floor. (Just kidding!)
P.P.S. I'll write, don't worry.

(Personally, I don't think her mother has any cause to worry. This thirteen-year-old will worry enough for them both, and then some.)

Another illuminating example of this control issue comes when a White dentist arrives home after a long day at the office. He is greeted with a warm kiss from his Blue interior designer wife, who has just taken a phone message and promised that her husband will call right back when he arrives home.

His initial response is "Thanks for the message. I'll call back in about half an hour." "Half an hour!" she replies. "I promised her you would call her immediately."

Three more times she hammers him while he tries to digest some of the evening paper. Finally, she threatens him, "Bill, either you call her right now or I'll just have to call her back and explain how you and I just don't see friendship and keeping promises the same way. After all, she is your friend and I did promise that you would call." Quietly, he hands her the phone, which infuriates her more. She calls and says, "Louise, I'm terrible sorry to have to call you, but I felt you should know I've given Bill your message and he will return it when he is good and ready." And he did. About half an hour later.

Both personalities are controlling, but Blues are more likely to try to control others, while Whites seek primarily to control only themselves.

EMOTIONAL	versus	EMOTIONAL AND LOGICAL

This represents a strong difference between the Blues and Whites. Blues thrive on emotional interaction. They focus on feelings (rational *and* irrational). Whites are able to work comfortably with both logical and emotional interaction. They focus on logical reasoning.

One couple (White wife, Blue husband) recently divorced and she remarked, "I could probably learn to love him again, but I can't take his excessive emotional behavior. Everything is emotional to him. I thought I had a problem our whole married life until I found out lots of people don't like to constantly deal with feelings. Actually, I was quite relieved to know I was just as normal as he was. I'm seeking a Red personality for my next relationship. I know how difficult they can be, but at least we can move from one issue to another without continually rehashing every negative thing I've ever done to him for the past twenty years."

IRRATIONAL	versus	IRRATIONAL
(unrealistic expectations)		(timid and fearful)

Blues want everyone to read their minds. They expect everyone to just *know* how they are feeling. They often say, "If I have to tell you, you don't really care." Unfortunately, that irrational thinking creates painful relationships for everyone involved with Blues. Typically, Whites feel guilty when they are unable to decipher the Blues' nonverbal clues as to how to behave and what questions are most appropriate to ask.

Blues fantasize a lot about how things *should* be, and then expect others to share the same fantasy and act accordingly. Whites come close to daydreaming the same way, but their fantasies generally pursue excitement and power rather than intimate relationships. Blues simply can't understand how anything would be as interesting or important to pursue as relationships. One White male said, "She expects me to read her mind because she spends every waking minute reading mine. She tiptoes around the house every morning getting ready for work because she knows *she* would appreciate the quiet. Who cares?! Certainly not me. I'm half deaf and never would have cared what kind of racket she made over the past ten years while she quietly moved in and out of the bedroom."

Whites behave irrationally out of fear. Whites often carry irrational ideas of others and what they are *certain* will happen if they confront someone or make a wrong decision. Some Whites become almost paralyzed and unable to take any risk because they somehow think they *know* what will happen. Healthy Whites readily acknowledge that they wasted many years being bashful or lonely because they perceived and projected problems that had not the least bit of rational justification. Some White mothers are scared to death they may physically abuse their children when no evidence or history of child abuse exists. White men often refuse to date because women will reject them, and yet they have never been rejected. It does become rather ridiculous to continue pursuing such irrational thinking, particularly when there is no historical or circumstantial evidence to support the perceived fear. Blue-White relationships must try not to encourage each other's irrational thinking.

ACHIEVER	versus	BALANCED

Blues are more inclined to stretch themselves in life toward increased productivity, while Whites are more content balancing their lives with work and play. One couple (Blue wife, White husband) found a successful solution with him sailing many weekends with friends while she corrected papers, designed lesson plans, and created new incentives for learning for her kindergarten class. She loved being well prepared for her students, and he loved developing his sailing expertise and friendships.

Blues are more determined to put whatever time and effort is required to be the best. Whites are more concerned with enjoying the total process of living, which includes a balanced support system of friends, family, self, and work. They are willing to sacrifice perfection and high achievement to have it all. However, they are vulnerable to pleasing others. On occasion, you find Whites working longer hours at the office in order to please the boss, until they are chastised by their spouses for not attending to home duties (children, the yard, or other household responsibilities). Then they frantically try to please their spouses, only to be once again drawn into longer hours on the job in order to meet the boss's demands. They are known to feel terribly torn between the components of their balanced lives and high frustration at being unable to satisfy anyone, including themselves.

Blues seem most content with their direction of high achievement. They value their choice of commitment enough to ignore outside influences on their priorities. One Blue woman returned from a slow-paced camping experience complaining about how bored she had been. "There was absolutely nothing to do. I finished my five books the first two days and looked blankly at the remaining five days with rather frustrated eyes. But my husband [White personality] and our daughter had the time of their lives hiking up trails and making new friends." She never suggested, or even seemed to consider, that her priorities might be somewhat limited to high achievement. She simply felt the environment wasn't conducive to her needs.

INTENSE versus RELAXED

"I know it isn't right, but I simply can't face my children another moment after we finally get dinner over with and the dishes washed. My [White] husband rescues me by always putting the children to bed. He reads them a story and says their prayers with them, and I sit quietly in my room listening to them ask Daddy why Mommy doesn't want to read the story, too. It kills me, but I really can't take them for one more minute." So goes the common complaint of involved Blue parents. They are so intense that they can easily overwhelm themselves with relationships and have to remove themselves for a while to gather their composure.

Whites seem to roll with life's twists and turns without often losing their perspective. Much of their success lies in their ability to exercise logical as well as emotional control. They are also less involved, and thus less intense, than their Blue companions. Blues appreciate Whites who get involved and share the burdens. When Whites take a more assertive position, Blues tend to calm down.

IMPATIENT	versus	PATIENT

Is it the perfectionism of the Blues that drives them to be so impatient? Is it their dominant personality? Blues tend to play the more patient role in Red-Blue relationships. However, in White-Blue relationships they generally are the more impatient of the two. They appear driven to assume the leadership role and to make things happen.

Whites are typically the most patient of all the personalities. "What difference will a few minutes make?" they say. Blues are usually prompt and expect the same of others. Whites do not give Father Time the power Blues do. They are not as concerned with punctuality. Whites are rarely irritated or distressed about family, colleagues, or friends arriving late. They see little value in getting all worked up over something you really can't change anyway.

CRITICAL OF SELF AND OTHERS	versus	TOLERANT OF OTHERS

Two friends were vacationing in Mexico when the White friend had her wallet stolen out of her purse while riding on a city bus. "I felt something tugging at my purse but never dreamed that someone would steal from me," she commented after learning that all their money and passports had been stolen. "We can replace the money, and I'm sure our passports will show up. After all, what would anyone want with them. Let's just drop by the American Embassy and explain our situation to the authorities. Everything will be fine." Her Blue friend remembered looking at her in utter amazement. "Vickie, we have just lost all our money and passports. We are in a country where the national pastime is *not* baseball and they don't speak English. We have no transportation, and we have *no* idea where the American Embassy is located. And you are telling me everything will be fine! Tell me, my friend, do you think it is possible that they took anything else with our money and identification like, for example, your mind?!" All criticism aside, they did locate the embassy, where they got help, and went on to have a delightful vacation. The Blue friend, however, remained terribly suspicious of all Mexicans for the rest of the trip, while the White friend repeatedly invited the local people to join them for dinner and teach them their cultural ways.

Blue parents tend to notice the one C on the report card, while the White parents compliment their children for attending class. Blue employees often notice their boss's lack of appreciation for all their hard work, while Whites accept that the boss deserves longer lunches because he is the boss. Generally speaking, Whites tolerate what Blues criticize.

| UNFORGIVING | versus | FORGIVING |
| AND RESENTFUL | | BUT REMEMBERS |

For Blues, getting mad is usually not enough. They wait to get even. They will often hold the grudge as long as they feel the other person needs to be punished. One Blue wife came to see me at sixty-five years of age prepared to leave her White husband because she perceived him as "cruel and unattentive." She revealed that he had missed their daughter's sixteenth birthday *and* her high school graduation. He, of course, could neither remember attending nor missing either. The irony, however, was that the daughter saw her father as more loving and supportive than her mother, and held absolutely no resentment toward her father for anything. The Blue mother had made herself miserable for years over an issue that had been long forgotten by the principal parties involved.

Whites are willing to forgive, but only after they have avenged any wrongdoing. Because they tend to be quiet, slow-paced revenge can take a considerable amount of time. One young White swimmer was verbally thrashed by her Red coach in front of all the other girls at an important swim meet. She said nothing to her coach. She simply listened. The final event of the meet was her best stroke. The score was tied. She could win or lose the event for her team. She led the other swimmers all the way to the finish. With a comfortable lead and only yards from touching the wall for a win, she suddenly stopped and stood up, disqualifying herself in the event. Her Red coach was livid. She simply looked up at him with a contented smile, which seemed to say, "Gotcha!" After that, she continued to swim for the team. Neither held the grudge. The wrong had been righted, and all could now be forgiven and forgotten. Blue-

White relationships are noted for holding resentments for longer than is healthy. They are also seen as most loving and genuine with their feeling once sincere forgiveness is sought (preferably on hands and knees!).

WILLING TO DEAL   versus   AVOIDS CONFLICT
WITH CONFLICT
ON PRINCIPLE

While it is true that Blues usually assume the leadership role in Blue-White relationships, they are not particularly interested in conflict. Blues are the moral guardians of society and will rise to the occasion when they feel an injustice has occurred. They are often highly principled people who will not tolerate wrong behavior. They will speak their minds and confront anyone when a situation flies in the face of truth and honesty. They are equally verbal when they feel they have been dealt with unjustly. Blues are known to act like cornered tigers, lashing out irrationally at someone they feel has perhaps erred in judgment or crossed them in some unforgivable way. In other words, when a Blue deems another's behavior to be unacceptable, verbal confrontation will generally take place.

Whites are less inclined to create a scene and stir up trouble for themselves. On one occasion, a White mother observed her young daughter being verbally abused by a cruel old man. At the time, she gave no indication that she was terribly disturbed. She did pull a face at the old man behind his back. She also brought the incident up to several other people two weeks later. However, she avoided conflict at the time of her displeasure. Whites do everyone a disservice with their unwillingness to respond.

In order to avoid conflict, Whites are notorious for saying "I don't care." One Blue woman remarked about her White husband, "I get so sick and tired of his 'I don't care' responses that it makes me furious whenever I hear it now. He really doesn't care whether the question concerns seeing a movie, going out to dinner, or even whether to get pregnant and have more children. All he ever says is, 'Whatever you would like to do is fine with me.'"

One day she was so frustrated with his answers that she asked him if they could blow their entire savings and go to Europe. As expected, he, half-listening, replied that he didn't care. She purchased the tickets the next day. They went to Europe, and now he appears to be somewhat more attentive and willing to express an opinion, regardless of the conflict it might create.

COMPLIANT . . . TACTFUL . . . WELL-BEHAVED . . . OBLIGING

Blues and Whites share all four of these traits. They appreciate and value each other for their willingness to extend the small courtesies and appropriate manners that Reds and Yellows struggle to understand or extend to others. These shared values help cement a warm and sincere relationship for Blue-White connections.

GIVES ADVICE AND   versus   GIVES ADVICE EXPECTS COMPLIANCE   ONLY WHEN ASKED

Blues tend to make stronger disciplinarians than Whites. Blues feel they have a great deal to offer, and willingly share it with others. When they give advice, they expect others to follow it.

Whites are more inclined to allow others to set their own boundaries. They are not prone to follow up their advice in order to ensure its application. They do not often give suggestions without some prodding by those seeking their advice. They may think a problem through and never say anything unless others specifically request their advice.

FEEL A LOT OF GUILT

Another trait Blues and Whites share is guilt. Actually, I think they have a corner on the market. Both are uncomfortable seeing anyone hurting, regardless of the reason for the pain. Both blame themselves for their inappropriate behavior and hold on to past regrets too long. They are both capable of becoming immobilized if their guilt is particularly serious. I worked with a Blue-White couple who had been separated for years but unable to file divorce papers because they both felt so guilty about dissolving the marriage. Neither could act because of their feeling of obligation to the children and each other. Yet, neither was willing to reengage the relationship because of the past emotional scars and dismal potential for future success.

CARING LISTENER   versus   EXCELLENT LISTENER

I think the major difference in the listening skills between Blues and Whites is their emotional attachment to the conversation. Both care about people, but Whites are more apt to hear the issues objectively, while Blues are instinctively drawn to the individual. Both are capable of giving their full attention to a discussion and responding with sincere concern for the individual and the content.

| COMPLEX AND DEEP WHEN SHARING FEELINGS | versus | EASY TO TALK TO; HARD TO GET FEELINGS FROM |

Blues' emotions run very deep. They are sincere and genuine when they share themselves with others. They are often insulted when others do not fully understand their complexity and concerns. They are typically left frustrated when there isn't time to finish a conversation. They are always concerned with the emotional content of the dialogue.

Whites are quite easy to talk to. They typically don't display much emotion. They prefer to sit quietly and listen to others. They are not likely to open up unless they are certain of the other's trustworthiness. They do not handle rejection well, and feel more comfortable holding their feelings inside. Many people find Whites desirable conversationalists because they would rather listen than talk. Blues and Whites are known for their sensitivity to others, and appreciate the increased warmth this specifically offers them in Blue-White relationships.

| LOVES DEEPLY AND HAS STRONG COMMITMENT | versus | LOVES EASILY AND HAS STRONG COMMITMENT |

Both Blues and Whites are capable of being highly committed to each other. They value security and find committed relationships to be the most natural way to enjoy life. They are often traumatized with the breakup of relationships with each other, and neither recovers easily, regardless of who terminated the relationship.

Blues are inclined to feel a deep emotional commitment to people, while Whites find it easy to accept and love those they meet. Blues are known for the lifelong guarantees on their love. While scars may develop with the relationship, Blues tend to feel strong loyalty to those select few to whom they commit. This does not come easily to Blues, but once it does the reward is a deep caring that often lasts a lifetime.

Whites are tolerant and accepting of theirs. Whites commit quietly to relationships. They feel the closest to those Blues who are gentle and kind.

Blue-White relationships are generally characterized by sincerity, stability, and quiet persuasion. Both colors tend to accept each other, and yet seek to promote positive changes in the relationship. Unlike most other combinations, Blue-White relationships tend to be gentle in their communication. They represent a most complementary sharing of similar values. They are also fortunate in having enough differences to broaden their capacity for successful enjoyment of each other and life itself.

MAKING THE MOST OF COMPLEMENTARY SIMILARITIES

Blues Need Whites:	Whites Need Blues:
To show them the good in others	To motivate them
To teach them relaxed attitudes	To be kind to them
To listen to them	To help them not to feel guilty
To respect them	To teach them creativity
To appreciate them	To encourage and believe in them
To calm their nerves	To direct them
To minimize their imperfections	To build their self-confidence
To carry out specific assignments	To nurture them
To be agreeable	To initiate activities
To be emotionally responsible	To accept them as they are

POTENTIAL CONFLICTS OF COMPLEMENTARY SIMILARITIES

Blues	Whites
Seek intimacy	Have difficulty expressing feelings
Committed	Uncommitted
Judgmental	Tolerant
Perfectionistic	Overwhelmed
Directed	Lazy
Passionate	Doubting
Detail conscious	Unaware
Crave oral communication	Comfortable with nonverbal communication
Unforgiving	Unforgiving
Irrational when angered	Uncommunicative when angered

*Blue-Yellow relationships allow
for the most intimate combination
of different-color personalities.*

BLUE-YELLOW RELATIONSHIPS

"HAND-IN-GLOVE"

Blue-Yellow relationships allow for the most intimate combination of different-color personalities. They represent the entire spectrum of emotions, and together they can experience explosive synergy. Blue-Yellow combinations are primarily concerned with quality relationships (genuine human connection). Blues most commonly represent the depth, sincerity, and compassion of intimacy, while Yellows display the excitement, warmth, and optimism of relationships.

Blues and Yellows tend to value each other but often experience difficulty accepting the other's vastly different perceptions of how life is best lived. For example, Blues believe that play comes after the work is done. Yellows regard work as necessary but play as far more valuable, and tend to give it first priority.

Blues are very steady, while Yellows are rather flighty. Blues prefer stability and Yellows seek change. Once again, the theory of "opposites attract" appears to work. They are as opposite as Red-White combinations, and yet they somehow feel strongly attracted. Perhaps each supplies what the other needs. Perhaps their differences afford them the opportunity to appreciate the other's strengths. Regardless of the reasons, Blues and Yellows frequently seek and enjoy each other's companionship. There is a strong bonding of the heart.

OVERVIEW

Blue Personality	Yellow Personality
MOTIVE	
Intimacy	Fun
NEEDS	
to be appreciated	superficial connections
to be understood	to be praised
to be good for self (morally)	to look good to others (socially)
acceptance	approval

Blue Personality	Yellow Personality
WANTS	
security	playful adventure
autonomy	freedom
to please others	to please others/self
to reveal insecurities (openly)	to hide insecurities (loosely)
BEHAVIORAL STYLE	
high complexity	low complexity
emotional heavyweight	emotional lightweight
purposeful and serious	playful and lighthearted
strong perfectionism	scattered productivity
highly controlling	refuses to be controlled
responsible	irresponsible
attention to detail	what detail?
sincere	superficial
low profile	high profile
stability	change
suspicious	trusting/naive
conscientious	flighty
emotional	emotional
cynical	innocent/naive
too sensitive	insensitive
doer	delegator/performer
creative	innovative
intense	carefree
impatient	good-natured
manipulative	seeks escape
demanding	obnoxious
direct communication (with feelings)	direct communication (with facts and feelings)
unforgiving of self	forgives self freely
willing to deal with conflict (based on principles)	avoids confrontation
strongly nonverbal	strongly verbal

Blue Personality	Yellow Personality
possessive	nonpossessive
tactful	tactless (uses humor)
behaved	rebellious
gives advice and expects compliance	gives advice but unconcerned with compliance
seeks advice from knowledgeable people	welcomes advice from others
aloof	inviting
critical of self and others	accepting of self and others
self-righteous	unpretentious
feels a lot of guilt	rarely gives or accepts guilt
blames self	blames others
negative	positive
emotionally cluttered	simple
caring listener	poor listener
complex and deep when sharing feelings	easy to share feelings with
gives with strings attached	gives freely
loves deeply and has strong commitment	loves easily but without commitment
lies to avoid hurting others and when embarrassed	lies to save face

BLUE-YELLOW INTERPERSONAL RELATIONSHIPS
(In-depth Presentation)

INTIMACY   versus   **FUN**

Yellows lighten the hearts of Blues, and Blues enrich the hearts of Yellows. They make a passionate team. Whether they are parent-child, friend-friend, husband-wife, or employer-employee, this combination usually experiences positive bonds of playful creativity and committed caring.

Blues are motivated by intimacy. Yellows are motivated by fun but need intimacy. Yellows are more inclined to seek intimacy than Blues are to pursue fun. Blues typically place little value on playtime, preferring to focus on the more serious aspects of life.

No other personality seeks fun the way Yellows do. Yellows often live to play. When Yellows become pressured at work or at home, energizing hobbies or short vacations replace their haggard looks with youthful vigor. Always reward a good dog with a pat on the head and a deserving Yellow with a vacation. Yellows can't understand why anyone would commit to anything that didn't include fun. They are equally confused by people who don't know how to relax on vacations. Blues have to have a reason to relax and play, while for Yellows, relaxing and playing *is* the purpose.

Blues commit themselves most completely to activities that enrich the Blue-Yellow relationship. They will take swimming lessons if their Yellow companion likes to swim. They give priority to being together in the relationship and schedule their various activities around enhancing intimacy within the relationship. Blue parents typically attend their children's school, sports, and other social functions, regardless of the inconvenience. Blue teachers often empathize with a student who is struggling with assignments. Blue spouses plan business or community obligations around birthdays and other special holidays so they can share memorable celebrations with their families. Blues feel deeply and enjoy committing to intimate relationships, regardless of the numerous expectations or difficulties.

Yellows operate on a superficial level most of the time. They are capable of feeling deeply but prefer a more limited emotional connection on a daily basis. Yellows are often accused by Blues of not really caring because they appear so superficial. Equally frustrating for the Blues is the Yellows' perception that Blues are so controlling. Yellows often remark that the price of being loved by Blues is, at times, too high. When they find a mutually satisfying level emotionally, no other mixed color combination can match their intimacy. They are funny, casual, sincere, accepting, endearing, and vibrant in their connection.

Blue-Yellow combinations
are primarily concerned
with quality relationships
(genuine human connection).

TO BE APPRECIATED   versus   TO BE PRAISED

When a Yellow wants to learn how to get along with a Blue, it's really quite simple. The first thing they must do every morning after they wake up is tell their Blue companion, "I love you and appreciate all you do for me." As long as Yellows are sincere, they will be on easy street for life. Blues thrive on emotional closeness and appreciation. They willingly forgo personal pleasure in order to meet needs of others. It means so much when others, however briefly, forgo personal pleasure to appreciate them. The theme for Blues could easily come from a song in *Camelot*. King Arthur suggests that the way "to handle a woman, is to love her, simply love her." Nothing could be more true for Blue men and women. They simply need to know you love and appreciate them in order for their lives to be complete.

Blues give at such a committed level that mere praise would generally not suffice. They are typically unimpressed by social acknowledgment, especially at a superficial level. Blues are more inclined to value a brief handwritten note of acknowledgment from someone who truly understands and appreciates their contribution.

On the other hand, Yellows typically throw things together at the last minute and come up smelling like roses. Appreciation isn't generally necessary for them. A congratulatory pat on the back and public acknowledgment (when appropriate) will sufficiently meet their needs.

TO BE GOOD   versus   TO LOOK GOOD
FOR SELF   TO OTHERS
(morally)   (socially)

Walt Disney's character Jiminy Cricket would call it a conscience. I call it character. Call it whatever you prefer, but in the end it means that Blues are more concerned with their moral obligations, while Yellows need social recognition. I remember consulting with a Blue patient directly after seeing a Yellow patient one day. Both patients had become drunk at their in-laws' twenty-fifth wedding anniversary celebrations. I was fascinated with how differently they approached their concern about their drunken behavior. The Blue patient needed to know if he should apologize for his drunken state. He was concerned that a proper son-in-law would have remained sober and helped host the party. The Yellow patient needed to know if I thought others in the family would think poorly of him. He was more concerned about tainting his social image with his in-laws than the inappropriateness of his behavior. The Blue suffered from moral guilt, while the Yellow suffered from social guilt.

Another illuminating example of the difference lies in the matter of weight control. Blues need to keep in shape so they will like the way they look, while Yellows need to look good for others. Yellows operate from personal vanity, while the Blues are primarily concerned with self-respect.

SECURITY	versus	PLAYFUL ADVENTURE

Blues are often envious of Yellows' self-esteem. Yellows carry this within themselves (often from birth). They do not seek validation from outside sources. They like themselves and usually feel confident that everything will work out in the end. This confidence allows them to seek adventure throughout their lives, while Blues continually grasp for the elusive feeling of security. Perhaps one reason Blues seek Yellows is the comfort they feel in connecting with someone who exudes confidence and security.

On the other hand, Yellows value the security they receive from Blues. Blues work very hard to offer security to those they love. Yellows intuitively sense the deep commitment that Blues offer, and generally strive to keep Blues in their life. Just prior to leaving on a business trip, a Blue woman discovered that her Yellow husband had worked out a business deal with his father behind her back. She could not tolerate his father. She threatened to leave her husband because she could no longer accept his interactions with his father. This carefree, lighthearted man was heartbroken. The thought of losing his wife became an obsession. He called her every night while she was away on business to the point of harassment. He wanted reassurance that she still loved him and would stay with him. Upon her arrival home at the airport, he met her with roses and a limousine. He read a poem he had written for her. Subconsciously, Yellows may seek Blues because they value security and know that of all the personalities, Blues are not only most likely to seek security, but to *offer* it as well.

Yellows love stretching themselves. They avidly pursue many facets of life. They are primarily interested in playful adventure and find extreme competition unappealing. Yellows risk freely. They will change jobs, residences, and friends more comfortably than Blues. They enjoy the thrill of trying something new and require constant challenges of a playful nature to hold their interest.

AUTONOMY versus FREEDOM

The words *autonomy* and *freedom* convey difference in purpose. Blues want autonomy to pursue a task. Yellows want freedom from completing a task as well as freedom to work on their own. In organizations Blues and Yellows find independent work situations very comfortable. Both Blues and Yellows prefer to be given their responsibilities and left to perform them in their own way and time. They accept direction but resist control. Blues enjoy the creative aspect of autonomy and thrive on the possibility of striving for perfection when no one else is able to force them to accept mediocrity. Yellows enjoy social interaction but prefer the freedom to work at their own pace without others setting deadlines and forcing unnecessary meetings. Both tend to find that teamwork often cramps their natural style.

EMOTIONAL HEAVYWEIGHT versus EMOTIONAL LIGHTWEIGHT

Blues tend to remain committed to the cause of intimacy regardless of emotional scarring, while Yellows are quick to seek refuge from personal disappointments. The animal kingdom offers us two role models. Blues are similar to the dog pursuing a rabbit. He is focused and determined. He is oblivious to any distractions. He tenaciously pursues his goal. Blues are predictably emotional and usually remain focused on the behavior throughout their life.

Yellows are like the butterfly, darting in and out with a look-and-see attitude. They never land anywhere too long and maintain a safe distance from other living beings. Beautiful, gentle, and exciting, they attract everyone's attention but generally make limited connections.

Blues are usually direct and consistent in their emotional intentions. Yellows are more vague and unpredictable. Both value sincere commitments, despite the differences in how they commit emotionally.

PURPOSEFUL AND SERIOUS versus PLAYFUL AND LIGHTHEARTED

Yellow: (to wife) Wouldn't it be fun to be in Paris this spring? Just think of how colorful and exciting it would be.

Blue: (to husband) I would love the romance of Paris in springtime. But I want to go when I know we are really in love. Just going to Europe for the sake of traveling doesn't excite me much.

Many Yellows could be nicknamed "the Yellow tease." They motion with one hand to come close and with the other hand to stay away. They seduce with their charm and innocence but are too easily frightened away. They shine like the sun and entice with their very existence, but quickly laugh it all off when the Blues in their lives become serious.

This is particularly frustrating for Blues, who rarely invest themselves lightly (particularly in relationships). They find the Yellows' casual attitude difficult to respect or depend on. Yellows are often baffled by the seriousness with which Blues approach relationships, and consider Blues to be too concerned and overzealous about their commitment. "All I wanted," Yellows explain while dating, "was to have some good, clean fun. The way Blues act, you'd think we were getting married or something."

STRONG PERFECTIONISM	versus	SCATTERED PRODUCTIVITY

Blues go through life noticing all details and maintaining a penetrating concentration. They willingly work out until they are practice-perfect. Blues value people who express the same commitment to perfection, regardless of their profession. They are often admired by others for their devotion to perfection. In relationships, however, this proves to be frustrating for both Blues and Yellows. Yellows become frustrated by the constant need Blues have to do everything perfectly. "Good enough" is exactly that for Yellows—good enough. For Blues, it usually means "settling for less."

Yellows are more inclined to like watching a player like Ilie Nastasie on the tennis courts. This lively Romanian player impressed tennis fans for years with his brilliant moments of tennis play and his equally brilliant childish antics on the courts, which he predictably displayed for the fans' amusement. He was clearly as interested in social approval as technical expertise.

This style of scattered productivity often proves terribly frustrating for Blues, who cannot understand how anyone, let alone this person they love (particularly spouse, child, or parent), can skate through life with little concern for accuracy and dedication to perfection. Blues need to understand that Yellows *will* be hostile and uncooperative, forsaking all their charismatic choices. Yellows, however, will generally balance playfulness with meaningful, productive moments.

CONTROLLING	versus	SEEKS FREEDOM
IN ORDER TO		
GET SECURITY		

Blue personalities tend to prefer a conventional, deliberate, and pre-dictable relationship. They have such strong needs for stability that they try to hold everything together in order to feel peace of mind. Blues are so appropriate and exacting that they often elect themselves to be the leaders of Blue-Yellow relationships. Yellows instinctively resist control. They refuse to give control to Blues without a price. Depending on the character of either person, this price could be extremely high.

Blues often appear controlling because they need to feel secure in the relationship, and they think this security comes from always knowing what Yellows are doing and where they are going. Blues also appear controlling because they feel it is essential that they remind Yellows about proper manners and appropriate public behavior. This instruction is typically construed by Yellows as unnecessary and demanding.

Yellows enjoy flexible, changing, and unstructured relationships. They reject hard boundaries ("be home for dinner every night by six") and find little need for stability. Freedom is essential to Yellows if they are to experience life at its best. Yellows prize the freedom to choose whom they will be with, where they will go, and how they will get there. Easily manipulated, they are quite receptive to the Blues, who allow them to choose their own options in life. Admittedly, with-out healthy character, Yellows do abuse their freedom and may find themselves unable to commit to relationships, pursuing instead a more self-centered (as opposed to cooperative) life.

| RESPONSIBLE | versus | IRRESPONSIBLE |

"Just tell me if you hear of anyone putting on a production of *The Wizard of Oz*," one Blue mother lamented to me. "I have the perfect person to play the part of the brainless scarecrow—my son!" She was so frustrated with his irresponsible behavior. "Seriously," she contin-ued, "it won't hurt my feelings. Just tell me straight out, is it possible that he will ever get a brain?" Her Yellow son was quite representative of many irresponsible Yellows. Yellows rarely stop and think before they speak or act.

Yellows are more vainly concerned with their physical appearance than the fact that their bedrooms are pigsties. Yellows are notorious for walking on expensive sweaters they may or may not have paid for with their own money. Yellow teenagers seem to epitomize the Yellow irresponsibility, because most teenagers are already that way during this exasperating transition from childhood to adulthood. Yellow babysitters are terrific at playing with the children but then prefer to talk on the telephone with friends rather than cleaning up the messes their good time with the kids left.

Yellows are more concerned with the speed with which they turn the corner than with the wear and tear on the car's tires. One Blue father was always concerned with the costs his Yellow son incurred. "From sheer negligence," he'd say, "you have cost me more than all your brothers and sisters combined." He always encouraged his son to get a good-paying job in order to survive on his own.

Yellows don't give adequate consideration to the long-term consequences of their behavior. They do not typically take good care of their belongings because they think only of the moment. Blues usually resist loaning camping equipment, cars, and other important possessions to Yellows.

On the other hand, Blues make marvelous companions for Yellows. Like Wendy in *Peter Pan*, Blues constantly work to help Yellows grow up and be responsible. They notice details and constantly acquaint Yellows with reasons why details (like stop signs, high school diplomas, and clothes hangers) exist.

SINCERE versus INSINCERE

Blues pride themselves on their sincere and loyal commitment to Yellows. One Blue client, Tom, came in and demanded an explanation for how his best friend John (a Yellow) could leave for southern California for a brief summer vacation and then decide to *stay* in Albuquerque, New Mexico, for his coming senior year in high school. "We were best friends," Tom explained. "I don't think he realized how much I invested in our friendship. And now, on a whim, he just up and leaves me for the thrill of a new environment. If that is all I meant to him, we must not have had a great friendship at all." Tom was devastated to think his friend would consider abandoning him after all they had shared through three previous years of high school.

Tom and John had great times while they were together. Now John was prepared to experience something new. It had just come up as a fluke, and he was game for anything. "After all," Yellows explain, "you only live once." This seems so insincere to Blues, who willingly sacrifice the thrill of it all for their committed relationships. Yellows feel different. They give what they've got while they are in the situation, and then comfortably move on when it changes.

LOW PROFILE　　　　　versus　　　　　HIGH PROFILE

Picture this: Two people apply for positions with a touring theatrical company. One specifically requests a position designing and sewing costumes behind the scenes, while the other expresses a strong preference to be onstage. Which one is most likely Blue, and which one do you suspect to be Yellow? The odds have it that Blues prefer the behind-the-scenes details, while the Yellows enjoy onstage exposure. One enjoys working with things, while the other prefers people.

SUSPICIOUS　　　　　versus　　　　　TRUSTING/NAIVE

"My wife is better than the FBI," one Yellow husband explained. "She knows everything I've done wrong since the day we began dating. I would hate to see the Wanted poster she would design if I were a criminal."

"It's true," she agrees. "We just got home from a vacation in Mexico with another couple. One day, our husbands wanted to go fishing. My friend's husband threw his wife a kiss from a distance and told her to eat dinner without him because he wasn't certain what time they would return. I demanded to inspect the boat for seaworthiness and got my husband's life jacket (which I had purchased and packed knowing he might want to go boating). I didn't trust him, the boat, or myself. Can you imagine my husband dying in a boating accident and leaving me to raise two kids by myself?"

Many Blues go through life too suspicious of others. They are rarely free to really enjoy pleasurable moments because they are so busy worrying about what may go wrong.

As much as Blues suffer from their suspicious minds, Yellows may suffer from their nondiscriminating natures. Too often wonderful Yellows allow negative friends to enter their lives and color them ugly. They never believe people could have such negative motives. They naively attach themselves to inappropriate people because, as Yellows say, the people are "fun" or "they really are good people once you get to know them inside."

Yellow innocence causes concern in Blue parents who value their child's refreshing enthusiasm but fear the inevitable consequences of not taking precautions. One Blue mother even sent her Yellow daughter away to a private school in order to break up a budding romance with a negative boyfriend. "Call me controlling or whatever you want," she cried. "I couldn't bear to see this perfectly charming child turn sarcastic, cold, and hardened right before my eyes."

It was a great move. No deception. Right up front, the young girl knew the reasons and, being Yellow, quickly found the exciting possibilities in being away from home and venturing out into the world on her own. She went to the private school and quickly found herself responding positively to new friends and her changed environment and lifestyle.

TOO SENSITIVE versus INSENSITIVE

To a Blue, everything is personal. They feel deeply responsible for whatever happens in their lives. Their extreme sensitivity can make them unpleasant to live with. If you arrive late, Blues may think you didn't really want to come. If you are angry, Blues typically feel guilty for possibly creating recent dilemmas in your life. Blues take many people and experiences too personally. With Yellows' carefree attitudes and flippant comments, Blues often struggle with Yellows' insensitivity. Blues tend to create many of their emotional traumas with their own hypersensitivity, but their difficulties often seem further complicated by Yellows' insensitivity.

One Blue woman was frightened about an upcoming river rafting expedition. She mistakenly asked two Yellow friends, who had been river rafting, if she would enjoy the experience. They flippantly reassured her, almost mocking her fear. She was furious when they wouldn't take her nervousness seriously. Her friends were insensitive. She was too sensitive. Perhaps nothing short of a violin serenade and a discussion of the need for increased life insurance would have made her happy. (And that probably would have depressed her.)

IMPATIENT versus GOOD-NATURED

Blue-Yellow relationships often find their behaviors in conflict. Blues want their families home every night for dinner, and Yellows want flexibility as to what time they will arrive home. Yellows want to be greeted with a smile and a kiss, while Blues want understanding for why they don't always present themselves with a smile at the exact moment Yellows decide to appear at the front door.

Blues struggle with the notion that they know what is best for everyone, especially Yellows. Yellows tend to forget time, people, commitments, and any other hassle that might complicate their lives. Children often adore Yellows for their casual style. This frustrates Blues, who are certain that the only reason Yellows are better loved is because they don't demand anything of anybody. Blues want things done right and done immediately. Yellows also want things done, but freely give allowances when unforeseen circumstances arise. (Unforeseen circumstances can be anything from a friend calling to play golf to a death in the family.) Yellows believe that most things aren't worth getting upset over and let them pass without giving them much thought. Blues notice everything (especially noisy children and late reports), and feel compelled to make everything an issue.

UNFORGIVING	versus	FORGIVING

This represents, perhaps, the best strength of Yellows and the greatest liability of Blues. Yellows do not generally dwell on the past. (They have a hard enough time remembering it, let alone dwelling on it.) Blues harbor tremendous anger, resentment, and bitterness over past negative encounters. They find it most difficult to let go of the feelings that Yellows rarely experience. If Yellows do feel deep anger or hostility, it seems to dissipate without much effort on their part. Their lives tend to be much less cluttered because of it.

One Blue patient told me how she had finally forgiven her ex-husband, who had left her for another woman. "I secretly hope someday to see him bald and fat with his stomach desperately hanging over his pants and underwear hanging out in back." With all sincerity, she then asked, "But don't you think I am finally forgiving him?"

Blues must learn to forgive, or they will frighten their Yellow companions away from any genuine sharing and intimacy. This, in turn, prevents Blues from experiencing their primary motivation in life—intimacy.

WILLING TO DEAL WITH CONFLICT ON PRINCIPLES	versus	AVOIDS CONFRONTATION

There are certain principles that Blues do not consider negotiable. They are willing to lay their reputations on the line for them. They will fight like a mother bear protecting a newborn cub rather than acquiesce in the name of peace. Blue spouses often find themselves angered by Yellows who won't engage in a good, wholesome argument. Blues feel that honest expressions of feelings show that one cares. Blues are more inclined to suffer a stressed relationship in order to make themselves clearly understood on important principles.

Yellows are more inclined to avoid the inevitable confrontation by laughing it off or quickly refocusing the conversation to a less controversial subject. Yellows are often seen as disloyal or "talking out of both sides of their mouths" because of their unwillingness to take a firm stand on issues. Yellows are, perhaps, too easily persuaded to abandon a particular philosophy or principle because it requires too much effort.

DISTANT   versus   INVITING

For many reasons, Blues are more intimidating than Yellows. Yellows have a winning way about them that invites people into their lives. "Everywhere I go, I meet the nicest people," one Yellow patient remarked. Life is much like a mirror, so Yellows seem to find invitations waiting for them wherever they go. Yellows warm up to people regardless of their age, race, or socioeconomic level.

Blues are more discriminating and judgmental. They are reserved and suspicious from a distance. They are most often loved only after a substantial period of time spent getting to know them. Blues feel "to *know* me is to love me." Yellows feel "to *love* me is to know me." Once Yellows feel invited into someone's heart, they willingly become vulnerable and expressive.

BLAMES SELF   versus   BLAMES OTHERS

Blues look inward to explain poor relationships, while Yellows, fearing the rejection created by owning up to their limitations, usually look elsewhere for places to put the blame. This often keeps Yellows from properly developing themselves. If they are not careful, Yellows can spend a lifetime explaining away their failures by placing responsibility elsewhere. Only when they can look within, and see the importance of responding to their limitations, will Yellows ever know the real power that comes from accepting responsibility for one's own actions.

One Yellow child repeatedly blamed his problems of school truancy, sexual-identity crisis, and auto theft on his controlling and demanding Blue father. He actually seemed to enjoy watching his poor father agonize over what he had done to his son, and how he should have done things differently. It took this Yellow child four years of frustration and personal disappointment before he began to see his part in the relationship. Eventually, he claimed some responsibility and began developing more appropriate living skills.

NEGATIVE   versus   POSITIVE

Blues seem to zero in on why something can't be done, while Yellows immediately see the reasons why it ought to be tried. Blues ask, "Why not me? I think I'd be the perfect choice!" Blues tend to see all the problems, while Yellows typically see all the possibilities.

CARING LISTENER   versus   POOR LISTENER

Yellows are usually out for a good time, and that rarely includes sincere listening. They are not interested in emotional details, and often find sitting and sharing the serious concerns of others to be quite boring. Blues enjoy the idea of deep conversation, and genuinely care about what the other person is trying to say. They are excellent at really listening rather than concentrating on what *their* comments will be.

Blues can be very disappointed in Yellows' superficial style of listening. They may even feel betrayed when Yellows hear only their words and neglect to focus on their feelings.

Yellows are typically frustrated with the storytelling of Blues. Blues tend to overkill their communication by relating every detail several times. You've heard, no doubt, the phrase "to make a long story short"; Blues prefer the other version, "to make a short story longer." Blues want to be understood and tend to keep talking in the superstitious hope that eventually they will be.

GIVES WITH   versus   GIVES FREELY
STRINGS ATTACHED

Blues are more inclined to give of themselves than Yellows are. However, when Yellows give, they give freely without expectation, while Blues often have strings attached. Many Blue personalities become angered at the shabby way they are treated after bending over backwards for others. Numerous individuals have shared resentments with me about guests who have stayed with them and been treated like kings and queens without even a word of appreciation. Yellows rarely feel the same depth of disappointment. Either they simply give less, or when they do give, Yellows don't attach any expectations to the gift.

LOVES DEEPLY	versus	LOVES EASILY
AND HAS STRONG		BUT WITHOUT
COMMITMENT		COMMITMENT

Blues have a strong loyalty to whomever and whatever they commit to. They are most comfortable in committed relationships and feel great apprehension about abandoning any commitments they make. One Blue colleague of mine experienced deep emotional turmoil while trying to decide whether to stay with her husband, who offered her good fun but no emotional depth, or to leave her marriage for a man she had loved deeply as a friend for years. In the end, there was no real decision. She loved her husband and could never leave him, regardless of the empty moments she endured.

In contrast, I remember heading for the ski slopes one time with a Yellow friend. He reminded me a great deal of Peter Pan, with his incessant acts of irresponsibility and his refusal to accept society's demands that he grow up. He claimed that he felt too restricted, confined, and committed in marriage. He wanted to play more than he wanted the responsibility of a wife and the children he had fathered.

Within a year of our conversation, my friend had abandoned his wife and two children for a more playful life. Yellows tend to be more vulnerable in the long run, because they lack the depth of commitment required to experience earned intimacy.

This exciting combination of opposites offers the possibilities that neither personality could experience on their own. They share a mutual admiration. Yellows prize Blues for their talent, creativity, sensitivity, loyalty, commitment, sincerity, and intimacy. Blues value Yellows for their vigor, optimism, acceptance, forgiveness, spice, candor, and intimacy. Both relish the Blue-Yellow relationships' strong intimate potential, and usually recognize the unique synergy afforded them together.

RELATIONSHIPS: THE COLOR CONNECTIONS

MAKING THE MOST OF COMPLEMENTARY OPPOSITES

Blues Need Yellows:

To keep a healthy "here
and now" perspective

To promote creative,
playful moments

To foster optimism and hope

To cherish and appreciate them

To remind them of their
intrinsic value

To make them laugh

To show them the lighter
side of life

To keep conversations flowing

To facilitate social relationships

To share intimate moments

Yellows Need Blues:

To give grounding and
direction

To teach compassion and
sensitivity

To notice details and specifics

To provide stability

To encourage them to
complete tasks

To remember important
events and facts

To laugh at them

To praise and notice them

To provide moral leadership

POTENTIAL CONFLICTS OF COMPLEMENTARY OPPOSITES

Blues

Very committed

Too sensitive

Generally work-oriented

Controlling

Detail-oriented

Serious

Takes on too many
responsibilities

Acts appropriately and properly

Too selfless

Requires long deliberation
in decision making

Yellows

Often flighty

Often sarcastic

Prefers playful activity

Obsessed with freedom

Lackadaisical

Lighthearted and carefree

Irresponsible

Often inappropriate and
ill-mannered

Self-obsessed

Makes decisions
spontaneously

Chapter Twelve

THE WHITE AND YELLOW CONNECTIONS

White-White combinations are
very tolerant of each other
and the world around them.

WHITE-WHITE RELATIONSHIPS

"PEACE AND TOLERANCE"

White-White relationships are readily identifiable by their peace. White-White combinations are relaxed and patient. They do not expend excess energy on trivial power struggles or concern with details. This combination tolerates differences. They are both more comfortable ignoring irritating behavior than making it an issue. Therefore, what often creates serious conflict for other personality combinations hardly affects the White-White connection.

Whites are not usually drawn to leadership. White-White combinations struggle without clearly defined leadership roles. Both typically wait for the other to take the lead. Whites are comfortable living as relaxed and unstructured companions. Neither is driven to plan or create strong goals for the future. Neither is upset if one decides to plan something or commit the other to a future goal.

White-White combinations are very tolerant of each other and the world around them. They are very flexible and accommodating. They allow for each other's independent preferences (personal hobbies or work schedules) and dependence (they listen to each other's concerns for hours). This personality combination understands the importance of having a safe port in the storm of life and offers that gift to friends, family, or colleagues.

While White-White color combinations are not common in marital relationships, they make for very agreeable friendships. Marriage poses leadership-role concerns; friendship does not. As long as the relationship is well structured and firmly established, this combination has little difficulty operating successfully. The two elements this combination primarily struggles with are *motivation* and *leadership*. Charactered Whites work very hard to develop self-motivation techniques and assertion skills. With these acquired skills in place, White-White combinations are more likely to succeed.

PEACE

Whites get along with each other. They are motivated by peace. Each brings the necessary tolerance and patience to relationships in order to ensure peace. This is a clear example of reaping what you sow. World geography gives an interesting illustration of this strong motivation in all Whites. White nations such as Canada or Finland are peace loving and rarely, if ever, start wars. They are, however, known to maintain strong defenses when attacked by other, more aggressive, nations. White companionships are similar to White nations in their behavior. They strive for peaceful coexistence. They are, however, quick to defend themselves when outside forces interfere with their relationship.

PATIENT AND TOLERANT

This combination is very slow to anger or feel prejudice. They are quietly accepting. They do not demand that other colors be as patient or tolerant. They simply role model their value system consistently and unobtrusively. White-White connections remind us of the lives of Mahatma Gandhi or Martin Luther King. Both men quietly challenged an angry world of prejudice and injustice without need for great fanfare or publicity. White-White relationships are unobtrusive. They live simply and allow others to simply live.

> *White-White relationships*
> *are readily identifiable*
> *by their peace.*

SATISFIED

Imagine a relationship that does not foster unnecessary disagreement or dwell on conflicts. Imagine White with White. These friendships rarely complain of having difficulty getting along with one another. In fact, they rarely even notice problems until other colors point them out. This combination is the least willing to expend energy on negative conflict. They are the satisfied ones.

UNPRODUCTIVE COMPLACENCY

Being unaware of others' faults is a blessing. Being unaware of reality is irresponsible. Many White-White combinations allow themselves to become very complacent in their relationship and ignore the circumstances outside that relationship. They are like the high school students who drop out before graduation and are surprised to find themselves undesirable in the workplace. White-White combinations often remain oblivious to changing external circumstances and end up with the short end of the stick. When push comes to shove, this combination is often too passive and unproductive, which may leave them unaware and vulnerable to a more assertive and changing environment.

This combination is notorious for leaving things that should be done today until tomorrow. They procrastinate and, without someone who is more determined, they are likely to put off important tasks. They tolerate each other's relaxed ways. This could result in a dangerous unproductivity. Hawaii, as a state, experienced the trauma many White-White couples do. Hawaiians remained complacent in their garden paradise until they suddenly realized that outside investors were buying their land right out from under them, leaving them with nothing to pass on to their grandchildren. White-White connections can remain so unproductive that they become victims of other, more determined, color combinations. They must learn to balance their relaxed and complacent preferential lifestyle with assertive productivity in order to successfully endure the ever-changing demands of daily living.

SELF-DOUBTING AND INDECISIVE

This combination suffers most from self-doubt. They are often second-guessing themselves about past decisions and personal capabilities. They tend to foster mutual self-doubt because usually neither is convinced that he or she has made the best choices. Whites are more likely to ask questions about decisions than to take a direct position in support of or in opposition to whatever decision was made. Each waits for the other to react in order to determine whether he himself was right or wrong. Often, neither gives a strong reaction, so questions about decisions remain unanswered. Self-confidence comes from within oneself. Confidence comes from succeeding. Whites either take risks or accept themselves, so self-doubt and indecision often remain stumbling blocks in White-White relationships.

RELUCTANT, TIMID, UNINVOLVED

Whites can be boring or appear to be boring because of their reluctant, timid, and uninvolved natures. White-White combinations can comfortably do nothing for a long period of time, yet drive everyone else around them into a frenzy.

One White-White couple dated for years before getting married. Their courtship consisted primarily of television watching and sleeping. One would often call the other late at night on the telephone and talk until one or both would fall asleep. Not to worry! They were terribly patient with each other. They fell out of love shortly after marriage, although they lived together five more years before terminating the relationship. After all, *who* would file the divorce papers? Both were reluctant to make the first move. Neither was involved in other relationships, and so their marriage continued, from a legal standpoint at least, until friends finally pushed the woman to pull the plug. Forcing issues in life can be traumatic to a White-White relationship. Unfortunately, their timidity often promotes unhealthy compromise rather than forcing them both to take a more responsible problem-solving position.

White-White relationships seek a peaceful coexistence. They prefer to float above life's hassles rather than face them directly. They are patient and tolerant of each other and their world. They remain gentle and satisfied observers of life but vulnerable to outside influences. This combination timidly avoids risks and decision making. They prefer a quiet, secure, and unobtrusive existence to a flashy, dynamic, and demanding life. Reflective as the water they represent, they flow deeply and evenly through their shared life experience.

WHITE-YELLOW RELATIONSHIPS

"GENTLE FUN"

This relationship is about the "nice guys" or girls. They are affable individuals, seeking an easy (as opposed to difficult) style of interaction with limited expectations. Neither chooses to hassle the other. Neither is particularly keen about directing the other, either. They can be excellent as friends, colleagues, or parent-child, but rarely find themselves in a committed, intimate relationship. Almost as if there is no compelling magnetism, they instinctively recognize the limitations of their companionship in surviving the rigors of daily living.

I was engaged twice to a wonderful, gentle, delightful girl but could never sign on the dotted line. I realize now that while there was a strong physical chemistry and an emotional comfort, our relationship felt incomplete. I am Yellow and she is White. At the time, I needed someone stronger and bolder to commit to me. Having developed my character over the years, I am certain we could now successfully complete the puzzle, because I've added new pieces that were not there in my innate personality.

Whites and Yellows accommodate each other. They do not generally motivate each other. Perhaps they lack the ferocity or drive Reds and Blues innately have to light each other's fires. As children, similar values and preferences for playful activity invite a natural blend. As friends in adolescence and early adulthood, their gentle natures make for a positive connection. As charactered adults, they appreciate each other's accepting and easy style. Theirs is a casual blending of two comfortably independent people.

OVERVIEW

White Personality	Yellow Personality
MOTIVE	
Peace	Fun
NEEDS	
power and control of self	superficial connection
to be respected	to be praised
to feel good within self	social acceptance
acceptance	approval

White Personality	Yellow Personality
WANTS	
independence	playful adventure
protection	freedom
to please self and others	to please others and self
to withhold insecurities	to hide insecurities (loosely)
BEHAVIOR STYLE	
stability	change
low profile	high profile
refuses to be controlled	refuses to be controlled
boring	exciting
passive	active
reluctant	engaging
loner	involving
tenacious	easily distracted
plowhorse	racehorse
feels deeply, finds expression of feelings difficult	emotional and expressive
logical in direct communication (with feelings and facts)	emotional, direct communication (with feelings and facts)
doer	delegator/performer
likes backstage	likes front of stage
patient	good-natured
nondemanding	obnoxious
relaxed	carefree
nonpossessive (unless threatened)	nonpossessive
craves peace	avoids confrontation
strongly nonverbal	strongly verbal
quiet manipulation	seeks escape
loves slowly, with strong commitment	loves easily but without commitment
consistent producer	scattered productivity
compliant with rules	defiant to rules

232

White Personality	Yellow Personality
tactful	tactless (uses humor)
gives advice only when asked	gives advice but unconcerned with compliance
seeks advice freely	welcomes positive advice
aloof	inviting
tolerant of others	accepting of others
feels inadequate	high self-esteem
holds guilt inside	rarely gives or accepts guilt
lies to avoid conflicts and repercussions	lies to save face and to keep from disappointing others
releases but remembers	forgiving

WHITE-YELLOW INTERPERSONAL RELATIONSHIPS
(In-depth Presentation)

PEACE   versus   **FUN**

Whites can't understand why Yellows must go to all the trouble they do in developing relationships, meeting personal commitments (mostly playful activity), or why they overextend themselves in the community, at school, or at work. Whites are more inclined to go with the flow and become frustrated when their Yellow friends over-book and/or try to drag them into all their unnecessary commitments. "If I had known life with you would be this hectic," one White woman exclaimed to her busy Yellow roommate, "I would have taken fewer classes and hired on as your personal secretary. This is absolute madness, with the whole world constantly calling us and men always tramping through our house. Do you suppose we could start charging rent or at least retain an answering service?" Whites try very hard to uncomplicate their lives, while Yellows keep committing, connecting, and conversing in order to make their life fun.

Whites are more interested in getting along with others than in having the last laugh. Whites quietly accept many of Yellows' limitations, while Yellows tend to tease White and poke fun at their limitations.

| POWER AND CONTROL OF SELF | versus | INTIMACY |

Whites are concerned with developing a safe environment, while Yellows risk more freely for an intimate relationship. Yellows are more outgoing, and their White companions remain more reserved. Whites are like cats, able to come and go comfortably on their own. Yellows are like dogs, always seeking to be noticed, petted, and played with.

| TO BE RESPECTED | versus | TO BE PRAISED |

Whites need to have their wishes respected. They resent being pushed into decisions they find uncomfortable. Whites appear (behaviorally) to need constant praise and attention. In reality, they want you to respect their pace in life and their preferences. Because Whites are not a verbal group, they resent always having to speak up in order to secure their right to be left alone, be with certain friends, or whatever else they want. Yellows could generally care less about respect. They want to be noticed and praised. They become frustrated with their White friends who don't talk but expect Yellows to know their desires and respect them. Perhaps one of the most difficult interactions for the White-Yellow combination is their differing needs for respect and praise. Whites are not known for their skill at or interest in praising others. Yellows are often disrespectful of others and typically overstep their acceptable boundaries with Whites.

| PROTECTION | versus | FREEDOM |

Yellows tend to be more confident than Whites. Yellows risk more freely, and therefore seem more comfortable with the unknown, while Whites prefer safer surroundings. Yellows often challenge their White friends to reach out and try wild and crazy experiences. Whites are more concerned with what will happen after the wild and crazy experiences. Yellows are more inclined to leave Whites hanging emotionally while they recklessly bound through life. Whites want to know they are secure and safe in the relationship.

STABILITY   versus   CHANGE

Whites and Yellows do not often see life through the same window. Whites want to see the same scene, and Yellows keep changing the picture. Whites appreciate the many opportunities Yellows bring to them but don't find it necessary to experience them all so rapidly or inconveniently. Yellows thrive on the fast pace and seldom feel inconvenienced as long as they're having a good time.

BORING   versus   EXCITING

If either has the inclination to fall in a rut, it's the Whites. Whites are often plagued by the *sameness syndrome*—same car, same books, same friends, same house. Yellows struggle with the exact opposite tendency—the *differentness syndrome*. Everything in their life is in a constant state of flux. They are always trying new foods, traveling to new places, meeting new friends, and buying new cars. Each can be quite beneficial to the other when they allow their differences to provide a positive balance. On the negative side, both can feel constantly harassed by the other's lifestyle.

RELUCTANT   versus   ENGAGING

Whites often need coaxing from their Yellow friends to try new experiences. Yellows willingly involve Whites in their activities. Yellows are so engaging and undemanding that Whites find them difficult to resist. If anything, Yellows get tired of having to convince Whites to stretch and risk a little more.

TENACIOUS   versus   EASILY DISTRACTED

Whites are like plowhorses. They are consistent and tenacious in their efforts to complete a task. They allow very little to distract them once they are committed to a cause. Yellows are less likely to commit over any length of time to relationships or activities. They float like butterflies, staying briefly in one place before they dart off to a more appealing location. Whites can become frustrated with the flighty, unreliable nature of Yellows but generally tend to remain tolerant despite the irritation.

FEELS DEEPLY, FINDS   versus   EMOTIONAL AND
EXPRESSION OF   EXPRESSIVE
FEELINGS DIFFICULT

Yellow teenage girl: (frustrated and pleading) But why won't you
    come and have dinner with my parents? They want so much to
    meet you!
White teenage boy: (frustrated and quiet) I really don't feel comfort-
    able meeting them yet. Maybe next month.

This White young man confided in me that he was afraid that his girlfriend's parents would ask him about his grades. He felt frustrated because they would be disappointed in him and in the future resist their daughter's decision to date him. Rather than being honest with her or them, he chose to avoid any communication and to stay away.

Whites often think deeply but choose not to say much because they feel awkward in their verbal skills. Instead, they ponder their feelings and share very little. Yellows get upset and emotional and say what they feel regardless of how eloquent it may or may not be. Yellows need both to express themselves and to hear what their White friends feel.

Yellows must learn to be patient with Whites. Whites appreciate Yellows just spending time with them, without expecting the Whites to speak. Whites require time. When they feel accepted, they are more likely to express themselves.

DOER   versus   DELEGATOR/PERFORMER

Whites are Indians rather than chiefs. They are not interested in great fanfare and complication. They generally feel more comfortable doing the work than delegating it to others. Whites are not strong verbal communicators, which typically limits their managerial skills. However, when Whites feel comfortable with these skills, they make excellent delegators because of their patience, tact, and tolerance for other employees.

Yellows like center stage. They enjoy opportunities to perform (no routine housework, please) and willingly delegate mundane work and details to others. Yellows are charismatic leaders with poor follow-through. They are aerodynamic motivators and often find themselves in the spotlight regardless of their actual job title. Whites and Yellows usually work well together because their role preferences lie in different directions.

PATIENT	versus	GOOD-NATURED

Two best friends spent a lot of their time together throughout their college careers. They were roommates and would often get together on campus to eat, see a movie, or study at the library. The White roommate would typically arrive up to one hour later than they had agreed upon. His Yellow friend would usually find a quiet place and study or share some good laughs with someone while he waited. They never became angry with one another. They simply ate later or took in a later movie. If Yellow became bored, he would go ahead alone, and neither was upset or concerned.

Yellows and Whites enjoy a rare capacity for tolerance and acceptance that no other mixed color combination shares. Both are slow to anger and quick to move on when slighted.

NONPOSSESSIVE	versus	NONPOSSESSIVE
(unless threatened)		

Neither personality is usually driven by a need to possess people or material things. Yellows live for the moment, rarely save money, and just need enough to survive. Yellows can always make new friends and, therefore, rarely feel threatened by losing people in their life. They can't really imagine losing friends, spouses, or children because so many people are so easily drawn to them throughout life.

Whites are gentle in their approach to other people. They are sometimes overwhelmed if they feel rejected and don't know how to respond. Whites typically have little concern for monetary advantages. They are easily satisfied and usually unwilling to expend the energy necessary to beat the competition and climb the ladder of corporate success.

White-Yellow combinations are very relaxed with each other. Neither places much demand on the other. Both are willing to live with less because their relationship is often comfortable without the pressure of always having to *be* or *have* more.

COMPLIANT WITH RULES	versus	DEFIANT TO RULES

Whites tend to obey laws, rules, regulations, and authority figures. Yellows often disobey laws, rules, regulations, and authority figures. This disparity can create tension between White and Yellows. However, Whites are so tolerant and tactful that they can often convince Yellows to rethink their unacceptable behavior. Yellows are sensitive to social approval. Despite their zest for doing wild and crazy things, they are open to positive social influences from those they value and respect.

| FORGIVING BUT REMEMBERS | versus | FORGIVING |

Both personalities are very forgiving. They tend to accept that everyone makes mistakes. Neither wastes much energy on holding grudges. Whites, however, are more likely to remember when they were crossed and steer clear of any similar situation that appears to be potentially dangerous. Whites are also known to feel transgressions against them deeply, but generally they find their desire for peace so dominant that it overrides any need for retribution.

Yellows forgive quickly. One Yellow woman confided a very personal problem to a White friend. The friend told others. The Yellow was terribly hurt but acknowledged not more than a day later that she would most likely confide in the same friend again.

Whites and Yellows rarely burden their relationship with emotional baggage. They focus on the positive aspects of the other's personality and appreciate his or her unique contribution.

| OVERWHELMED | versus | POSITIVE |

When crises arise Whites often feel overwhelmed. Yellows typically see the silver lining in the dark clouds. Whites tend to see only a few options when seeking solutions. Yellows often find unlimited possibilities. Whites *seek* magical rescuers (the white-knight syndrome), while Yellows *feel* magical in problem resolution. Usually, Whites are pessimists, and Yellows assume the role of the optimist.

| DEDICATED ONLY WHEN INTERESTED | versus | LACKS DISCIPLINE |

Whites are particular about their commitments. They can be lazy and do not necessarily feel any compulsion to be productive. With this relaxed attitude, Whites find it difficult to commit themselves to people or to activities that have little or no interest for them. Whites are often difficult to motivate and keep motivated. Yellow parents and spouses are often frustrated trying to get White children and companions to take responsibility for themselves or stay interested. However, once a White connects with some activity or work assignment, he or she is generally dedicated and loyal.

Throughout their lives, Yellows have trouble with discipline. Consistency is a foreign concept to Yellows. They tend to stay with something as long as it is fun. Most achievements in life require a commitment of consistent effort and pain. Fun is not generally a major ingredient in the initial stages of achievement. This explains why many Yellows settle for the simple life. They prefer to play and often lack the desire and commitment of stretching.

EXCELLENT LISTENER   versus   POOR LISTENER

Yellows are restless, and Whites are calm. Listening requires patience and a willingness to put others before oneself. Yellows tend to do neither well. Whites are comfortable sitting with another person for hours while they discuss details of how they feel. Yellows constantly interrupt. Yellows hurry the conversation along, often finishing the speaker's sentence. Whites enjoy a slower pace and encourage the speaker to move at his pace, accepting long pauses without questioning or rushing the thoughts. Whites find Yellows quite abrasive in this behavior and tend to stay quiet until (or unless) the Yellow learns to appreciate and practice the art of listening.

BLAMES SELF   versus   BLAMES OTHERS

When something negative happens, Whites usually blame themselves, and Yellows blame others. The following example reflects their styles.

White: How could I have been so stupid? I would have handled it
    differently.
Yellow: Why didn't you take care of the problem? You should have
    handled it differently!

Neither response is positive. Whites often struggle with low self-esteem because they assume responsibility for creating (or at least contributing to) most problems. Yellows are naively overconfident and tend to be limited in their emotional growth because they assume no responsibility for creating or contributing to most problems.

TOO SENSITIVE   versus   INSENSITIVE

Whites tend to feel bad easily. They are especially vulnerable to Yellows' flippant criticisms and overall naive insensitivity. Yellows do not think of others' feelings when they make rude or playful comments. Whites are not inclined to respond. They are more likely to hold the pain inside and quietly shy away from further social interaction. Often Whites silently blame themselves and simultaneously feel hurt that others don't understand their pain. Yellows typically misread Whites' behavior as, "They're okay. They're always quiet like that." Yellows do not pay much attention to others' needs or behaviors as long as Yellows are having a good time. They are often totally surprised to find out later that they have offended Whites.

MAKING THE MOST OF COMFORTABLE OPPOSITES

Whites Need Yellows:	Yellows Need Whites:
To excite them	To calm them
To encourage them	To listen to them
To accept their low profile	To praise them
To be kind to them	To play with them
To be intimate with them	To be tolerant of them
To keep confidences	To share confidences with
To promote activities	
To share a peaceful relationship	To share a peaceful relationship
To be sensitive to their self-doubts	To accept them

POTENTIAL CONFLICTS OF COMFORTABLE OPPOSITES

Whites	Yellows
Nonverbal	Crave praise
Directionless	Directionless
Passive	Passionate
Enjoy private time	Like social scene
Lackadaisical	Lackadaisical
Quiet	Loud
Softspoken	Obnoxious
Boring	Exciting

Yellow-Yellow relationships
are as striking as neon lights
on a street corner at night.

YELLOW-YELLOW RELATIONSHIPS

"SPARKLE AND SHINE"

Yellow-Yellow relationships are as striking as neon lights on a street corner at night. They sparkle and shine for everyone to see. People rarely mistake this combination for anything else. Like two playful pups, they chase each other through life, oblivious of the rest of the world around them. They are playful and fun. This combination definitely knows how to have a good time.

Yellows enjoy their mutual friendships. They are not typically drawn to each other in committed marital relationships. Friendships are generally convenient, while marriage is not. As long as two Yellows can get themselves to the same place at the same time, they will always enjoy a good time together. Marriage requires much more than merely agreeing on a place and a time. Someone has to tell the playful pups when the work needs to get done. When there is no one but the playful pups, they rarely have a healthy balance between work and play.

Yellows live on raw energy. They can go for hours without revitalizing themselves. They travel well together. They party well together. They laugh well together. What they don't do well together is work—homework, housework, or detailed deadline work. They are easily distracted from labor and easily find numerous reasons why it is an excellent time to take a break from the rigors of work. They focus their energy on playful productivity such as recreation, conversation, and creative exploration. They prefer to use their energy in twos or more and rarely opt to be alone.

Yellow-Yellow combinations draw people to them like magnets. They are leaders and yet tend to be overwhelmed once they attract the interest of others. They lead most comfortably in play activity. Therefore, their greatest influence on others is most often expressed in the playful world of fun.

FUN

Yellow-Yellow combinations generally agree that the more, the merrier. They want to share their fun with everyone as long as others don't demand too much of their time. They also struggle with people they think are too conventional in their thinking. Yellow-Yellows rarely place limits on the fun zone in their relationship. As long as everyone is having a good time, everything else can wait. This relationship shares the fantasy that all roads eventually lead to Disneyland, a ski resort, or the beach.

NEEDS ATTENTION

Each requires a lot of the other's attention. Actually, this works out because Yellows seek instant and simple praise rather than deep appreciation. They are naturally optimistic and praise each other easily. They can accommodate each other's needs by pausing briefly in their self-centered monologues to notice the other. Neither is generally offended or concerned by this limited attention. A good time and praise is usually enough to keep Yellow-Yellows from feeling neglected in the relationship.

FREEDOM

This combination regards freedom as a sacred principle in their relationship. Neither tries to attach strings or commitment (a less than sacred word). Yellow friends accept whatever time they have to share together and share it to the fullest. Neither wants or intends to commit to much beyond the present. Yellows can drop out of each other's lives for years and easily pick up where they left off when they get together again. They don't feel neglected or particularly frustrated by losing touch over the years. Both value the freedom to move in and out of the relationship and don't attach strings to their relationships. They are more likely to simply accept each other at face value.

HIGHLY VERBAL

Talk, talk, talk! Yellows can talk about anything or nothing equally well. They appreciate superficial as well as serious discussions. Put them at a party, a funeral, or in their kitchen and they will find things to converse about. Neither is strong on listening skills, which doesn't seem to deter their interest in conversation. However, it does preclude much depth or meaningful direction in ongoing relationships, because their poor listening skills often make them miss many important insights. Constant dialogue is not lacking in their relationship, and both willingly share responsibility for promoting and sustaining positive chatter.

UNCOMMITTED

This color combination promotes play and fears commitment. They have the perception that freedom and playful activity are necessarily incompatible with commitment. In light of this dilemma, Yellow relationships typically choose their freedom and neglect commitments. This attitude makes interaction of an intimate or responsible nature unlikely. They typically wear out, which is disappointing in relationships requiring a long, enduring commitment.

IRRESPONSIBLE

Yellows expect others to handle the details and loose ends. When the other person is another Yellow, the details are often neglected and loose ends never tied together. Neither takes his or her role very seriously, so their relationship is often burdened with last-minute mixups and other problems that reduce the quality of their shared life experience.

This is well illustrated by two Yellow friends who were baby-sitting together one evening. The girl fell asleep at 5:00 P.M. and woke up at 7:00 P.M. Meanwhile, her friend had made popcorn. He and the kids were enjoying popcorn and a movie when she awoke. She assumed they had already eaten dinner because they were eating popcorn. He assumed popcorn was enough. Needless to say, neither was asked to baby-sit again. Ignoring details is not always serious, but repeated negligence can be dangerous, if not life threatening.

OPTIMISTIC

This color combination believes most anything can be accomplished with time or help or something—perhaps just hope. They are eternal dreamers and optimists. They always seek the silver lining in the cloud or find some value in the pit in a cherry. Pollyanna times two is tough for anyone. Yellows don't get depressed easily, and if they do, they don't stay depressed for long. In a Yellow-Yellow relationship, each supports the other with hope and positive reinforcement.

CURIOUS AND INQUISITIVE

Yellows ask the darnedest questions at the darnedest times. They simply want to know things and usually forget important social protocol when asking. The answers are not as important as the process of discovering the answers. Yellows find it great fun to look for clues to explain human behavior. They enjoy each other's free-spirited (often bordering on the obnoxious) pursuit of insight and understanding.

ENTERTAINING

Yellows love to entertain and be entertained by each other. They are performers. They entice each other with spontaneous surprises (show tickets, weekend retreats, cards, or flowers). They enjoy carefree experiences and light moments of laughter and intimacy. This combination is far more inclined to spend money and time on action-filled opportunities (trips and recreations) than material possessions (expensive gifts and household fixtures). They live for the present, and both appreciate experiences that offer immediate pleasures.

Yellow-Yellow combinations adore each other. They value their relationship and find each other spontaneous and refreshing. They enjoy their freedom, and struggle with necessary commitments and responsible behavior. As they are living for today, they have little interest in yesterday's regrets or tomorrow's concerns. Yellows gravitate toward each other and often remain playful companions for life. They casually enter and exit each other's lives with little concern for the long term.

This combination loves life best when it is shared with others. They appreciate each other's positive and hopeful natures. They are fun and superficially attentive to one another. Intimacy remains an important, yet fleeting, concern in a Yellow-Yellow relationship. They value their connection to other people and particularly enjoy sharing special moments with other Yellows.

Energetic and highly verbal, Yellows ignite each other with constant chatter and inquisitive interaction. These shared behavior styles make this combination enjoyable to observe. In the long run, Yellow-Yellow connections are enviable playmates but unlikely marital companions. Whatever relationship they experience together will never be dull or lack excitement. They are a fun, dynamic duo who vigorously pursue the good life with refreshing curiosity and optimism.

Chapter Thirteen

THE RAINBOW CONNECTION: BUILDING SUCCESSFUL RELATIONSHIPS

Each of us is 100 percent responsible
for the quality of relationships we create.

There you have it. It doesn't matter whether we are discussing personal or business relationships. If you are engaging a certain personality, you now have a clear picture of what natural strengths and limitations you will create and face in your relationships.

I have always told businesspeople who are recruiting new staff to apply the Color Code so they will know generally what they can expect from the relationship. And anyone getting married or rearing children without identifying their core color must prefer high-stakes gambling to a sure bet. Knowing who you are and the personality you are engaging with offers you tremendous advantages in making your best possible connection.

You always deserve what you get when you marry or when you work for the same company over one year. Great managers and positive business relationships are not created by sheer luck. They require hard work and equal partnership in providing essential personality gifts for success. They seek (albeit often subconsciously) someone to balance them and fulfill their needs. Bad managers and poor business relationships aren't just bad luck, either. Someone looked the other way rather than focusing on the negative truth about why they engaged each other. We must take 100 percent responsibility for our relationship choices, or we can never feel empowered to experience the tremendous magic that healthy relationships can bring in completing our lives.

We understand the Reds enjoy power. We accept the sincerity of the Blues, the gentle touch of the Whites, and the charisma of the Yellows. Furthermore, we have discussed how daring Reds interact with reluctant Whites. We see now how committed Blues and carefree Yellows work together.

We established that each color represents natural strengths and limitations. We reviewed the desirable and undesirable traits that come when a person of one color interacts with someone of another. Each combination offers a unique blend. For example, two Red individuals interact with one another differently than a Blue and Red couple does. A business composed mostly of Yellows and White will operate differently from a business composed of Yellows and Blues.

Let's investigate the fascinating world of relationships a little further. There are some general themes that may prove helpful in understanding specific dynamics of the rainbow connections. These insights will save individuals countless hours of emotional grief or financial waste in needless hiring and firing of employees if they understand how the concepts play out in relationships.

HEAVYWEIGHT VERSUS LIGHTWEIGHT PERSONALITIES

There are general similarities and differences that we should delineate before focusing on specific combinations. For example, Reds and Blues are the heavyweight personalities, while Whites and Yellows reflect the lightweights. They represent the hunters and the hunted in nature. The lion pursues the antelope. The wolf pursues the lamb. There is an offense and defense in sports. The tackle pursues the quarterback in football. In tennis, the person at the net attacks the person at the baseline. In business, the sales representative pursues the customer.

In life, the Reds and Blues assume the roles of lion and wolf. They are the football tackles and tennis players who charge the net. They are the sales representatives. The Whites and Yellows are the antelope and lamb. They are the football quarterbacks and tennis baseliners. They represent the customers and the consumers. Each role is invaluable.

We could not be as successful without both types. Each requires the other. Both have strengths and limitations that enable them to survive as well as contribute. *Opposites do, in fact, attract each other.* Each enhances the other's life. Each would be lost without the other. They give credibility to each other. Each serves as a role model for the others for specific areas of character building. Each color gives balance in the full spectrum of relationships.

INTIMACY

Blues and Yellows are intimacy-oriented. Blues and Yellows are motivated by intimacy and prefer an emotional connection in securing a strong bonding with others in life. Celebrating romantic occasions, holding hands for no apparent reason, and remembering early days of intimacy between a couple are most common for Blues and Yellows. Both colors want to be told often of their romantic allure. In business, they appreciate being noticed, and often decide whether to stay in a particular job based on the shared intimacy at work.

Blues and Yellows understand their needs for intimacy at a much more subconscious level than they realize. For example, one major reason Yellows are so demonstrative is their inner desire to be touched. Many Yellows never understand why they are so physical, but, in truth, they may be simply reaching out for what they need.

POWER

Reds and Whites are power-based. Reds and Whites expend a lot of energy preserving the balance of power in the relationship and other practical issues. One White woman demanded that her Red husband repay her the money he had borrowed immediately. I suggested that her timing was not the best for the relationship. She said, rather blandly, that it needed to be done since it was already overdue, and, besides, she was trying to learn how to be assertive. Actually, she was striving to balance the power.

Reds and Whites want the conveniences of companionship without all the complex emotional strings attached. Subconsciously, they understand each other's style and often position themselves to maintain control of their relationships. Reds are far more direct in their pursuit of power than Whites. Whites often use a passive-aggressive approach. (Passive-aggressive behavior refers to accepting certain slights without negative reaction and then later aggressively getting even using a totally different set of circumstances.)

An example of passive-aggressive behavior is the mother who tells her son he can go outside and play football, *but* he can't get his clothes dirty. When the son comes home filthy, she gladly tosses the clothes in the washer but neglects to fix his dinner until much later than usual that evening. She is terribly upset by his behavior, but rather than confront him at the time, she gets even later in an unrelated incident.

COMMUNICATION STYLE

Methods of communication differentiate styles. Reds and Yellows are more inclined to tell people things to do, while Blues and Whites are more likely to ask people for their opinions. Whites and Blues are comfortable seeking advice, while Reds and Yellows prefer to give the solutions. Reds and Yellows tend to blame others. Blues and Whites blame themselves. Reds respond best to direct, logical communication. (Whatever you do, don't cry!) Blues prefer a softer, emotional style of feedback. They tend to be hardest on themselves with their perfectionistic tendency. Negative feedback offered empathetically is most effective for Blues. Whites cannot be yelled at. They prefer a gentle honesty with low conflict profile. Yellows enjoy a casual (even humorous) style when receiving feedback. They appreciate warmth and reassurance.

SELF-ESTEEM

All colors seek self-satisfaction and self-esteem with a unique flair. Self-esteem has become a particularly interesting component of personality in this century. Parents want to know how self-esteem and productivity are connected. Teachers want to understand how learning and self-esteem interact. One of the most significant findings in the color theory is the difference in how each personality reflects self-esteem.

Reds and Yellows appear to be born with higher self-esteem than Blues and Whites. Blue and White children tend to have self-defeating attitudes. They criticize themselves and feel inadequate. Most Red and Yellow children tend to project themselves, criticize others, and openly display more positive self-regard. All personalities, however, come with some positive self-regard and some negative feelings of insecurity.

Reds appear to the the most self-assured of all the colors, and yet they tend to be the most insecure. Perhaps they are not originally less secure, but since they work so hard to disguise their insecurity, they often delay character development, which can come only by exposing oneself emotionally (being vulnerable) and taking responsibility for one's insecurities. Unfortunately, Reds hide their insecurities so well that few people recognize that they need to grow up emotionally. They are often allowed to slide emotionally because they are so stubborn. Most people are unwilling to invest the energy necessary to deal with them. Reds willingly dive from the highest diving board and scale the most difficult mountain in order to maintain their competent and secure image.

Yellows often manage to maintain a superficial social snobbery, thus protecting themselves from real, intimate exposure of their insecurity. Whites and Blues are far less likely to make the effort to hide their insecurities.

Consequently, when we look at self-esteem, we consistently come up with the supposition that Reds and Yellows appear stronger than the Blues and Whites. Perhaps the Reds and Yellows maintain strong self-images because society (especially parents and teachers) perceives the initial behavior of Reds and Yellows as strong and treats them accordingly. As a result, Reds and Yellows theoretically develop even greater self-regard. The Blues and Whites openly reveal their insecurities, and society often responds with a protective, coddling, or condescending manner. This encourages a potential lifetime pattern of self-degradation and/or martyrdom.

Unfortunately, Reds and Yellows often fall prey to a "self-satisfaction syndrome." Perhaps they feel so good about themselves that they simply slide through life rather than working to earn a deeper self-respect. This self-respect only comes from confronting personal inadequacies and choosing to contribute to others. On the other hand, Blues and Whites may develop deeper self-esteem later in life because they recognize and acknowledge their deficiencies and put forth the effort necessary to feel better about themselves. Unfortunately, some may feel overwhelmed by their feelings of inadequacy and live their entire lives with fear and guilt complexes.

All personalities find true self-esteem only after honest self-analysis followed by a loving commitment to promoting the well-being of themselves and others. Self-esteem is gained slowly and often painfully by risking exposure to others. Many individuals are willing to have shallow relationships in order to avoid disclosing negative personality traits and/or character flaws. Charactered people value self-esteem enough to continue to risk it throughout various phases of life.

INVOLVEMENT VERSUS ISOLATION

Reds and Yellows are alert and focus directly on practicalities and tasks. (Remember, for Yellows *task* often means *play*.) Blues and Whites tend to think in terms of the past and the future, while Reds and Yellows concern themselves predominantly with the present. Blues and Whites are the daydreamers and are often preoccupied.

We need to allow Reds and Yellows their task-orientation. Blues and Whites deserve time for creativity or quiet reflection. We enhance relationships when we encourage opportunities for individuals within the relationship to pursue their style of life. It might be more destructive than productive to demand that a Yellow reflect quietly for too long if the individual isn't prepared for such an experience.

Educators (typically Blue) can hinder Red students if they refuse to afford them task leadership opportunities. Most Blues will feel frustrated if they are not allowed their time to meditate and plan prior to taking action or making a decision. Whites typically become silently stubborn when they are ordered to move faster or to act too aggressively on a project. Each color responds most effectively when allowed, within reason, to use his or her preferred style.

THERAPEUTIC INTERVENTION STYLE

Every psychotherapist has the opportunity to serve in the role of a "change agent." In order to be effective, the approach should match the specific needs of the patients. There is a high correlation between the patient's personality and the style of intervention. Reds and Blues are far more resistant to change, while Yellows and Whites are initially more receptive to the change process. Resistance is less direct and abrasive for Blues than Reds. The intensity of the resistance is, however, fairly equal. On the other hand, Yellows are more likely to say they are receptive to change than the Whites are. However, both generally appear receptive and willing to adapt their lifestyles.

Just the reverse is true of these personalities when it comes to follow-through and completion of the change process. Reds and Blues are far more likely to successfully commit themselves to the changing process once their resistance is removed. Yellows and Whites are more inclined to slip back into old behavior patterns or feel unmotivated to complete the change process.

Therapeutically, Blues and Reds demand answers. They want specific methods, solutions, and direction once they decide to change. They request behavioral therapy that focuses on specific homework assignments and expectations. The most frustrating aspect of therapy for them is coming to the realization that the therapist will not and cannot necessarily design a specific behavioral process with long-term success for them. What they actually need most is an attitudinal adjustment.

Attitudinal therapy forces them to examine their motives and clear up unhealthy perceptions. Reds suffer most often from inaccurate emotional messages such as hidden insecurities, blocking communication, or layers and years of denied anger. Blues suffer most often from irrational thinking. They have usually relied so heavily on their "emotional muscles" that their ability to think rationally is seriously impaired. This process of attitudinal readjustment takes much longer and requires more patience than the behavioral process. Consequently, Reds and Blues often become frustrated with psychotherapy.

Conversely, the therapeutic approach for the Whites and Yellows is more direct and behavioral. It is the kind of therapy Reds and Blues would really prefer. Generally, Yellows and White have positive and receptive attitudes, but their discipline and motivation often leave a lot to be desired. They require constant support with new techniques for effectively tackling life. It is particularly challenging to work with a couple requiring different approaches (e.g., a Yellow-Red couple). The Red often complains that the therapist attacks him or her too much in the session. The Yellow complains that he or she has more homework than the Red after the session is over.

Yellows and Whites need to see themselves completing goals and disciplining themselves consistently over a long period of time in order to increase their self-esteem and to develop healthy lifestyles. Giving a Red or Blue more hobbies or tasks will do little to increase self-esteem. They are already driven to achieve and produce, and probably don't feel that what they do is good enough. They need to increase their awareness of self-flagellating (Blue), or arrogant (Red) feelings and thoughts in order to be more accepting of themselves and others.

To sum up, Reds and Blues want immediate action and behavior modification. They most often get a time-consuming attitudinal adjustment and must struggle with it. Yellows and Whites want a relaxed, attitudinal approach. They get a direct process, requiring commitment and behavior modification, and they find it taxing to endure. Once they accept a "no pain, no gain" philosophy, they can modify their behavior.

Blues and Whites are less verbal, while Reds and Yellows generally share strong verbal skills. (The strong, silent type is a White.) Reds and Yellows also tend to think very quickly on their feet, while Blues and Whites spend a lot of time kicking themselves for not having had the best retort at the time of the conversation. Their creative wit often lets them come up with great lines. Unfortunately, the thought is two days too late.

It has been suggested that *an unexamined life is hardly worth living*. Knowing ourselves makes our journey through life much more meaningful for ourselves and others. It also enhances our opportunities to change those limitations that inhibit our ability to contribute. It enhances our opportunities to develop the strengths that define our uniqueness in how and what we contribute. With luck, you will be receptive to learning about yourself and understanding those around you as we look at specific color combinations.

IT IS IMPORTANT TO UNDERSTAND THE CHARACTERISTICS OF *ALL* THE PERSONALITIES IN ORDER TO APPRECIATE HOW WE AND OTHERS SEE THE WORLD. Nothing in nature operates well in a vacuum. Each personality relies on the others to fully experience its true color. Learn about the personalities without judgment. Seek to appreciate the unique strengths and limitations in others. Strengthen your inherent limitations in order to get along better with others. Limitations can become strengths. Strive to recognize the natural bonding or resistance that various personalities experience. In accordance with the prayer of St. Francis of Assisi, "Grant that (we) may not so much seek to be understood as to understand."

The following diagram illustrates the similarities and differences among the personalities in the total color spectrum.

PERSONALITY CONNECTIONS

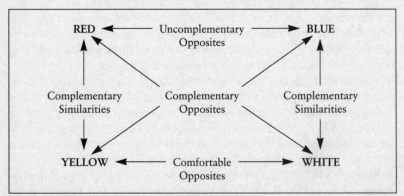

252

Let me explain this diagram. By definition, *complementary* suggests "an adding to the effect of" or "supplying what is lacking." By the literal definition, then, each color complements every other color with its innate strengths. However, this diagram presents a looser definition in order to help us understand the realities of color combinations, rather than simple theory.

Some colors are more alike than others. Reds and Yellows share strong verbal skills, insensitivity, and positive-action orientation. Blues and Whites are similar in their nonverbal preference, sensitivity, and desire to accommodate others. When an individual's personality is a combination of Red-Yellow or Blue-White, they find the blend very comfortable.

Some colors are opposites but appeal to each other for a sense of completion and to make them feel whole. Reds and Whites enjoy a practical orientation to relationships and rely on facts and common sense to light their way. They share similar perceptions of power, excitement, and leadership. Blues and Yellows mutually seek intimacy, romance, and fantasy. Both sets of colors offer a natural balance within themselves. Consequently, Reds-Whites and Blues-Yellows are most inclined to find themselves in committed relationships with each other. However, when *one* individual has either of these blends within himself/herself, he/she finds a perpetual split in focus and must commit to the dominant motive in order to find harmony within his/her attitudes and behavior.

Some colors do not find their blending naturally complementary and/or innately comfortable. Red-Blue and White-Yellow combinations find themselves in this category. Reds and Blues generally experience the greatest conflict because (1) they are such strong personalities, and (2) their innate impulses, one to power, one to intimacy, provide an awkward blend. People with a Red-Blue personality experience the same awkwardness within themselves as two individuals with Red and Blue personalities feel in their relationship. They must work harder on their character in order to facilitate the potential strength of this uncomplementary connection.

White-Yellow combinations do not offer each other completion. They are both easygoing and unlikely to commit to business or to marriage because without a lot of character development, both lack the necessary strength to be successful in a shared, committed relationship. As uncomfortable as Red-Blue combinations are, they are far more likely to connect than Whites and Yellows. However, an individual with the White-Yellow blend enjoys strong people skills and rarely feels much inner conflict because each personality is innately gentle.

The film classic *Gone With the Wind,* derived from the equally enduring Pulitzer Prize–winning novel, offers us a vivid presentation of the colors in relationships. The leading characters represent the different personalities and provide us with a visual portrayal of how the colors interact.

Scarlett O'Hara was a Red. Influenced by power and a strong will to be right, she brilliantly orchestrated her survival during the Civil War. Her great love was Rhett Butler, whose charismatic and flamboyant lifestyle illustrated the Yellow personality. His attraction to Scarlett was eventually doomed because she would never give the emotional connection he craved.

Ashley embodied the loyalty and high moral standard of the Blue. He consistently rebuffed Scarlett's romantic overtures, despite his attraction to her, because he sensed her emotional insecurities and that she would be inadequate to his needs for genuine intimacy.

Melanie, on the other hand, offered peace and support to all three characters. She represented the White. She never suspected Ashley or Scarlett of anything less than moral and proper behavior. She defended Scarlett against her enemies. She warmly received Rhett into the family. She loved Ashley to her dying breath. Interestingly, Rhett and Ashley (Yellow and Blue) were quite compatible despite their different backgrounds.

Each character embodies the essence of personalities within relationships. Their colors defined their preferences, limitations, and motivations. Their relationships were decided before they ever met.

Now let's look at specific relationships. The following comparisons offer a quick guide to how the different personalities interact in their most raw and natural forms. If you have a developed character, you may find that some of the statements no longer completely reflect your current style. Simply make a note of how your character development has replaced innate personality limitations and added new dimension to your life. With rare exception, the *motives,* the *needs,* and the *wants* remain in place. What you are trying to do here is to identify how you (and those you care about) are *motivated* and what style you should choose to use while interacting with others.

This is your opportunity to see yourself and the way your relationships connect. Review the motives, needs, wants, and behaviors and determine your own compatibility.

RAINBOW

Look for the various combinations you encounter in your life. Ask yourself why you seek the combinations you do. Consider how the color combinations of your parents and yourself affected your life. Reflect on the relationship between your employers (or employees) and yourself. Seek to understand how your personality influences and is influenced by others. How do the different combinations affect you? Which combination do you find most intimidating and why? Which combination feels most comfortable to you? Why do you respond to certain colors more than others? Why is a clean home so important to one individual and relatively meaningless to another? Does your yeller and screamer really mean the awful things she or he says? How do we accept or redirect laziness in others? Why do I link up with people who spend money lavishly, while I save everything I earn?

Consider the wonderful possibilities you can use these insights for in your life. Whether you are selecting a candidate for a job or trying to make sense out of a parent-child relationship, the rainbow connection is invaluable. Determining the depth of one's character is important to understanding people as unique individuals. However, we can rest assured that everyone operates best within his or her own personality. Therefore, despite the obvious limitations each color has, we can generally trust that we will behave, at least to some degree, in a manner consistent with our defined personality color group.

Each personality combination brings with it a unique set of strengths and limitations. Developed character and an understanding of innate personalities allow us to deal with the specific needs of each possible combination, whether it be in the role of friend, lover, parent, employer, or child. Learning to facilitate relationships without jeopardizing our integrity is essential to our success in life.

Part Four

❈❈❈

BUILDING
CHARACTER

Chapter Fourteen

CHARACTER:
HOW TO BECOME
YOUR BEST COLOR

If you want to be all you can be, like a finely tuned athlete,
you must choose to commit to the whole process,
not just the convenient parts you like.
Becoming your best self means becoming charactered.

Picture this. You have arrived at the airport and identified the correct gate where you will board your flight. (We have correctly identified your innate personality.) You have surveyed the other passengers and flight crew. (We have clarified the roles that various color combinations offer in relationships.) Now it is time to take off and fly. This is where becoming your own best color begins. It's like taking off and completing your flight. Why else would you come to the airport if not to complete the journey to your final destination?

However, as odd as that seems in the airport metaphor, it is not uncommon for people to show up for life and never complete the experience they came here to have. Some never gain an accurate self-awareness. Others figure themselves out but never apply their awareness to their business or personal relationships. Still the majority of people fail most often to complete the process of becoming fully human—fully alive. They never become their best selves.

The Color Code offers you a very clear structure for identifying yourself correctly, building successful relationships, and becoming a legitimate, fully actualized person. All you have to do to begin the final process is accept 100 percent responsibility for yourself. This section is not about anyone else but you. If you want to become all you can be, like a finely tuned athlete, you must choose to commit to the whole process, not just the convenient parts you like. Becoming your best self means becoming charactered. It means developing muscles (strengths) you never realized you had before and accepting pain (stretching, risking, getting out of your current comfort zone) as inevitable.

People behave in four basic patterns. They are charactered, healthy, unhealthy, or psychologically sick. While we may operate in all four patterns at any given time, most people commonly find themselves in one of three blends of these basic patterns. They live predominantly in the realm of charactered-healthy, healthy-unhealthy, or unhealthy-sick.

The *charactered* pattern refers to people who identify, value, develop, and embrace the positive strengths outside their innate core color. *Healthy* describes people who exude the positive strengths that come within their natural and innate core personality. *Unhealthy* defines people who live their lives out predominantly in the negative limitations that are natural to their innate core personality. *Sick* patterns refer to people who embrace negative limitations that do not innately come with their personality but have been developed in their lives. People in this pattern are terribly difficult to deal with because there is absolutely no rhyme or reason to match their personality with the attitudes and behavior they display.

While we can never change our innate driving core motive, we can develop any strengths of any of the other colors. This is becoming charactered. In order to free ourselves of our innate limitations and become our best selves, we must develop strengths from the other colors. Simply staying within our own personalities will not suffice. Building character is the only way to override the innate limitations that already exist in our personality (unhealthy pattern) or the limitations we learn through unfortunate life experiences and/or dysfunctional relationships (sick pattern).

Character is a powerful phenomenon with complex beginnings. We can explain personality as innate, but character defies such a simple explanation. Our understanding of character begins with an accurate definition.

> *Personality is a gift.*
> *Character is a victory!*

It takes character for a Red personality to *tolerate* differences, or a Blue personality to take time to *play,* or a White personality to *assert* himself or herself as a leader, or a Yellow personality to *commit* to an intimate relationship. When we push our OVERRIDE button, these behaviors go against the natural grain of our innate personality and require developed character in order to exist.

Individuals develop character strengths and limitations just as they are born with personality strengths and limitations. Furthermore, it appears that some character traits are most innately compatible with certain personalities. Every individual has obvious strengths and limitations that he or she must deal with from birth. Though we may not be born with a particular character trait, we do appear to be more receptive and/or vulnerable to one or another depending on our given personality color.

We have defined character and linked common character flaws

THE SEVEN MOST COMMON CHARACTER STRENGTHS OF EACH COLOR

RED	BLUE	WHITE	YELLOW
loyal to tasks	loyal to people	tolerant	positive
committed	committed	patient	forgiving
visionary	quality-oriented	cooperative	friendly
logical	sincere	accepting	optimistic
leader	honest	objective	trusting
focused	purposeful	balanced	appreciative
responsible	moral	excellent at listening	open

THE SEVEN MOST COMMON CHARACTER LIMITATIONS OF EACH COLOR

RED	BLUE	WHITE	YELLOW
proud (arrogant)	self-righteous	timid	uncommitted
insensitive	judgmental	silently stubborn	inconsistent
poor at listening	easily depressed	emotionally dishonest	obnoxious
tactless	controlling	lazy	irresponsible
rebellious	unforgiving	uninvolved	rebellious
critical of others	suspicious	dependent	self-centered
impatient	irrational	directionless	permissive

with each personality. Personality limitations are capable of inhibiting others' character development. Notice particularly those areas where *your* personality may be inhibiting another's character development. Look for any specific behaviors in any colors that are currently inhibiting your character-building process. The following list delineates common and specific ways each personality inhibits the character development of others.

INHIBITING BEHAVIORS

REDS

1. Have a tendency to be overbearing and inflexible (which limits depth of shared feelings and/or perceptions in conversations).
2. Often have exaggerated ego needs (which often create an unnecessary power struggle).
3. Known to make sarcastic and unkind remarks in order to maintain control (which drives others around them into a defensive posture).
4. Typically are too task-oriented. They forget the spirit of living and remain too strict in their orientation to life. (If I suggest that a Red patient buy flowers for his wife, he may do so, but rarely for the enjoyment—he completes the assigned task rather than feeling the spirit of the giving process.)
5. Often are judgmental of others' weaknesses (which causes others to hide their insecurities for fear of rejection or ridicule). Doesn't bring out the creative best in others.
6. Tend to resent being questioned and need to always be right. (Typically others learn to lie or pretend they agree with a Red to his face and mock him behind his back.)
7. Often are unappreciative of others. They don't give compliments freely, which frustrates others who crave their approval and/or acceptance. This also backfires on Reds who would enjoy intimacy but rarely get it because they don't generate it themselves.

BLUES

1. Tend to take things too personally (which often causes others to lie in order to protect the insecure and overly sensitive Blue).

2. Often have too many unrealistic expectations (which makes others feel inadequate, unnecessary, or unloved).
3. Typically place themselves last on their list of priorities, presenting bad role models for self-esteem.
4. Often are too critical of others who choose to live life with a more relaxed or aggressive style (which causes others to feel unable ever to please them).
5. Tend to be too demanding of others' manners (which causes others to rebel against manners altogether).

WHITES

1. May be too easily overwhelmed by life (which causes others to pity Whites).
2. Can be too fearful of expressing themselves honestly (which causes others to lose respect for them).
3. Often are too timid to take a stand (which causes others to feel a need to always protect them).
4. Tend to be too insecure to set goals and pursue them (which causes others to resent being held back by their lack of initiative and cooperation in accomplishing joint endeavors).
5. Can be too independent to promote teamwork.
6. Often are too silently stubborn (which angers others and often causes them to ignore Whites and go their own way).
7. Appear to be too helpless and inadequate (which causes others to want to rescue them).

YELLOWS

1. May appear to be too flighty and uncommitted (which causes people to feel Yellows don't really care about them or anything).
2. Can be too flippant and make rude comments (which hurts feelings and/or causes others to not take them seriously).
3. Often are too irresponsible with jobs (which causes others not to trust them to come through).
4. Can be unwilling to learn many living skills (which causes others to lose respect for them or become overly protective of them).
5. Sometimes refuse to accept committed leadership roles (which causes others to carry more than their fair share).

6. Can be emotionally dishonest in order to avoid conflict (which causes others to believe things that aren't really happening and/or keeps intimacy on a superficial level).

We have briefly reviewed how the personality limitations of each color actually bind the character development of others. We can easily see the value of building our character. Now we can choose a healthy character-building process that will enable us to balance ourselves and experience the greater meaning life offers to those of us who are willing to reach out and stretch.

HOW TO BUILD YOUR CHARACTER

It is predominantly character, not personality, that ultimately determines the quality of our lives. Character is essentially anything we learn to think, feel, or do that is initially unnatural and requires an effort to develop. Character is reflected in the changes we make in our values and beliefs through our lives.

There are several components that are essential for character development. The first component is *free will*. The second component is *selecting positive influences in our lives*. The third component is *identifying positive life principles*.

> *If free will were not at the very core of our human existence,*
> *we would be trapped within the limitations*
> *of our innate personalities.*

FREE WILL

If free will were not at the very core of our human existence, we would be trapped within the limitations of our innate personalities. There would be no personal development or possibility for change. Developing our character is a way we can balance our personalities. Unless we build character, we must remain unfulfilled and limited. Developing our character allows us to most fully enjoy an exciting and productive life.

Character is usually shaped best in an atmosphere of free will, which lies at the root of every healthy character-building program. One young woman was forced by her father to practice piano every morning for two hours before school. She appeared very charactered to those who witnessed this daily ritual. However, healthy character is reflected by consistent commitment to positive life principles. This young woman grew to hate the piano. She also hated her father for demanding that she practice so much. She even hated herself for allowing him to control her life. Unfortunately, she had developed an unhealthy character by committing to the negative motive of pleasing others at all costs and resenting and blaming everyone for her miserable life. Similarly, her father had erred in demanding that his daughter develop character by working on his values rather than her own. He was shocked when she voiced her hatred for him, confessed that she was bulimic, attempted suicide, and vowed never to play the piano again. Neither the father nor the daughter had effectively identified positive life principles and consistently committed themselves to them. Both had accepted unhealthy character.

SELECTING POSITIVE INFLUENCES IN OUR LIVES

We are often told that we preach our greatest sermons by the lives we lead. Example is often all a child knows for its first few years of life. As we continue the aging process, we choose examples to follow. After years as a psychotherapist, I am convinced that with the exception of self, the most influential factor in childhood character development is the example and influence of parents. As teenagers, we are highly influenced by our peers. As adults, we are most influenced by our spouses. Playing a strong supporting role, however, are siblings, extended family, and friends. We must continually ask ourselves whom we seek as role models and who may be looking to us for mentoring.

IDENTIFYING POSITIVE LIFE PRINCIPLES

Life principles are those positive principles common to everyone. They may include living and being loved, the need for food and shelter, or the importance of feeling there is purpose in our lives. They may be theoretical or philosophical in nature. They help us to become more effective and charactered. They include the knowledge that:

- Every person can offer unique strengths to a relationship.
- Individuals who have personal confidence feel little need for power plays with others.
- People who like themselves find it easier to like and accept others than do those who feel inadequate.

- When we spend energy belittling others and blocking their development, we limit our own growth.

Life principles enhance our color by giving us insight into how others perceive things. These same life principles assist us in overcoming our inherent personality limitations by developing initially uncomfortable, yet positive, attitudes and behaviors based on principles that apply equally to all people.

In order to build character, we must identify and commit to those life principles that will maximize our color strengths and minimize our limitations. Regardless of our color, these life principles will guide us through the challenging process of character development.

Character building requires attitudinal and behavioral commitments. In order to be effective, character building must become specific and personal. For some, it may include the act of letting go or forgiving another for something that was said or done. For others, it may require a physical act such as refusing an alcoholic beverage. It may mean initiating a physical embrace with another person, or it might be as simple as giving a compliment to a deserving family member or a coworker.

The character-building process requires us to *identify healthy life principles; accept them into our lives; commit to living them consistently;* and *share them with others.*

> *We must continually ask ourselves*
> *whom we seek as role models*
> *and who may be looking to us*
> *for mentoring.*

Life principles will benefit all colors in their own development as well as in becoming less inhibiting of the relationships they encounter with other colors. Key life principles include:

Life Principle 1

Personal truths must be identified, pursued, and blended with universal truths if we are to have a balanced life.

Life Principle 2

Charactered people take responsibility for their own attitudes and behaviors.

266

Life Principle 3

We must stretch and risk personal discomfort in order to make alien attitudes and behaviors become natural.

Life Principle 4

Charactered people actively love themselves and others.

Life Principle 5

Our strengths must be shared with others in order to benefit us fully.

Life Principle 6

Everything has its price. Charactered people choose wisely and pay their debts.

Life Principle 7

Trust is vital to the positive human experience. We are all interdependent in varying degrees.

LIFE PRINCIPLE 1

Personal truths must be identified, pursued, and blended with universal truths if we are to have a balanced life.

Personal truths differ from universal truths in their focus. Personal truths may include careers we choose, friends we enjoy, hobbies we pursue, or the amount of sleep we require. Personal truths are those unique and healthy lifestyles we individually prefer, regardless of our personality color. When we think *everyone* should drive fast or slow on the freeway, we cause accidents. When we think *everyone* should be academically educated, we deprive our skilled laborers of earned self-respect.

Some of us would be miserable if we were psychotherapists or medical doctors. Others would be miserable as plumbers or auto mechanics. Unfortunately, we may disguise our own professional and personal insecurities by criticizing the occupations of others. We think this enhances our occupations. Personal truths suggest that one occupation is not necessarily better than another as long as both render an honest service. *Charactered individuals understand this concept. Simple, innate personalities do not.* We can waste so much energy trying to force personal truths into universal truths. We develop character when we identify universal truths and embrace them. We also foster effective human relationships when we understand and accept others in light of their personal truths.

You love to snow ski. I prefer tennis. You relax by reading novels. I relax with music. You prefer living single. I want children in my life. One person works in order to play, another individual thrives on the work itself. These are all examples of personal truths that simply suggest that each of us has our own road in life. We're not right or wrong for having different preferences. Personal truths are directly connected to our personal preferences. They do not necessarily apply to humanity in general. Being true to oneself often means valuing oneself enough to pursue the lifestyle of one's choice.

In order to build our character we decide on many personal truths and commit time and energy to developing them. Personal truths range from wanting better communication in our family to wanting to take a step up the career ladder. Only we know what is true for us. We must keep revising some of these truths in order to stay current with our changing life situations. We may want to make a list of at least ten personal truths we want to utilize in our lives. We should pay particular attention to our specific needs and values when we design our lists. This list is most effective when it focuses on our "wants," rather than our "musts" and "shoulds."

All of us want to feel loved and to be valued by others. We appreciate our lives more when they include a sincere element of purpose. Friendship is a mutual experience for two sacrificing individuals who willingly give priority to their relationship. These statements reflect some feelings and realities that are *universally true*.

The charactered person seeks a healthy blend between his/her personal values and the values of the universe. An individual may love his/her free time but forgo some in order to comfort a sick friend. Another person who values peaceful relationships may be forced because of integrity to confront a situation. Life is a series of choices. It is motivating and thus productive to maintain a proper perspective about our life. Balancing personal daily commitments with universal ones remains the most challenging and creative high-wire act any of us attempts.

We should seek help with our balancing act from within ourselves and from others. We are advised to listen to our internal intuitive senses. We also benefit by listening to sound suggestions from others who may have greater life experience than we do. Setting up positive support systems of family and friends, and keeping ourselves emotionally healthy so that we are receptive to intuition, are essential for successfully balancing on the high wire in life.

> *Unhealthy judgment of others*
> *comes from one's personal inadequacy.*

LIFE PRINCIPLE 2

Charactered people take responsibility for their own attitudes and behaviors.

Character building requires that we take responsibility for our attitudes and behavior. The emphasis for *charactered* people is in the action word *take*. They take responsibility while others passively accept or even deny it. Immature people often say, "I'm just that way. I've always been that way, and I will always be that way." *We must be cautious that we never use the colored personality labels as a way to excuse ourselves, to judge others, or to limit or trap anyone.*

If we hope to be charactered, we must be able to present ourselves with a given personality (style), but simultaneously accept responsibility for healthy attitudes and behaviors that may not be associated with our given personality. For example, I am a Yellow *personality*. We present ourselves as fun, full of optimism, and playful. However, as a *charactered* Yellow I recognize our tendency to be irresponsible. I try to pay equal attention to our optimism, our playful personality, *and* our irresponsible nature. A spontaneous, friendly Yellow who also commits willingly to an intimate relationship with sensitivity and honesty is a wonderful blend of a healthy *innate personality* and *developed character.*

Charactered people don't use personality color labels to limit themselves or others. They simply use the labels to help them understand and accept basic differences and similarities in all of us. They use these insights to build rather than block human relationships.

LIFE PRINCIPLE 3

We must stretch and risk personal discomfort in order to make alien attitudes and behaviors become natural.

Some individuals say they are unable to identify their personality from the available options. One individual was confused as to whether his personality was Red or Blue. We briefly discussed his dilemma. Suddenly, he said, "I have always been a strong, dominant man. My wife has been dead for several years. I'm just beginning to realize how she influenced my life. My wife was an invalid for most of our married life. Twenty years before she died, she had a serious stroke that limited her physically and forced me to shoulder many of the burdens usually shared by a couple. She had been so good to me that I initially felt obligated (admittedly resentfully) to take care of her. Through the years, however, my feeling turned to devotion, and I genuinely cared for this special woman. Her handicap allowed me to stretch. Eventually, I actually learned how to love."

This charactered man is innately a Red personality. He exemplifies many of the strengths we admire in Reds. However, he was able to replace his innate Red limitations with positive Blue attributes, giving him the enviable combination of Red and Blue strengths. Charactered individuals either rise to the tasks placed before them or honestly acknowledge their inadequacies. This man rose to his task with success. Charactered people learn to grasp every opportunity (positive or negative) encountered and to give the best that is in them.

Charactered people invite risk into their lives. They want to experience change. Their self-respect is heightened as they face life's discomforts with sincere purpose and clear motives. They do not passively wait for life to test their strength. They seek the opportunities and confront complacency in their daily lives with personal integrity. They are deeply committed to stretching themselves regardless of the inconvenience or discomfort.

LIFE PRINCIPLE 4

Charactered people actively love themselves and others.

Recently, an article in the newspaper caught my attention. The article mourned the loss of a school crossing guard. She was killed by a car only seconds after pushing seven youngsters to safety. Many remembered her for her unselfish love of children. Giving her life for them made a remarkable statement about her commitment to the children she had loved for so many years. However, one child captured a far more endearing expression of her love. The child said, "She'd ask how our classes were going. She was so nice, never grumpy or grouchy."

I once asked a group of parents how many would be willing to die for their children. Every parent raised a hand. Then I asked how many of them would be willing to commit to a daily expression of love for their children and mates with declarations of love; positive comments; quality time for social activities, reading, or games; and by touching them with their hands, their voices, and their eyes. No one raised a hand. "Are you kidding?" one man asked. "I have to earn a living too, you know!" "At least you are honest," I remarked. "But it appears that your perception of being a husband and father is some-what typical. Many of us may be saying we would rather die than live for our mates and children!" The crossing guard remembered by the children had captured the total picture. In her daily living she had communicated her love before she had died expressing it.

There comes a time in life when the children leave home, and some mothers find themselves at a loss for meaning in their lives. This is referred to as the empty nest syndrome. Actually, dads are often left in worse shape. Mother had expressed her love daily. Dad had been busy earning money to pay the bills and missed opportunities to develop his relationship with the children.

"I should have seen it coming when they were teenagers," one father lamented. "That was my first clue that they were more interested in friends and clothes than they were in me. Instead of thinking about some creative options for getting closer, I retreated to my work and television. I think I was scared of them. I didn't understand them. I refused to go to parenting classes. I wouldn't even take up a mutual hobby with my kids. I just expected my wife to handle them. Now they're gone and I can't bring them back." Then he shrugged his shoulders and asked rhetorically, "What am I saying, bring them back? How can they come back to a place where they have never been? I mean they have never been with me, and I've never been with them. Not really. We're strangers who shared most everything life offers except ourselves."

It's interesting that men are more affected than women by the empty nest syndrome. Many men actually break into tears during interviews as they recall the lost opportunities for loving their children. Parenting requires a commitment to daily expressions of love and to being a quality role model for children.

We may limit the lives of those we love by expecting them to love us the way we are. We limit the character building of those we love when we tell them what they must be and how they should perform because we don't trust them to make the right decisions. Some husbands and wives want to change each other. Some employers hound employees. Some parents overprotect children because they haven't learned to trust either themselves or their children. We may restrict and monitor the lives of those we feel responsible for. This is not love.

Love is accepting and encouraging others. Too many of us think we are especially wonderful lovers because we love others the way *we* would like to be loved. Unconditional love is always expressed in the language of the receiver, not of the sender. One woman shared her grief in realizing that all her life she had loved on her terms and simply ignored the needs of others. For example, when she was giving a dinner at her home, she was more concerned about how beautiful the house looked and how delicious the food was than about her guests. She almost canceled a dinner party one evening because she was so worried about herself. Fortunately, just prior to the event, we had a counseling session. We discussed her dilemma, and she agreed to pick some things up at the local delicatessen and simply enjoy her guests. The evening was a smashing success, and she began to realize how her entire life had been dedicated to looking good rather than loving others.

She also told me that she had not given her best friend a Christmas gift the previous year because she couldn't find the perfect gift. Rather than trying to look good and be perfect, she could easily have invited her friend to a special dinner or suggested they meet at a fast-food restaurant just to get together. Something personal would have been appreciated by her friend. Unfortunately, she was concerned only with her needs and never realized that being concerned with only her needs would never allow her to genuinely say "I love you" to others.

Our love is most helpful when we accept and encourage others as *they* need to be accepted and encouraged. It is critical that we recognize the importance of *accepting* each individual as he or she is. Remember, we did not select our personalities. They came with us at birth. Each of us is struggling to identify, understand, and accept ourselves. Perhaps the most valuable gifts we can offer our friends, children, and companions are acceptance, approval, and appreciation of their unique expressions of self. We can also help by having patience with them as they go about the arduous task of character building.

Any discussion of acceptance immediately brings up the issue of self-esteem. How well one accepts and appreciates himself or herself has a direct effect on how well one *can* accept, approve of, and/or appreciate others. Unhealthy judgment of others comes from one's personal inadequacy. This is perhaps best illustrated by teenagers. Teenagers are known for their cruelty to peers. Who can't recall being on the hurting end of an unkind comment during those years?

Ask most junior and senior high school students what they value most. The two most commonly stated attributes are looks and athletic ability. *LOOKS AND ATHLETIC ABILITY?* Is there a more awkward, acne attacked, body-changing time in life? They value what so few of them have at that time.

We are most likely to criticize the very thing we crave most. For example, if I am an individual who needs emotional stroking, I am more likely to expect others to provide what I lack than would another individual who feels relatively secure and doesn't require excess emotional support. We often criticize others for our own inadequacies.

We have often been told that in order to love others, we must first love ourselves. Loving ourselves means we value and accept ourselves as we are, with the understanding that we are endeavoring to improve our faults. When others misunderstand or mistrust our love, it is our self-love that allows us to continue loving them because we know our motives are pure. We can genuinely accept that while we may choose to love, others may not yet be willing to be loved. Loving ourselves frees us from attaching strings to our caring for others. When we are too needy, we may be kind and caring toward others, but the underlying motives are selfish. We are trying to control the behavior of those we are being good to. We may appear to give freely, but there are actually conditions that others must meet in order for us to continue to "love" them.

For example, arrogant people and people who grovel for approval are all suffering from the same need. They are insecure. At times, they may seem to be loving by taking care of others (arrogance) or by telling others how they only wish they were as bright or attractive or rich as they are (groveling). Arrogance and groveling come from insecurity. Neither are examples of humility. Self-respect produces a humble (teachable) nature that allows us to love unconditionally.

Humility requires an accurate perspective on ourselves and others. It requires that we value ourselves enough not to need validation from others. It suggests we are receptive to others' feedback as a way of maintaining an accurate perception of ourselves and our interpersonal relationships.

Seeking feedback constantly from our children, coworkers, employees, and friends regarding our motives is a growth process. Only insecure individuals fear the answers to "How am I doing as a parent, employer, or friend?" Secure individuals appreciate truth and opportunities to correct any misunderstandings.

We cherish friends who accepted and approved of our awkward self-discovery, who believed in us and shared that belief without reservation. We value those parents, teachers, friends, and children who taught us and nurtured us in the skills of living and the art of loving. We value those who offered us the numerous opportunities that have enabled us to build a strong platform to leap from childhood into adulthood.

In all these experiences we are often simultaneously restless and at peace. We love ourselves, yet we seek further life challenges to deepen our ability to love. We have wisdom, yet feel terribly ignorant about the mysteries of life. We are heartened by meaningful friends who remind us there is always time for those who love us and for those who are willing to be loved.

> In order to be effective,
> character building must become
> specific and personal.

LIFE PRINCIPLE 5

Our strengths must be shared with others in order to benefit us fully.

Developing a character begins with desire. The desire is expressed with an action. Character begins with what we think and do when no one else is around, but true character goes beyond personal commitment. *Fully developed character inevitably expresses itself in the giving of service to others.* It may begin as a mental battle, then proceed to an outward search for more knowledge and understanding. Character is not what we have, nor what we do. It is what we are that determines our worth.

Personality can be expressed without reference to others. Character must eventually affect others' lives as well as our own. We may be able to practice in the privacy of our homes, but we cannot fully develop our character alone.

Do we not have a mutual responsibility to love and accept love from everyone we encounter? How we model love for others often has a significant impact on them and their ability to love others. As we express our love, others watch us and learn from our ways.

We may ask, "Who are our role models? Who are the individuals we most admire?" We find them historically and when we are open and honest. We find them in our current everyday lives.

Florence Nightingale forsook wealth and physical comfort in order to pursue a need she felt deep within her soul. She felt driven to try to care for thousands of men, to share their emotional devastation and fear while they died with her at their side. She became the mother of the profession we know and appreciate today as nursing.

Father Damien, the Catholic priest who gave up everything to minister to the lepers on the Hawaiian island of Molokai, fully embraced the principle of sharing for character building. He fought numerous battles with the church bureaucracy to acquire supplies for his congregation. Eventually, he contracted leprosy and died with the people he had lived for and had loved.

Mahatma Gandhi gave over his entire being to the cause of freedom. His theory and example of nonviolent revolution eventually allowed him to break the bonds of English subjection for millions of Indians. When he was repeatedly encouraged to write about his life he gave his greatest statement of character: "My life is my message."

These historical examples of charactered role models, who shared their strengths for the good of others, may help us identify and appreciate those individuals (including ourselves) in our everyday lives who share themselves for the benefit of all humanity. Recently, some historians seem determined to discredit public figures by dredging up all their character flaws. I have little doubt that we could find fault with any public role model if we looked hard enough. This merely verifies my contention that character building is no easy task. However, we must celebrate the wonderful contributions these charactered individuals made to their fellow man, despite their obvious human limitations.

LIFE PRINCIPLE 6

Everything has its price. Charactered people choose wisely and pay their debts.

The price for reading this book can be calculated in various ways. It may help change aspects of our lives. For example, it may encourage an individual to address existing problems in a relationship that have previously been ignored. It may cause pain with the realization that we have been ignoring the development of our character. It costs us time to read when we could be engaging in other activities. It may directly influence our relationships with those we love. Remember Amelia Earhart's challenge "Courage is the price you pay for peace"? If you are not at peace with yourself or your relationships, this book may cause significant shifting in how you courageously challenge the status quo. Any movement on the part of one individual will always impact others around them.

Similarly, there is a price for those who may choose not to read this book. They may miss helpful insights that would enhance their personal and professional lives. They may miss learning about concepts that would open doors for future relationships. One can only imagine the prices we have all paid with our decisions in life. The prices we pay, good or bad, are not ours alone. Everyone connected with us gains or suffers as well.

One individual has been involved in an extramarital affair for many years. He says he wishes to leave his wife and yet continues to live a double life. His lover explains the price she pays: "I can't continue to live like this. We can't go any further with true intimacy because we are living a lie. I want memories of us sharing the holidays with family and friends, but I have to settle for a phone call after his wife goes to sleep." The man's wife necessarily suffers as well. She experiences the loneliness that comes when one's companion is psychologically withdrawn from a relationship, whether he or she ever acknowledges it or not. Everything has a price. We never pay the price alone.

The effect of our character is much like the ripple effect caused by throwing a pebble in a lake. The intensity of our impact increases with greater character. We are rewarded when we commit to integrity. A scattered life offers mixed messages and little intensity, because it lacks identified purpose. Likewise, we must recognize the high price of a charactered life. It necessarily prohibits a totally carefree and peaceful existence.

LIFE PRINCIPLE 7

Trust is vital to the positive human experience. We are all interdependent in varying degrees.

I have often asked students at the university to guess how many lives touched them prior to our 8:00 A.M. class. The answers usually range from zero to three. That's when the fun begins. The eyes light up and the minds grasp for answers as we consider the clothes they put on (who raised the animals, processed the chemicals, sewed, and sold their clothing?) Who directly and indirectly furnished their breakfast? Who drove with them or against them in traffic? Who designed, built, and repaired their cars? Who set the stoplights, paved the roads, and painted road signs? And we've only just begun! Somehow, we typically perceive ourselves as independent agents and seldom recognize that we are connected to others. When we have agreed to sincerely see ourselves as we are and develop a vision of what we hope to become, taking classes, risking new friendships, seeking therapy, reading books, and learning new hobbies can assist us. By appreciating our own contributions to humanity and those positive additions others make to our lives, we can see the value of the life principle known as *interdependence*.

It is not enough to simply choose our *preference* of interest. We commit to a broad spectrum of character development, or we suffer the consequences of a limited life. We will find certain areas easy and inviting. Others may require assistance from people we meet throughout our lives. Typically, the most common categories of interdependence are social, intellectual, emotional, financial, physical, and spiritual. Spirituality has received an unfortunate rap in its association with organized religion. Spirituality runs far deeper than religion. Spirituality is the light in our eyes reminding the world that we are well rooted and "at home" with our purpose in life.

The character-building process begins within us. We are the ones who allow ourselves to feel guilty, arrogant, uncommitted, or withdrawn. We are responsible for choosing the friends we keep and accepting the life we live! Uncharactered parents, siblings, teachers, and/or other role models may have been teachers who taught us limitations rather than strengths. They may have shown us disappointment rather than creative optimism. Our lives may have crossed one of those tragic souls who, in fearing themselves, taught us to fear our potential. However, all of us can seek and find examples of healthy, charactered role models. Choosing positive role models is crucial to charactered living. Becoming a healthy role model is equally essential to our own personal success.

The power of pure motives and healthy life principles is phenomenal. We can never underestimate the value of clearing our energy sources in order that we become free—free to love, free to change, free to accept ourselves at our worst as well as at our best. We can set our goals and commit to a charactered life congruent with those goals. As highly charactered people, we have pure motives. We examine our reasons for behaving or thinking in a particular way. We accept and encourage the best in everyone we encounter. We are emotionally and spiritually alive. We are mentally alert and physically disciplined. We honor our commitments.

Examples of charactered individuals are: the parent who promotes opportunities and independence but accepts and approves of each child's preferences; a busy parent who freely gives her own vacation and/or playtime to children; a student who risks a lower grade point average to try a more difficult course; a lawyer who defends a client he or she believes in regardless of fee or notoriety; a corporate president who fosters excellence in his or her product and remains equally concerned about employee morale; a teacher who seeks alternative ways of learning in an attempt to reach struggling students.

We can broaden our vision. We can sacrifice life's trivial distractions in order to remain focused on our true purpose in life. *When we seek with pure motives, we can balance our lives by developing all strengths expressed uniquely by each personality.* We can exchange our limitations for strengths and enrich our own lives as well as the lives of others we touch. It is an interesting irony that often highly charactered individuals' personalities are difficult to decipher because they have so artistically and skillfully blended the strengths of others with their own innate strengths. In other words, when our character and personality are blended, our innate personality is no longer always easily recognized.

Character is one of the three major aspects we must balance in our individual lives and relationships, along with passion and personality.

PASSION

CHARACTER　　　　　　　　PERSONALITY

Passion expresses feelings we have no control over. It comes from deep within our subconscious mind. We may feel passionate toward ourselves, another person, or toward a particular hobby or course of study. Passion reflects an unusually strong bonding of emotion. It feels clean and unencumbered. It just feels right and good. This explains why some people are so hard to let go of in relationships, whether they are right for us or not. It explains why some of us may be attracted to certain hobbies and careers that others do not find particularly inviting or worthwhile.

Character represents the responsible attitudes and behaviors we select for our lives. Healthy character is always rooted in truth. We can continue to develop it throughout our lives by striving to adhere to various life principles essential to successful lives, regardless of our culture's influence.

As we balance these three components of relationships, we will feel the confidence that comes from expressing committed, quality lives.

Truth lies within all of us. Nothing and no one can release truth within us without our consent. Even if we are arrogant, critical, devious, or uncommitted, we can ultimately seek, hear, and accept that truth. (Our innate personality, or style, is not undesirable. The unique qualities in each personality offer us opportunities to mix and blend with each other. There are many variations of successful living. It is quite natural for a person to continue developing his or her life with unique preferences.) We must learn to recognize our true motives and commit to healthy life principles. In our quest for truth and character, we feel the ultimate joy known only to those individuals who are willing both to risk pain and accept happiness. As we work toward developing a life built on both a *positive personality* and a *developed character,* we experience the most passion.

ADVANTAGES OF BUILDING CHARACTER

Character defines the type of positive or negative connection we make with ourselves and others throughout life. It is developed over years by personal design and commitment to life principles. Once established, it cannot be easily altered. We must be patient with the process. Character development often changes and takes numerous twists in its process. However, once the various aspects of character are established, they become as solid as our given personalities at birth. My next book, *The Character Code,* will offer more specific steps to assist you and enhance your character-building journey.

Knowing that our character will eventually become as solid as our personality should motivate us to enrich ourselves by balancing our life experiences. With luck, we will seek those positive attributes we observe in others. The search for this balance eventually provides greater meaning to our own lives.

> As we work toward developing a life
> built on both a positive personality
> and a developed character,
> we experience the most passion.

Personality is the style we use to present our thoughts and actions to others. Character is the core of life principles behind those thoughts and actions we present. Many naturally vibrant individuals have allowed themselves to put their best "personality" foot forward, rather than taking a more balanced stance on one "personality" foot and on one "character" foot. We are much stronger and more valuable when we add to the color of our innate personality by developing the best character traits we observe in others. Once we have identified our existing personality and character traits, we can begin to work on designing whatever image we prefer. We can't alter our innate personality. It is, however, tremendously important for us to keep striving to develop our character.

Character allows us to recognize our flawed human nature. We recognize the many times we have made poor decisions. Yet we continue to pick ourselves up and try, with renewed determination, to overcome our limitations. We want our lives to count for something— to matter. We want others to know we have lived for a greater purpose than merely to have survived this existence, after all. This feeling can come only with developed character. Personality alone can never offer such a powerful sense of destiny.

AFTERWORD

*Look at your journey
as the ultimate purpose of life.*

Life is a series of mountains to climb. *The Color Code* is simply a beginning. It may, however, represent a significant step in your life's journey. Your new identification as a Red, Blue, White, or Yellow may encourage further questions and insights about your life. You have identified how your color fits in the puzzle of relationships. You may want further help addressing concerns you struggle with in the process of mixing colors and creating your rainbow connections.

During every mountain-climbing experience, there are wildflowers and beautiful sunsets. They are available for every climber to see and enjoy. They represent truths in all of our lives. Whether we choose to see them or not, they exist. Truths in life, like wildflowers and sunsets on our mountain climb, can be pointed out—taught. If we refuse to see them, however, we will remain ignorant and blind. Yes, we will still climb the mountain, but the quality of our mountain-climbing experience remains limited and disappointing.

As we go through life, superficial people may ask us to lead them up the mountain, knowing we have been there before. Limited by our own choosing, we can only take them directly to the top. We are unable to see and point out the wildflowers and beautiful sunsets because we have neglected to see them ourselves on previous climbs. Until we choose to see and hear quality truths in life, we necessarily remain unable to offer them to others.

Quality people (whether in the role of parent, child, friend, lover, or employer) demand a more balanced mountain-climbing experience. Yes, they desire to reach the top. For them the climb must include the truths and available beautiful aspects they instinctively know or have been taught can be experienced on the climb, as well. Merely surviving the ordeal will never fully suffice. They expect to live their lives, herein symbolized by a mountain climb.

Our personal happiness and our success at building our character will be determined by our willingness to observe, conceptualize, and apply what we learn. Depth, breadth, and height are gained accordingly. Limitations are placed on us primarily by ourselves. If our goals are flexible and our expectations are reasonable, we can attain and maintain a positive self-image.

Look to your journey as the ultimate purpose of life. We can never again live our lives quite the way we do today. As we look within ourselves and identify who we are, we can feel joy in knowing we have substance and value. We can commit to replacing personality limitations with charactered life principles. We can commit to relationships with passion, and feel the strength expressed in the rainbow connection. The first step is being able to say, "I know who I am and what I am, and I know who and what I want to become." These perceptions may change as we grow, but the essential attitudes of humility and positive goal setting remain healthy catalysts in our life journey.

A common sign of an unhealthy person is defensiveness. Insecure people get stuck on the mountain, refusing to seek higher levels of awareness. Consequently, having to deal with a new color (one with explicit limitations as well as strengths) often overwhelms a weaker person and causes him or her to resist any new and challenging input. These are *frightened individuals* who refuse to be labeled or to see themselves as flawed in any way. They may react to new information about themselves with any number of attitudes and/or behaviors. Common defenses include: attacking the presenter of the material, ignoring the material, quickly pointing out a friend who could really use the information, pretending to accept the material but having no intentions of pursuing it in their lives, or suggesting the timing is somewhat difficult and they will get back to you when there is a better time to discuss it.

Unfortunately, they are reacting the only way they know how. They are simply protecting the little self-regard they feel is left them. If only they would risk the little self-regard, they might see the vast self-love they could generate if they would just invest the effort. We all deserve to travel through life with an abundance of self-love, rich with positive experiences and caring friends and family. Defensive people cut themselves off from what they deserve. They will discover that only when they are willing to see themselves accurately and get on with the process of growing up (character building) can they experience the mountain climb at its best.

While reading *The Color Code*, you have experienced a new identity, and your journey to self-actualization has begun. With your commitment to developing your new identity you will experience many opportunities to appreciate yourself and others. Life's greatest moments are never more clearly experienced than in our genuine connection to ourselves and others. Our success comes with these rare yet magical moments. These moments occur throughout our lives as we honestly assess ourselves and lovingly value others.

Unconditional love is experienced when we accept and encourage others as *they* wish to be accepted and encouraged. Loving requires trust and risk. Loving allows for the limitations of those we love. It prevents our expectations from exceeding their abilities. We must believe in others' abilities to make healthy decisions. We accept and encourage their choices, regardless, at times, of how healthy or unhealthy their choices may be.

There are occasions when criticism is appropriate and helpful, but it must always stem from a pure motive in order to affect the individual for whom the criticism is intended. We must care and truly value the individual before we are in a position to offer criticism.

Enjoy your climb up the mountain. I have enjoyed the part of the trip that we have made together. As a Yellow, it has been challenging to commit myself so completely to something other than play. As with anything worthwhile, the slopes are high, but the sunsets—yes, the sunsets—have been even more rewarding than I could have dreamed.

I value intimacy, learning, and creating new insights. Unfortunately, distributing my thoughts in a book is less personal than I would like. However, I invite your feedback so that I can share in your life's journey as you have shared in mine. Happy mountain climbing. I hope that we will continue to cross each other's paths on our ascents to the top.

How Can You Order Recommended Books, Tapes, and Seminars?

They are available from

Hartman Communications
515 South 700 East, Suite 3I • Salt Lake City, UT 84102 • Phone: 1-800-761-0001

The Color Code by Taylor Hartman, Ph.D.
Paperback $13.00 (Utah residents add $.86 tax)
The most accurate work on personalities and relationships available. Inspires and motivates quality lifestyling. Vital to understanding personal development and successful interpersonal relationships.

Color Your Future by Taylor Hartman, Ph.D.
Paperback $12.00 (Utah residents add $.79 tax).
The most revolutionary psychosocial-spiritual book in existence on becoming a fully charactered individual. Presented with refreshing style and candid professionalism, this six-step guide gives tremendous counsel for identifying and embracing a quality life.

Sandcastles by Taylor Hartman, Ph.D.
Paperback $12.00 (Utah residents add $.79 tax)
While his first two books defined who we are and the development of our character, this book guides us through the building of a relationship.

Dealing Effectively with Different Personalities
Six Tape Cassettes $75.00 (Utah residents add $4.95 tax)
Powerful six-tape cassette program complete with excellent recommendations for understanding and successfully relating to each individual color. Numerous examples are provided to assist you in immediate application. Each tape focuses on one of the Four Color Personalities, plus entertaining live presentation overview of Color Coding concepts and the six steps to becoming a genuinely charactered individual.

Hartman Personality Profile (Adult or Youth Profile available)
Self-Scoring Profile $9.95 (Utah residents add $.66 tax)
This easy-to-administer and self-scoring Personality Profile has already become the standard for accurately measuring an individual's personality. Profile includes questions, scoring, methodology, honest overview of personalities, and explanation of Profile results. (Please specify Adult or Youth Profile and quantity.)

Hartman Character Profile (Adult only)
Testing Profile $9.95 (Utah residents add $.66 tax)
This powerful testing instrument accompanies the Hartman Personality Profile. Insightful with its clarity on what strengths and limitations an individual has developed from other personalities, as well as their own. Profile includes questions, scoring, methodology, honest overview of character development, and explanation of Profile results.

Code Cards (pocket-sized reference cards)
Card Set $12.00 (Utah residents add $.79 tax)
New quick reference cards that give a review of each personality's strengths and limitations, tips on things to do and not to do to effectively build relationships, time management tips for each Color, and verbal and non-verbal clues that can be used to determine a person's personality. Easy application and very user-friendly.

Satisfaction Guaranteed: Quality performance of our services and products is vital to us at Hartman Communications. We believe in you and want to earn your trust as we develop a mutually beneficial relationship. If at any time, for whatever reason, you feel the quality of our services or products has been compromised, we will make full restitution and guarantee your complete satisfaction.

Telephone Orders: 1-800-761-0001. Please have credit card number, expiration date, name, mailing address, and daytime telephone number ready. *Merchandise is mailed within three working days.*

E-mail: info@hartmancommunications.com

Mail Orders: Make checks payable to Hartman Communications. Send order form with check to:
Hartman Communications, 515 S. 700 E., Suite 3I, Salt Lake City, UT 84102

Fax: (801) 531-1826

Quantity	Description	Price	Amount
	PLEASE INCLUDE SHIPPING CHARGES. UTAH RESIDENTS MUST PAY 6.6% TAX	(Up to $30) $7.00	SHIPPING _____
	ORDERS CAN BE FAXED TO (801) 531-1826	Up to $60) $10.00	TAX _____
		(Over $60) $15.00	TOTAL _____

NAME: _____   PHONE _____

ADDRESS: _____

CITY _____   STATE _____   ZIP _____

VISA/MASTERCARD/AMERICAN EXPRESS/DISCOVER _____   EXP. DATE _____

THE HARTMAN COLOR CODE SYSTEM

Sales and Training of Color Code
Copyrighted Materials and Programs

Hartman Communications is the exclusive worldwide agent authorized to train, teach, and license Dr. Taylor Hartman's Color Code program. The unauthorized use of copyrighted materials and programs in any format is strictly prohibited. Inquiries regarding the sales and training of Color Code concepts should be directed to Hartman Communications.

HARTMAN COMMUNICATIONS TRAINING APPLICATIONS

* Conflict Resolution
* Sales and Relationships
* Teambuilding
* Charactered Leadership
* Corporate Culture Creation/
  Enrichment
* Executive and Personal Coaching
* Interpersonal Skills Effectiveness

* New Employee Orientation/
  Culturization
* Strategic Hiring, Firing, and Retention of
  Employees
* Train-the-Trainer Certification Courses and
  Customized Delivery Methods for Your In-
  House Corporate Trainers
* Other Topics Can Be Customized Upon Request

HARTMAN COMMUNICATIONS

Personal Retreats in Sundance

Dr. Taylor Hartman and his wife, Jean, personally supervise these 3-day retreats at their center in Sundance, Utah. Intimate (only 12 guests per session) and extremely enlightening, these retreats are equal to 6 months' therapy. People come from all over the world and every walk of life for this rare experience. Individuals and/or couples are welcome.

On-Site Training

Hartman Communications provides outstanding, experienced presenters for in-house programs. The Color Code System is easily integrated into existing training programs, providing the "missing link" for better teams, improved customer service, quality management, and increased sales, thereby maximizing productivity and enhancing profits. The Color Code System also helps resolve many of the Cultural Diversity issues within the workplace, and provides a means to recognize the value of individual contribution.

Train-the-Trainer

Hartman Communications will certify individuals to train within an organization or to teach the Color and Character Coding concepts on an independent level. For detailed information regarding costs, dates, options, and to fill out an application, visit www.hartmancommunications.com.

Convention, Conference, or Meeting Speakers

Dr. Taylor Hartman may be retained as a keynote speaker. In addition, Hartman Communications provides other outstanding speakers who present the Hartman Color Code concepts in one-hour, two-hour, half-day, and full-day sessions.

FOR ADDITIONAL INFORMATION, WRITE OR CALL:

Hartman Communications • 515 South 700 East, Suite 3I • Salt Lake City, UT 84102 • 1-800-761-0001 E-mail: info@hartmancommunications.com